EXPANDED and UPDATED

LAWRENCE BLOCK'S
writing the novel
from Plot
to Print
to Pixel

A LAWRENCE BLOCK PRODUCTION

WRITING THE NOVEL
FROM PLOT TO PRINT TO PIXEL
Copyright © 2016, Lawrence Block

This edition has been expanded and updated from the original *Writing the Novel From Plot to Print*, first published in 1978.

All Rights Reserved. No part of this book may be reproduced by any means mechanical or electronic without express permission from the publisher, except by a reviewer who may quote brief passages in a review.

Cover and Interior design by QA Productions

lawrenceblock.com

LAWRENCE BLOCK'S
writing the novel
from **Plot**
to **Print**
to **Pixel**

Contents

- **1** **Introduction** to the expanded and updated edition.
- **7** **Introduction** to the 1978 edition.
- **13** **Chapter 1** Why Write a Novel? The advantages, commercial and artistic, of writing a novel as opposed to short fiction. The novel as a learning experience. As a vehicle for self-expression.
- **33** **Chapter 2** Deciding Which Novel to Write. What to do when you don't have a specific novel in mind. How to pick your type of novel.
- **49** **Chapter 3** Read... Study... Analyze. How to read, as a writer. Taking books apart to see how they work. Applying these principles in structuring your own novel.
- **61** **Chapter 4** Developing Plot Ideas. How to encourage ideas to bubble up from the unconscious. How ideas come together to create plot. Ways to sharpen up a plot.
- **81** **Chapter 5** Developing Characters. Drawing characters from real life. Making up characters from the whole cloth. How to make your characters memorable.
- **97** **Chapter 6** Outlining. First, learn about outlines, by writing one of an existing book. How to write an outline of your own. How to expand it step by step into a book. Advantages of not using an outline. Avoiding outline-enslavement.
- **115** **Chapter 7** Using What You Know... and What You Don't Know. How to put the background you have to work in your novel. Capitalizing on your own experience. Research—how and when to do it, how and when to do without it.
- **133** **Chapter 8** Getting Started. Beginnings. How to open the book up, when to begin at the beginning and when not to.
- **143** **Chapter 9** Getting It Written. How to harness self-discipline for the long haul of novel-writing: Take it a day at a time.

157	**Chapter 10** Snags, Dead Ends and False Trails. What to do when a wheel comes off.
169	**Chapter 11** Matters of Style. Grammar, diction, usage. Dialogue. First vs. third person. Single vs. multiple viewpoint. How to handle transitions, descriptive passages.
185	**Chapter 12** Length. How long is long enough? Length as a market consideration. Writing the right length for your particular book.
195	**Chapter 13** Rewriting. All at once or as you go along? Structural revision. Stylistic polishing. How rewriting sharpens prose.
209	**Chapter 14** Getting Published. Difficulties facing the first novelist. Queries. Finding an agent, if you think you need one. Dealing with editors. Subsidy publishers.
225	**Chapter 15** The Case for Self-Publishing. How self-publishing has become respectable and affordable. My own experiences with self-publishing, early and late. The economics of the indie world.
237	**Chapter 16** The Case Against Self-Publishing. Will your mother be impressed? Will you feel you've really arrived? Do you want to spend the requisite time on non-writing tasks? Do you want to spend the money?
243	**Chapter 17** How to Be Your Own Publisher. Getting your manuscript edited, copy-edited, and proofread. Formatting your book for electronic publication. Designing a cover. What to do yourself, how to find experts to do it for you.
261	**Chapter 18** Doing it again. Moving on to the next book. Special aspects of sequels and series books. Ghostwriting and co-authoring.
277	**Chapter 19** Now it's up to you. A summing up. A passing of the torch. Good luck!
279	**Acknowledgements**, Then and Now.

Introduction to the Expanded and Updated Edition

When *Writing the Novel from Plot to Print* was first published, Jimmy Carter was halfway through his four years as President of the United States. Mamie Eisenhower and Nelson Rockefeller were still alive. So was John Wayne. So too was Mary Pickford.

And I was forty years old. And you, Gentle Reader, may not even have been born yet.

The world has changed in the years since 1978, and you don't really need me to count the ways. The small world of publishing has changed at least as much as the greater world, to the point where a latter-day Rip Van Winkle, newly risen from a 37-year slumber, would wonder what the hell was going on. Five or six major houses instead of fifty or sixty? Ebooks? Online booksellers? Self-publishing? Phones you tuck in your shirt pocket, and whole books you can read on them?

And computers, for heaven's sake! Why, if Rip wanted to write about what he saw, he'd need a typewriter. And where would he find one outside of an antique shop?

You get the point. Being a writer is vastly different now. So how could a 1978 book about the writing of novels have anything to offer to today's reader?

Well, here's the thing—when all is said and done, the novelist's task is pretty much the same as it always has been. The important element of writing has always consisted of taking the right words and putting them in the right order, and that's every bit as true whether you're cutting them into clay tablets with a stylus or talking them onto a screen with the aid of voice-recognition software. You have to tell your story, and everything follows from what you write and how you write it.

And the elements that make a story work, that make characters come alive on a page or screen, have not changed much since Shakespeare's day, or Chaucer's.

Writing the Novel from Plot to Print remained continuously available from its original publisher, first as a hardcover volume and then as a trade paperback, until just a few years ago. By the time Writer's Digest Books finally allowed it to go out of print, I'd made it electronically available from Open Road as an ebook. All these years after its initial appearance, I continue to get letters—well, emails nowadays—from writers who tell me how valuable they have found it.

May I take a minute or two to review how it came about in the first place?

In the spring of 1976 I sold a piece to *Writer's Digest*, the monthly magazine for writers. I was in Los Angeles at the time, in mute testimony to H.L. Mencken's observation that a Divine Hand had taken hold of the United States by the State of Maine, and lifted, whereupon everything loose wound up in Southern California. The article I sold them was a reply to the perennial question, *Where do you get your ideas?*, and no sooner did they accept it than I got an idea on the spot.

My idea was to sell them on the idea of hiring me as a columnist. They already had a couple of columnists, but nobody was writing about fiction, and that was the chief interest of most of their audience, so the need seemed to be there. Rather than press my case through the mail, I waited until I could do so in person; my daughters flew out in July to spend the summer with me, and we stayed that month in LA and passed the month of August on a leisurely drive back to New York, where they lived with their mother—and where I had lived, until that Divine Hand sent me spinning.

I mapped out our route east so that I could work in a lunch in Cincinnati with John Brady, then the editor at *Writer's Digest.* He'd bought my article, and now he bought my lunch, and over lunch he bought my idea for a fiction column, to run six times a year, alternating with their cartoon column. I got back to New York and sent in the first column, and by the time I'd written the third one they'd booted the cartoonist. My column, called simply *Fiction,* would appear in the magazine every month for the next fourteen years.

I'd been doing it for a little over a year when Brady got in touch. Their book division felt the need for a book telling how to write a novel. And they liked the way I wrote about writing, and wanted me to do the book for them.

I was living in New York again, in an apartment on Greenwich Street. (It's no more than a two-minute walk from where I live now, all those years later, but I've had a slew of addresses in the interim.) I wrote the book and sent it off, and the folks in Cincinnati liked it just fine, and proposed a title: *Writing the Novel from Plot to Print.*

I didn't like it at the time, feeling that it made the whole process sound more mechanical than I thought it to be. I'd made a particular point in my book of not telling the reader, *"This is the way to do it."* There were, as I saw it, at least as many ways to do it as there were writers, and arguably as many ways as there were books. But they really liked the title, and I went along with it, and I have to say it seems OK to me now.

The book, after all, has had a nice run. I guess the title hasn't hurt it any.

Twenty years ago, Writer's Digest Books wanted me to revise *Writing the Novel.* They felt it was dated. I talk about the Gothic novel, for example, and while books fitting that pattern may continue to be written and read, the category by that name has long since ceased to exist. If I could go through the book and update it, then they could bring out a new edition with the words "updated new edition" on it, and increase sales accordingly.

I thought about it, and ultimately decided against it. The book seemed to be one readers find useful, and the techniques and principles discussed struck me as essentially timeless, as pertinent in 1995 as they had been in 1978.

And the whole idea of updating a book bothers me, anyway. I knew a writer once who'd updated a novel, or tried to; it was being reissued after fifteen or twenty years, and he'd gone through it page by page, upping the cost of a telephone call from a nickel to a dime (this was a few years ago), changing the stars of a movie his character watches from William Powell and Myrna Loy to William Holden and Gloria Swanson (yes, this *was* a while ago), and otherwise altering the book's temporal setting.

Well, it didn't work. One way or another, every word in that book was attached to the year when it was written. It had a certain integrity, and you altered it at your peril.

Writing the Novel is not a novel, and thus may not need to adhere to the same standard of artistic integrity, but it's nonetheless a creature of the time of its writing, and my inclination was to leave it alone. I'm also predisposed to avoid work, and this looked to me to be work to no purpose.

Now, twenty years after I decided the book wasn't broke and didn't need to be fixed, it is in fact that much older and that much further out of date. But it still ain't broke, as I can tell by the enthusiastic word-of-blog I keep encountering on the Internet, and I'm still predisposed to avoid work.

Still, if the book doesn't need fixing per se, neither does it have to go on looking like something chiseled out of a time capsule. I don't want to sit down and rewrite it, changing William Powell and Myrna Loy to Michael Cera and Ellen Page, or Smith-Corona to iMac, or Britannica to Wikipedia, or—well, you get the point. But shouldn't there be a way to retain what works while bringing the book into today's publishing universe?

Toward that end, here's what I've done: I've kept the original text of *Writing the Novel* intact, except for the occasional alteration of the occasional infelicitous phrase. And for that original text I've used this nice traditional typeface, which has the great virtue of readability.

And I've added new material in this nice modern sans-serif typeface, to set it apart and make it easy to tell today from yesterday. Sometimes, when I write about ebooks and self-publishing and such, the new material will reflect the manner in which the world has changed. And on other occasions, when I reflect further on a point, it's because I myself have changed. All those years have come and gone, and it would be odd if I didn't see some things a little differently now.

Of course, when all is said and done, it's still only a book. I can but wish it does for you all a book of this sort can possibly hope to do. May my words, old and new, help you speak in your own voice, map out your own route, and find your very own way to your very own book.

Before we get started . . .

One thing I'm not going to do is change language that in recent decades has come to be decried as sexist. I have used the masculine pronoun when a third-person singular pronoun was called for. Thus *he* = he or she, *him* = him or her, and *his* = his or hers.

Thus: "Everyone has a right to his own opinion."

And, presumably, to his own grammar as well. The alternatives are ones I find unacceptable: "Everyone has a right to their own opinion" is a phrase I grew up regarding as illiterate, and "Everyone has a right to his or her own opinion" is cumbersome and dopey.

If this bothers you, consider that the use of the masculine pronoun is not a philosophical statement but a convenience and a convention, that it has less to do with gender than with grammar.

Times change, and so does language, and there are indeed sentences I might structure differently now. But I wrote them close to forty years ago, and to revise them this long after the fact seems to me as ill-advised as updating Huckleberry Finn and renaming the fellow sharing Huck's raft as African-American Gentleman Jim.

There's a point further on when I discuss the argument that computers are responsible for authors writing longer and longer books. I don't believe I can blame my Mac for the fact that the present work has grown from 66,000 to 93,000 words.

There is, to be sure, a great deal of new subject matter. And there's also the tendency I share with not a few others to grow more garrulous with age.

But even the title's longer!

And it needs the extra couple of words. Because print is no longer the last word in our new world, so why should it be the last word in the title?

Writing the Novel from Plot to Print to Pixel. It has a nice ring to it, don't you think? Even if you, like this author, are a little vague on just exactly what a pixel is . . . .

Introduction to the 1978 edition

This is a book designed to help you write a novel. It contains the distillation of my own experience of twenty years as a published novelist, plus a considerable amount that I've learned from other writers. My goal throughout has been to produce the sort of book I might have found useful when I set out to write my own first novel.

But there are no guarantees. Just because you've bought this book, just because you've studied it diligently, does not mean for a moment that your success as a novelist is a foregone conclusion. You may never write so much as the first paragraph of a novel. You may begin work on a book and find yourself unable to complete it. Or you may labor long and hard on a book, working your way through outline and first draft and final polish, only to discover that you've turned a perfectly good ream of paper into something commercially unviable and artistically indefensible.

These things happen. That they happen constantly to neophyte writers should hardly be surprising news. What may be more of a surprise is that they happen to seasoned professional novelists as well.

They even happen to me. Over the years, I've published, at last count, twenty novels under my own name, plus perhaps five times that number under various pseudonyms. You would think that all that furious typing would have resulted in my having learned something, that while I might not know how to tie my shoes or cross the street I ought certainly to have the mechanics of writing a novel down cold by now.

But in the past two or three years I've had perhaps half a dozen ideas for novels that got no further than the first chapter. I've written three novels that died after I'd written over a hundred pages; they repose in my file cabinet at this very moment, like out-of-gas cars on a highway, waiting for someone to start them up again. I very much doubt they'll ever be completed.

That's not all. During that same stretch of time I've seen two novels through to completion and succeeded only in producing books that no one has wanted to publish—and, I've come to believe, for good and sufficient reason. Both were books I probably shouldn't have tried writing in the first place. Both failures constituted learning experiences that will almost certainly prove beneficial in future work. While I could by no means afford the time spent on these books, neither can I properly write that time off as altogether wasted.

But how could an established professional write an unpublishable book? If he's written a dozen or two dozen or five dozen publishable ones in a row, wouldn't you think he'd have the formula down pat?

The answer, of course, is that there's no such thing as a formula. Except in the genuinely rare instances of writers who tend to write the same book over and over, every novel is a wholly new experience.

In *Some Thoughts I Have in Mind When I Teach,* Wendell Berry makes the point that

> *No good book was ever written according to a recipe. Every good book is to a considerable extent a unique discovery. And so one can say with plenty of justification that nobody knows "how to write." Certainly nobody knows how other people ought to. For myself, though I think I know how to write the books I have already written—and though I guess, wrongly no doubt, that I could now write them better than I did—I am discomforted by the knowledge that I don't know how to write the books that I have not yet written. But that discomfort has an excitement about it, and it is the necessary antecedent of one of the best kinds of happiness.*

Some of the books I write involve series characters. I've done three books, for example, about a burglar named Bernie Rhodenbarr; in each of them he becomes the prime suspect in a homicide investigation because of his activities as a burglar, and in order to get himself out of the jam he has to solve the murder himself. There is, clearly, a similarity to the structure of all three of these books which at a cursory glance might well look like a formula.

But each plot is significantly different and each book, let me assure you, has presented its own specific problems. You might think the books would become easier to write. The third, just recently completed as I write these lines, was by a fair margin the most difficult of the three.

As a noun, *novel* means a book-length prose narrative. As an adjective, it means "of a new kind or nature." The dual definition is historic, of course, deriving from a time when the novel was a new fictional form. Still, I see it as a happy accident, for every novel *is* novel.

I would suppose that a majority of this book's readers have yet to write a book-length work of fiction. It is commonplace to hear that the first novel presents special problems to author and publisher alike. But in a larger sense every novel is a first novel, presenting no end of unique problems, carrying enormous risks, and offering immense excitement and other rewards.

If you're unprepared for the risks, perhaps you'd like to rethink this whole business of novel-writing. If you're unwilling to live with the possibility of failure, perhaps you'd be more comfortable writing laundry lists and letters to the editor.

If you really want to write a novel, stick around.

• • •

My own literary résumé has grown since this book's first edition. I don't honestly know how many books I've added to the list, but it must run to around fifty new titles. The Bernie Rhodenbarr series has gone from three books to eleven, the Matthew Scudder series from three to eighteen. A few years ago a friend pointed out that he and I had reached that stage in our careers when the ethical act was not to write the book but to spare the tree—and I've gone on to cause the premature death of many more trees.

It would be pleasant to report that there have been no more false starts or abandoned manuscripts since 1978. While I think the percentage of aborted novels has dropped off significantly, my perception may be colored by their relative invisibility in the age of the computer. There are no trunks or cartons crammed full of failed books, simply because those unfortunate creatures never make their way onto paper. They live out their days as files on a hard drive—and, as one generation of software follows another, they become files I'm no longer able to open.

No loss . . .

• • •

One thing you won't find in this book is an explanation of *the* way to write a novel.

Because I don't believe there is one. Just as every novel is unique, so too is every novelist. The study I've made of the writing methods of others has led me to the belief that everybody in this business spends a lifetime finding the method that suits him best, changing it over the years as he himself evolves, adapting it again and again to suit the special requirements of each particular book. What works for one person won't necessarily work for another; what works with one book won't necessarily work with another.

Some novelists outline briefly, some in great detail, and a few produce full-fledged treatments that run half the length of the final book itself. Others don't outline at all. Some of us revise as we go along. Others do separate drafts. Some of us write sprawling first drafts and wind up cutting them to the bone. Others rarely cut three paragraphs overall.

Some months before I wrote my own first novel—of which there will be more later—I read a book which purported to tell how to write a novel. The author taught writing at one of America's leading universities and had written a couple of well-received historical novels, and he had set out to tell the great audience of would-be novelists how to go and do likewise.

His method was a dilly. What you did if you wanted to write a novel, I was given to understand, was to trot down to the nearest stationery store and pick up several packs of three-by-five file cards. Then you sat at a desk with the cards and a trayful of sharp pencils and got down to business.

First you went to work on your character cards. You wrote out one or more of those for each and every character to appear in the book, from the several leads to the most minor bit players. For the major characters, you might use several cards, devoting one to a physical description of the character, another to his background, another to his personal habits, and a fourth, say, to the astrological aspects at the moment of his birth.

Then you prepared your scene cards. Having used some other cards to rough out the plot, you set about working up a file card for every scene which would take place in your novel. If one character was going to buy a newspaper somewhere around page 384, you'd write out a scene card explaining how the scene would play, and what the lead would say to the newsdealer, and what the weather was like.

There was, as I recall, rather more to this method. By the time you were ready to write the book you had innumerable shoeboxes filled with three-by-five cards and all you had to do was turn them into a novel—which, now that I think of it, sounds rather more of a challenge than converting a sow's ear into a silk purse, or base metal into gold.

I read this book all the way through, finding myself drawing closer to despair with every passing chapter. Two things were crystal clear to me. First of all, this man knew how to write a novel, and his method was the right method. Secondly, I couldn't possibly manage it.

I finished the book, heaved a sigh, and gave myself up to feelings of inadequacy. I decided I'd have to stick to short stories for the time being, if not forever. Maybe someday I'd be sufficiently organized and disciplined and all to get those file cards and dig in. Maybe not.

Couple of months later I got out of bed one morning and sat down and wrote a two-page outline of a novel. About a month after that I sat down to the typewriter with my two-page outline at hand and a ream of white bond paper at the ready. I felt a little guilty without a shoebox full of file cards, but like the bumblebee who goes on flying in happy ignorance of the immutable laws of physics, I persisted in my folly and wrote the book in a couple of weeks.

Shows what a jerk that other writer was, doesn't it? Wrong. It shows nothing of the sort. The extraordinarily elaborate method he described, while no more inviting in my eyes than disembowelment, was obviously one that worked like a charm—*for him.*

Perhaps he said as much. Perhaps he qualified things by explaining that his method was not *the* way to write a novel but merely *his* way to write a novel. It's been a long time since I read his book—and it'll be donkey's years until I read it again—so I can't trust my memory on the point. But I do know that I was left with the distinct impression that his method was the right method, that all other methods were the wrong method, and that by finding my own way to write my own novel I was proceeding at my own peril. It's unlikely that he put things so strongly, and my interpretation doubtless owes a good deal to the anxiety and insecurity with which I approached the whole prospect of writing a book-length work of fiction.

Nevertheless, I would hate to leave anyone with the impression that the following pages will tell you everything to know about how to write a novel. All I'll be doing—all I really can do—is share my own experience. If nothing else, that experience has been extensive enough to furnish me with the beginnings of a sense of my own ignorance. After twenty years and a hundred books, I at least realize that I don't *know* how to write a novel, that nobody does, that there *is* no right way to do it. Whatever method works—for you, for me, for whoever's sitting in the chair and poking away at the typewriter keys—is the right way to do it.

• • •

The book was *How to Write a Novel,* by Manuel Komroff; a professor at Columbia University, he was a prolific writer of fiction and nonfiction. His book, published in 1950, is available from used booksellers for between $10 and $25.

CHAPTER 1

Why Write a Novel?

If you want to write fiction, the best thing you can do is take two aspirins, lie down in a dark room, and wait for the feeling to pass.

If it persists, you probably ought to write a novel. Interestingly, most embryonic fiction writers accept the notion that they ought to write a novel sooner or later. It's not terribly difficult to see that the world of short fiction is a world of limited opportunity. Both commercially and artistically, the short-story writer is quite strictly circumscribed.

This has not always been the case. Half a century ago, the magazine story was important in a way it has never been since. During the 1920s, a prominent writer typically earned several thousand dollars for the sale of a short story to a top slick magazine. These stories were apt to be talked about at parties and social gatherings, and the reputation a writer might establish in this fashion helped gain attention for any novel he might ultimately publish.

The change since those days has been remarkable. In virtually all areas, the short fiction market has shrunk in size and significance. Fewer magazines publish fiction, and every year they publish less of it. The handful of top markets pay less in today's dollars than they did in the much harder currency of fifty or sixty years ago. Pulp magazines have virtually disappeared as a market; a handful of confession magazines and a scanter handful of mystery and science-fiction magazines are all that remain of a market once numbered in the hundreds. Whole categories of popular fiction have categorically vanished; the western, the sports story, the light romance—these were once published in considerable quantity, twelve or fifteen stories per magazine, and now they have simply gone the way of the dodo and the passenger pigeon.

The remaining pulps are scarcely worth writing for. Consider the plight, for example, of the writer of detective fiction. Twenty years ago, the two leading magazines in the field paid five cents a word for material, and their rejects sold quite readily to any of a batch of lesser markets. Now, at a time when the erstwhile nickel candy bar has gone to twenty cents, those two magazines still pay the same nickel a word—and only a single cent-a-word publication exists to skim the cream of the stories they reject.

The outlook is not much more promising for writers of "quality" fiction. Very few magazines publish stories of literary distinction and pay a decent price for the privilege. After a piece has made the rounds of *The New Yorker, Atlantic, Harper's,* and a few others, its author is reduced to submitting it to the small literary magazines that pay off in contributor's copies or, at best, token payment. It is not merely impossible to make a living in this fashion; it is very nearly impossible, over the course of a year, to cover one's mailing expenses.

On the other hand, one can make a living writing novels.

I'm not going to make you drool by rattling on about the stratospheric sums certain writers have received of late for their novels. The earnings of bestsellers, the fortunes paid for film and paperback rights, have relatively little to do with the average writer, be he neophyte or veteran. James Michener once remarked that America is a country in which a writer can make a fortune but not a living—i.e., a handful of successful writers get rich while the rest of us can't even get by. There's some truth in this— the gap between success and survival is, I submit, an unhealthily yawning one—but there's some hyperbole in it as well. A writer can indeed make a living in America; if he's a reasonably productive novelist, it can even be one we'd characterize as comfortable.

Financial considerations aside, I have always felt there are satisfactions in the novel which are not to be found in shorter fiction. I began as a writer of short stories, and to have written and published a short story was an accomplishment in which I took an inordinate amount of pride. But genuine literary achievement, as far as I was concerned, lay in being able to hold in my own hands a book with my own name on the cover. (I was to hold a dozen of my own books before one of them was to bear my own name, as it turned out, but that's by the way.)

Short-story writing, as I saw it, was estimable. One required skill and cleverness to carry it off. But to have written a novel was to have achieved something of substance. You could produce a short story with little more than a cute idea backed up by a modicum of verbal agility. You could, when the creative juices were flowing, knock it off start-to-finish on a slow afternoon.

A novel, on the other hand, took real work. You had to spend months on the thing, fighting it out in the trenches, line by line and page by page and chapter by chapter. It had to have plot and characters of sufficient depth and complexity to support a structure of sixty or a hundred thousand words. It wasn't an anecdote, or a finger exercise, or a trip to the moon on gossamer wings. It was a *book*.

The short-story writer, as I saw it, was a sprinter; he deserved praise to the extent that his stories were meritorious. But the novelist was a long-distance runner, and you don't have to come in first in a marathon in order to deserve the plaudits of the crowd. It is enough merely to have finished on one's feet.

These arguments presented above would all seem to urge the writer to turn eventually to the novel. But it's my contention that the beginner at fiction ought to focus his attention on the novel not sooner or later but right away. The novel, I submit, is not merely the ultimate goal. It is also the place to start.

At first, this may well seem illogical. We've just seen the short story likened to a sprint, the novel to a marathon. Shouldn't a marathon runner work up to that distance gradually? Shouldn't a writer develop his abilities in the short story before attempting the more challenging work of the novel?

Certainly a great many of us do begin that way. I did myself, as far as that goes. In my earliest efforts, it was extremely difficult for me to sustain a prose narrative for the fifteen hundred words necessary to constitute a proper short-short. Over a period of time I became increasingly at ease writing full-length short stories, and then I finally wrote my first novel. Other writers have followed a similar path, but perhaps as many have leaped directly into the novel without any serious effort at short stories. There doesn't seem to be any traditional path to follow in becoming a writer. Whatever road leads to the destination turns out to have been the right road for that particular traveler.

With the understanding, then, that all roads lead to Rome, here are some of the reasons why I believe a writer is best advised to begin with a novel.

Skill is less at a premium. This may seem paradoxical—why should a novel require less skill than a short story? You'd think it would be the other way around.

Don't you have to be a better craftsman to manage a novel? No, I don't think you do. Often a novelist can get away with stylistic crudity that would cripple a shorter piece of fiction.

Remember, what a novel affords you as a writer is *room*. You have space to move around in, space to let your characters develop and come to life, space for your story line to get itself in motion and carry the day. While a way with words never hurts, it's of less overwhelming importance to the novelist than the sheer ability to grab ahold of the reader and make him care what happens next.

The bestseller list abounds with the work of writers whom no one would want to call polished stylists. While I wouldn't care to name them, I can think offhand of half a dozen writers whose first chapters are very hard going for me. I'm perhaps overly conscious of style—writing does radically change one's perceptions as a reader—and I find their dialogue mechanical, their transitions awkward, their scene construction clumsy, their descriptions imprecise. But if I can make myself hang on for the first twenty or thirty or forty pages, I'm often able to lose my excessive awareness of the trees and start to perceive the forest. The author's pure storytelling ability grips me and I no longer notice the defects of his style.

In shorter fiction, the storyline wouldn't have this chance to take over. The story would have run its course before I ceased to notice the author's style.

Similarly, some novels triumph over the style in which they are written because of the grandeur of their themes or the fascination of their subject matter. The epic novel, presenting in fictional form the whole history of a nation, catches the reader up because of the sheer power of its scope. Leon Uris's *Exodus* is a good example of this type of book. And Arthur Hailey's books exemplify the novel that conveys an enormous amount of information to the reader, telling him almost more than he cares to know about a particular industry. This is not to say that these novels, or others of their ilk, are stylistically clumsy, but merely to point out that style becomes a considerably less vital consideration than it must be in short fiction.

The idea is less important. I've known any number of writers who have postponed writing a novel because they felt they lacked a sufficiently strong or fresh or provocative idea for one. I can understand this, because similar feelings delayed my own first novel. Logic would seem to suggest that a novel, by virtue of its length, would require more in the way of an idea than a short story.

If you're having trouble coming up with ideas, you may well be better off with a novel than with short stories. Because each short story absolutely demands either a new idea or a new slant on an old one. Often the short story amounts to very little more than an idea fleshed out and polished into a piece of fiction. This is particularly likely to be the case with the short-short, which is typically not much more than a fifteen-hundred-word preamble leading up to a surprise ending, an idea thinly cloaked in the fabric of fiction.

Novels, on the other hand, are time and again written with no original central idea to be found. Every month sees the publication of new gothic novels, for example, and the overwhelming majority of them hew quite closely to a single plotline—a young woman is in peril in a forbidding house, probably on the moors; she is drawn to two men, one of whom turns out to be a hero, the other a villain. Another category, the historical romance of the *Love's Tender Fury* variety, has an initially innocent heroine getting ravished in various historical periods and with varying degrees of enjoyment.

Westerns typically adhere to one of five or six standard plotlines. Similarly, there are a handful of basic book types in the mystery and science-fiction fields. And, in the world of mainstream fiction, consider how many novels each year deal with nothing more original than the loss of innocence.

This is not to say that the novel does not demand ingenuity. It is this quality which enables the novelist to take a standard theme and hang upon it a book which will seem quite fresh and new to everyone who reads it. As he writes, characters come to life, scenes acquire dimension upon the page, and a wealth of original incident serves to make this particular book significantly different from all those other novels to which it is thematically identical.

Sometimes these elements of characterization and incident which make a novel unique exist in the forefront of the author's mind when he sits down to the typewriter. Sometimes they emerge from his creative unconscious as he goes along.

I enjoy writing short stories myself. They offer me considerable satisfaction, for all that their production is economically unsound. I very much enjoy being able to sit down at the typewriter with an idea fully formed in my head and devote myself to a day's work of transforming that idea into a finished piece of fiction.

The enjoyment's so keen that I'd do this sort of thing more often—except that each story requires a reasonably strong central idea, and the idea itself gets used up in the space of a couple of thousand words. I simply don't get that many ideas that I find all that appealing.

Ed Hoch makes a living writing nothing but short stories, and he manages this superhuman feat because he seems to be a never-ending fount of ideas. The development of short story ideas and their speedy metamorphosis into fiction is what gives him personal satisfaction as a writer. I sometimes find myself envying him, but I know I couldn't possibly come up with half a dozen viable short story ideas every month the way he does. So I take the easy way out and write novels.

You can learn more. Writing has this in common with most other skills: we develop it best by practicing it. Whatever writing we do helps us to become better writers.

It has been my observation, however, that there is no better way to learn how to write than by writing a novel. I learned quite a bit by writing short stories. I learned much more when I wrote my first novel, and I have continued to learn something or other with virtually every novel I have written since.

Short story writing taught me quite a bit about effective use of the language. I learned, too, how to construct a scene and how to handle dialogue. Everything I learned in this fashion was valuable.

When I wrote a novel, it was as if I were working out now with heavy weights; I felt growth in muscles I had not previously been called upon to use at all.

Characterization was at once a very different matter. Before my characters had existed to perform specific functions and speak specific lines. Some were well drawn, some were not, but none had the sort of fictive life that transcended their role on the page. When I wrote a novel, the characters came to life for me. They had backgrounds, they had families, they had quirks and attitudes that added up to more than the broad lines of caricature. I had to know more about them in order to make them maintain vitality over a couple of hundred pages, and thus there was more substance to them. This is not to say that my characterization in my earliest novels was particularly good. It was not. But I learned immeasurably from it.

I learned, too, how to deal with time in fiction. My short stories had often consisted of a single scene, and rarely of more than three or four scenes. The novels I wrote seemed to cover a matter of days or weeks, and of course consisted of a great many scenes. I learned to deal with any number of technical matters—viewpoint shifts, flashbacks, internal monologues, etc.

You can earn while you learn. It's curious how many writers tend to expect instant gratification. We've barely rolled a sheet of paper into the typewriter than we expect to see our efforts on the bestseller list.

It seems to me that other artists are rather less impatient of tangible success. What painter expects to sell the first canvas he covers? More often than not he plans to paint over it once it's dried. What singer counts on being booked into Carnegie Hall the first day he hits a high note? Every other artistic career is assumed to have an extended and arduous period of study and apprenticeship, yet all too many writers think they ought to be able to write professionally on their first attempt, and mail off their first stories before the ink is dry.

There must be reasons for this. I suppose the whole idea of communication is so intrinsic a part of what we do that a piece of writing which goes unread by others is like Bishop Berkeley's tree falling where no human ear can hear it. If nobody reads it, it's as if we hadn't even written it.

Then too, unpublished writing strikes us as unfinished writing. An artist can hang a canvas on his own wall. A singer can croon in the shower. A manuscript, though, is not complete until it is in print.

At first glance this desire to receive money and recognition for early work would look like the height of egotistic arrogance. It seems to me, however, that what it best illustrates is the profound insecurity of the new writer. We yearn to be in print because without this recognition we have no way of establishing to our own satisfaction that our work is of any value.

I would not for a moment advise a new writer to expect to get any recognition or financial gain out of a first novel. Unless you are fully prepared to spend months writing a book with no greater reward than the doing of it, you would very likely be better off getting rid of your typewriter and taking up some leisure pastime which places less of a premium on achievement.

This notwithstanding, there is no gainsaying the fact that any number of first novels are published every year. Publishers typically bitch about the difficulty of breaking even on a first novel, conveniently ignoring the several first novels per season to achieve bestseller status. True, most first novels are not published. True too, most that are sell very poorly. The wonder is that any are published at all.

Thus it is possible to make certain gains, in money and in recognition, while acquiring those skills which can only be acquired through experience. And this sort of paid apprenticeship is far more readily accessible to the novelist than the short story writer.

It wasn't always this way. When the newsstands teemed with pulp magazines, the pulps were precisely where the new writer earned a living—albeit a precarious one—while developing his skills and refining his technique. A similar kind of magazine apprenticeship is standard procedure to this day in the field of nonfiction; article writers earn while they learn by writing for house organs and trade journals before they are ready to write either nonfiction books or articles for more prestigious magazines.

Some of the surviving fiction magazines are certainly open to new writers—*Ellery Queen's Mystery Magazine,* for example, makes a special point of publishing first stories, having printed over five hundred maiden efforts to date. But ever since the decline of the pulps in the 1950s, there has not been sufficient depth to the magazine fiction market for a writer to serve out his apprenticeship there.

In contrast, the market for original paperback fiction continues to be quite strong, and quite receptive to the work of beginners. The relative viability of the various categories of category fiction—suspense, adventure, western, science fiction, gothic, light romance, historical romance—runs a cyclical course, but there are always several categories which constitute a healthy market.

I served my own novelistic apprenticeship in the field of paperback sex novels. In the summer of '58, I had just finished my first novel and was wondering what to do next. My agent was marketing the book; I had no idea whether it would sell or fail completely.

The agent got in touch with me to say that a new publisher was entering the field of sex novels. Did I know what these books were? Could I read a few and try one of my own?

I bought and skimmed several representative examples in the field. (If I had all of this to do over again, I'd spend more time on this analysis, as detailed in Chapter Three.) I then sat down at the typewriter with the assurance of youth and batted out three chapters and an outline of what turned out to be the start of a career.

I didn't know how many sex novels I was to write in the years to follow. For quite a while I was doing a book a month for one publisher with occasional books for other houses as well, along with a certain amount of more ambitious writing. I suppose I must have turned out a hundred of them. Maybe not—I really don't know, and my copies of most of the books were lost in the course of a move some years ago. Let's just agree that I wrote a lot of them and let it go at that.

I learned an immeasurable amount from doing this. Bear in mind that these books were written in more innocent times; while they were the most inflammatory reading matter then on the market, they can barely qualify as soft-core pornography by contemporary standards. Unprintable words were not to be found, and descriptive passages were airbrushed like an old-fashioned *Playboy* centerfold.

The books had a sex scene per chapter, but the scene couldn't take up the whole chapter. There was plenty of room left for incident and characterization, for dialogue and conflict and plot development, room in short for a story to be told with periodic interruptions for sexual titillation. Without the sex, surely, the books would have had no reason for existence; the stories in the main were not strong enough to carry the books unassisted. (Though I can think of one or two exceptions, books where a character took over and came to life, so that the sexual episodes seemed almost like annoying interruptions. But this was rare indeed.)

This was a wonderful apprenticeship for me. I was by nature a fast writer, gifted with the ability to write smooth copy in a first draft; thus I could produce these books rapidly enough to make a satisfactory living.

(They did not pay much, nor were there royalties to be had or subsidiary income to anticipate; it was indeed like working for the pulp magazines, with all sales outright.)

I learned a tremendous amount about how to write fiction, learning by the irreproachable method of trial and error. I could fool around with multiple viewpoint, with various sorts of plot structure, could in fact try whatever I wanted as long as I continued to write the books in English and keep the action coming. I got any number of auctorial bad habits out of my system. And, as I've said, I earned while I learned.

I'm acquainted with quite a few writers who started out by cultivating this particular secret garden. There were a number who never went on to anything else; they earned some easy money at sex novels until the novelty wore off but lacked the particular combination of talent and drive which it evidently takes to establish a writing career. The rest of us moved on, sooner or later, to other things. I don't know anyone who doesn't regard the experience as valuable.

In my own case, I suspect I found the sex-novel groove too comfortable and stayed with it too long, past the point where it was able to teach me much. I probably should have tried stretching my literary muscles a little sooner. On the other hand, I was painfully young then in virtually every possible way. The sex books put bread on the table and gave me the satisfaction of regular production and regular publication at a stage when I was incapable of writing anything much more ambitious. I can hardly regret the time I devoted to them.

Is the sex novel field a good starting place for a beginner today? I'm afraid not. Their equivalent in today's market is the mechanical, plotless, hard-core porn novel, written with neither imagination nor craft and composed of one overblown sex scene after another. The books I wrote were quite devoid of merit—let there be no mistake about that—but by some sort of Gresham's Law of Obscenity they've been driven off the market by a product that is indisputably worse. Any dolt with a typewriter and a properly dirty mind could write them; accordingly, the payment is too low to make the task worth performing. Finally, the books are published by the sort of men who own massage parlors and peep shows. You meet a better class of people on the subway.

There's no need, though, to be nostalgic for the old days, be they the old days of pulp magazines or the old days of soft-core sex novels. There always seems to be an area in which to serve out a writer's apprenticeship. We'll see how to choose your own particular area in the next chapter; meanwhile, let it be said that for the foreseeable future it's almost certain to be a novel of some sort.

The suggestion that a beginner ought to begin as a novelist is a radical one. The natural response is to offer some immediate objections. Let's consider some of the most obvious ones.

Isn't it harder to write a novel than a short story?

No. Novels aren't harder. What they are is longer.

That may be a very obvious answer, but that doesn't make it any less true. It's the sheer length of a novel that the beginning writer is apt to find intimidating.

As a matter of fact, you don't have to be a beginner to be intimidated in this fashion. My suspense novels generally stop at two hundred pages or thereabouts. On the several occasions when I've begun books I knew would run two or three times that length, I had a lot of trouble getting started. The very vastness of the projects put me off.

What's required, I think, is a change in attitude. To write a novel you have to resign yourself to the fact that you simply can't prime yourself and knock it all out in a single extended session at the typewriter. The process of writing the book is going to occupy you for weeks or months—perhaps for years.

But each day's stint at the typewriter is simply that—one day's work. And that's every bit as true whether you're writing short stories or an epic trilogy. If you're writing three or six or ten pages a day, you'll get a certain amount of work accomplished in a certain span of time—whatever it is you're working on.

I remember the first really long book I wrote. When I sat down to begin it I knew I was starting something that had to run at least five hundred pages in manuscript. I got a good day's work down and wound up knocking out fourteen pages. I got up from the typewriter and said, "Well, just 486 pages to go"—and went directly into nervous prostration at the thought.

The thing to remember is that a novel's not going to take forever. All the old clichés actually apply—a journey of a thousand miles begins with a single step, and slow and steady honestly does win the race.

Consider this: If you write one page a day, you will produce a substantial novel in a year's time. The writer who turns out one book a year, year in and year out, is generally acknowledged to be quite prolific. And don't you figure you could produce one measly little page, even on a bad day? Even on a *rotten* day?

> *When I write a short story I can hold the whole thing in my head when I sit down at my desk. I know exactly where I'm going and it's just a matter of writing it down. I don't have that kind of grasp on a novel.*

Of course you don't. Nobody does.

The chapter on outlining will offer some suggestions in this regard. Meanwhile, there are two things to keep in mind.

First of all, recognize that the total control you have over short stories may be largely illusory. What you really have is confidence—because you *think* you know everything about the story by the time you set out to write it.

But, if you're like me, you keep surprising yourself at the typewriter. Characters take on a life of their own and insist upon supplying their own dialogue. Scenes that looked necessary at the outset turn out to be superfluous, while other scenes take a form other than what you'd originally intended for them. As often as not, midway through the story you'll think of a way to improve elements of the plot itself.

This happens to a much greater extent in novels. And it should. A work of fiction ought to be an organic entity. It's alive, and it grows as it goes. Even the most elaborately outlined novel, even the product of those authors who write outlines half the length of the final book, must have this life to it if it is going to live for the reader. The writing of fiction is never purely mechanical, never just a matter of filling in the blanks and tapping the typewriter keys.

A second thing to realize is that you do not have to grasp the whole book at once because you are not going to be writing the whole book at once. Novels are written—as life is lived—One Day At A Time. I've found that all I really have to know about a book in order to put in a day's work on it is what I want to have happen during that day's writing.

I get in trouble when I find myself starting to project. As soon as I step back and try to envision the novel as a whole, I'm likely to be paralyzed with terror. I become convinced that the whole thing is impossible, that there are structural flaws which doom the entire project, that the book can't conceivably resolve itself successfully. But as long as I can get up each morning and concentrate exclusively on what's going to happen during that particular day's stint at the typewriter, I seem to do all right—and the book takes shape, page by page and chapter by chapter.

Many of the books I write are mystery novels of one sort or another. Books of this type have two storylines which unfold simultaneously. First, there's what happens before the reader's eyes from the first page to the last, the record of action as perceived by the viewpoint character or characters. Underlying this plot is the mystery storyline itself, that which is happening (or has happened previously) and is withheld from the reader until the book's climax.

Years ago, I took it for granted that a writer had to have both of these storylines fully worked out in his head before putting a word on paper. I've since learned that it's occasionally possible to write an elaborately complicated mystery novel without knowing the identity of the villain until the story is almost at an end. In *Burglars Can't Be Choosers*, I was within two or three chapters of the finish before a friend's chance remark enabled me to figure out whodunit; I had to do some rewriting to tie off all the loose ends, but the book worked out fine.

Suppose I spend a year writing a novel and it proves to be unsalable. I can't risk wasting that much time, so wouldn't it be safer to stick to short stories?

Would it? Let's assume that you could write twelve or twenty short stories in the time it would take you to write a novel. What makes you think you'd have a better chance of selling them? The nature of the market is such that you'd probably have a better chance placing one novel for publication than one out of twenty short stories. And, assuming you wouldn't sell either the novel or the short stories, why would a batch of unsalable short stories feel less like a waste of time than an equally unsalable novel?

Nevertheless, the fear of wasting one's time keeps a lot of people from writing novels. But I don't think the fear is justified even when it proves true.

So what if a first novel's unsalable? For heaven's sake, most of them are, and why on earth should they be otherwise?

Any of several things may happen to the person who produces an unsalable first novel. He may discover, in the course of writing the book, that he was not cut out to be a novelist, that he doesn't like the work or doesn't possess the talent.

I don't know that it's a waste of time to make this sort of discovery.

On the other hand, the author of an unpublishable first novel may learn that writing is his métier, that he has a burning desire to continue with it, and that the weaknesses and flaws which characterized his first book need not appear in the ones to follow. You might be surprised to know how many successful writers produced hopelessly incompetent first books. They were not wasting their time. They were learning their trade.

Consider Justin Scott, whose first novel I read in manuscript several years ago. It was embarrassingly bad in almost every respect, and hopelessly unpublishable. But it did him some good to write it, and his second novel—also unsalable, as it happened—was a vast improvement over the first.

He remained undiscouraged. His third novel, a mystery, was published. Several more mysteries followed. Then he spent over a year writing *The Shipkiller,* a nautical adventure story on a grand scale which brought a six-figure paperback advance, sold to the movies for a handsome sum, and did well enough in the stores to land on several of the bestseller lists.

Do you suppose Justin regrets the time he "wasted" on that first novel?

Maybe I haven't started a novel because I'm afraid I wouldn't finish it.

Maybe so. And maybe you wouldn't finish it. There's no law that says you have to.

Please understand that I'm not advocating abandoning a novel halfway through. I've done this far too often myself and it's something I've never managed to feel good about. But you do have every right in the world to give up on a book if it's just not working, or if you simply discover that writing novels is not for you.

As much as we'd all prefer to pretend our calling is a noble one, it's salutary to bear in mind that the last thing this poor old planet needs is another book. The only reason to write anything more extensive than a shopping list is because it's something you want to do. If that ceases to be the case you're entirely free to do something else instead.

I'm inclined to hope you *will* complete your first novel, whatever its merits and defects, whatever your ultimate potential as a novelist. I think the writing of a novel is a very valuable life experience for those who carry it through. It's a great teacher, and I'm talking now about its ability to teach you not about writing but about yourself. The novel, I submit, is an unparalleled vehicle for self-discovery.

But whether you finish it or not remains your choice. And failing to begin a task for fear of failing to complete it doesn't make abundant sense, does it?

Okay, I'm convinced. I'm going to sit down and write a novel. After all, short stuff isn't significant, is it?

It isn't, huh? Who says?

I'll grant that commercial significance singles out the novel, and that long novels are automatically considered to be of more importance than short ones. I'll admit that, with a handful of exceptions, short story writers don't get much attention from literary critics. And I won't deny that your neighbors will take you more seriously as a writer if you tell them you've written a novel. (Of course if that's the main concern, just go ahead and tell them. You don't have to write anything. Lie a little. Don't worry—they won't beg to read the manuscript.)

But as far as intrinsic merit is concerned, length is hardly a factor. You've probably heard of the writer who apologized for having written a long letter, explaining that he didn't have the time to make it shorter. And you may be familiar with Faulkner's comment that every short-story writer is a failed poet, and every novelist a failed short-story writer.

I'm not sure the desire to be significant is a particularly useful motive for writing anything. But length is no guarantee of significance and brevity no hallmark of the trivial. Sonnet, short story, thousand-page novel—write whatever it is you want to write, and that's the long and short of it.

All right. Significant or otherwise, what I want to write is a novel. But what novel should I write? All I've got is a desk and a typewriter and a ream of paper and an empty head. What do I do now, coach?

Well, for openers, why don't you turn the page?

• • •

Well, not so fast. Maybe you shouldn't turn the page just yet.

I've mentioned Ed Hoch, who spent a whole career writing short fiction. While he did manage a handful of novels, it was the short story that brought him true satisfaction and considerable recognition. He wrote almost a thousand of them, and for thirty-four years he had a story every month in *Ellery Queen's Mystery Magazine.*

I had at most a nodding acquaintance with Ed back in the late '70s, but we became friends over the years, and it was my great pleasure to present him with the Grand Master Award at the Mystery Writers of America annual awards dinner. Ed Hoch died in 2008; seven years later, publishers are still bringing out new collections of his stories.

I also mentioned Justin Scott, who has never stopped evolving as a novelist, writing under his own name and as Paul Garrison. Most recently, he has become very successful co-writing a series of historical thrillers with Clive Cussler.

The gist of this chapter, the arguments for writing novels rather than short stories, still strike me as sound. If anything's changed over the years, it's the need to make this point in the first place. In recent years I've added *anthologist* to my box of tricks, and have had occasion to solicit stories, new or previously published, from writers of my acquaintance. What I was surprised to discover was how many of them had never even attempted a short story.

As I've said, I began as a short-story writer, and I must have published twenty of them before I wrote my first novel. Until I'd developed my muscles with short fiction, I could not have dared to undertake a novel.

A century ago writers like Damon Runyon and O. Henry wrote short stories exclusively—because that's where the money was. By the time I began writing this had changed considerably, with paperback books having taken the place of all-fiction magazines, and television weakening the grip of the general magazines. A professional writer was advised to aim for a career as a novelist.

But short stories were still the natural place to begin. One could learn how to write, and earn a few dollars while enjoying the sight of one's words in print in a magazine. Fewer markets exist now for short stories, and the few that actually pay for submissions don't pay very much. If one was well advised to write novels thirty-plus years ago, the advice is if anything more pertinent today.

And yet, curiously, I find myself rather less adamant on the subject. There are arguments to be made for an apprenticeship as a writer of short stories.

On the happily rare occasions when I've led workshops for writers, I've insisted that the participants work not on a novel but on individual short stories. I did so because it struck me as tedious beyond belief to sit listening to writers reading portions of the same unending novel week after week. But if they brought in a new story every week, we'd have something to talk about.

Um, what are you trying to say, LB?

Perhaps that, just as there's no one way to write a novel, neither is there one way to grow into a writing career. Some writers will do well to plunge right into a full novel. Others will be more comfortable writing short stories.

But as for you, Gentle Reader, it's evident that you have at the very least a passing interest in writing a novel. Otherwise you wouldn't have picked up this book.

So. *Now* you can turn the page.

Chapter 2

Deciding Which Novel to Write

You may not need this chapter. A certain proportion of novelists start off knowing pretty much what book they want to write, and you may very well be one of them. Although the precise shape of the plot and the structure of the book may be vague in your mind, it's possible that you know certain things about the book. You know that it is a novel, for example, and you know what it's about.

Perhaps the book you have decided to write is based upon your own life experience. Maybe you've endured something that strikes you as the raw material for a novel—a hitch in the military, a stretch in the slammer, or four years in a coed dormitory, say. Colorful or bland, anyone's life can be turned into arresting fiction if it is incisively perceived and dramatically portrayed.

Similarly, you may be caught up in the notion of a novel that has nothing whatever to do with your visible life experience. Something from your reading or fantasy may have stimulated your creative imagination in such a way that you have a book to write firmly in mind. Perhaps your lead is a member of the Children's Crusade, or an intergalactic explorer, or a contemporary private detective with a taste for Armagnac and a collector's passion for oriental snuffboxes. Or your central character might as easily be a realistic contemporary figure with whom you identify on some inner plane—an abused child, an ex-athlete recovering from a failed marriage, a nun breathless with adoration. The possibilities are quite literally infinite; the only requisite is that there's a character or conflict or fundamental situation somewhere along the line that makes you want to write a novel about it.

If this is the case, you have a slight advantage; you at least know what you want to write about, and the knowledge puts you one important step closer to the act. Skip ahead to the next chapter, if you're so inclined.

During the first of my several vexingly undistinguished years as a college student, a cartoon hung for months on the English Department bulletin board. I returned to that campus twenty years after my precipitous departure from it, a prodigal son come home to teach a writing seminar, and as I walked across the greensward that cartoon came vividly back to me.

It showed a sullen eight-year-old boy staring down an earnest school principal. "It's not enough to be a genius, Arnold," the man was saying. "You have to be a genius *at* something."

I recall identifying very strongly with Arnold. I had known several years before college that I wanted to be a writer. But it seemed it wasn't enough merely to *be* a writer.

You had to be a writer *of* something.

Some people get the whole package as a gift. Not only are they endowed with writing talent but they seem to have been born knowing what to write about. Equipped at the onset with stories to tell, they have only to get on to the business of telling them.

Some people, in short, have it easy.

But some of us don't. We know *that* we want to write without knowing *what* we want to write.

It's encouraging to note that we're in the majority, that most writers have been obsessed with the idea of becoming writers before the nature of what they might write about revealed itself to them. It's easy to accept this premise about the nuts-and-bolts commercial writer, but the same initial uncertainty is every bit as likely to characterize the early years of writers with impeccable critical reputations. The identification of self as writer comes for most of us before we know what sort of writer we'll be or what we'll write about, and that seems to be just as true whether our ultimate literary product is *Moby-Dick* or *Trailer Trollop*.

(This might be a good place to suggest, incidentally, that fiction writers of every stripe have a great deal more in common than the disparity of our work might suggest. The fact that we write unites us far more than the nature of what we write separates us.)

Let's suppose, then, that all you know at this point is that you want to write a novel. Why you have this curious urge is not terribly important. It's enough that you have it in good measure. Whether you'll prove to have other elements essential to novelistic success—talent, perseverance, resourcefulness—is not something you have to know at this stage. Indeed, it's not something you're in a position to know. You'll find out in due course.

How do you decide what novel to write?

It seems to me that this question can best be answered by asking a few others. First of all, what kind of novel do you like to read? I would not go so far as to say that we can only produce the sort of fiction that we most enjoy reading ourselves.

I've known of too many instances where this is simply untrue. When I was knocking out soft-core sex novels, for instance, I did not commonly spend my free hours reading other people's soft-core sex novels. And I've observed that a substantial number of people who write westerns are very much averse to reading in the genre. Contrariwise, most mystery and science-fiction writers seem to enjoy reading in their respective fields.

When I was starting out, confession magazines constituted the most receptive market for new writers. They paid fairly well, too. Their numbers have shrunk since then and their rates of payment have actually declined, illustrating once more how the short story writer's lot has gotten worse over the years, but back then they were an excellent place for a neophyte to get started.

Because I once read a lot of them, I came to understand what a confession story was, the basic structure of its plot, and what made one story good and another unacceptable. During the year I spent working for a literary agent, the two confessions I yanked out of the slush pile both sold on their initial submissions, and the author of one of them came to be a leader in the field, ultimately going on to make a name for herself in the field of romantic fiction.

Well, I was game. Confessions back then paid several times what I was earning for suspense short stories, so on several occasions I went out and bought or borrowed confession magazines and set about reading my way through them. I never quite made it. I could not read one of the damned things all the way through without skimming. I couldn't concentrate on what I was reading. And I couldn't shake the conviction that the entire magazine, from front to back and including the bust-developer ads, was nothing but mind-rotting swill.

Nor, consequently, could I produce a confession story. The ideas my mind came up with were either mind-numbingly trite or at odds with the market's requirements. I never did turn one of these ideas into a story that I stayed with beyond a couple of tentative pages, never completed a confession until one bizarre weekend when I wrote three of them to order for a magazine editor with a couple of holes to fill and a deadline fast approaching. I managed to get them written simply because I'd accepted the assignment, and he printed them because he had to, and that was not the easiest money I ever made in my life, let me tell you.

How much do you have to like a type of novel in order to have a chance of success at it yourself? Well, let's suppose you sit down one weekend with a stack of gothics or male adventure novels or light romances or whatever. If you have to flail yourself with a whip or whip yourself with a flail in order to get them read, fighting a constant urge to hurl the books across the room, and if your ultimate response is something along the lines of "This stuff is garbage and I hate it," I think you might want to look a little further.

On the other hand, if you find the stories reasonably riveting even though you never lose sight of the fact that you're not reading *War and Peace,* and if your final reaction is more in the vein of "This stuff's garbage, all right, but it's not *bad* garbage, and while I might not want word to get around, I've got to admit that I sort of like it," then perhaps you've found a place to start.

There are other questions to ask yourself. Here's one—how essential is it for you to be rewarded for your work? And what sort of reward's most important? Money? Recognition? Or simply seeing your work in print? While the three are by no means mutually exclusive, and while the great majority of us want them all—in large portions, thank you—each of us is likely to find one of the three of maximum importance.

When I was fifteen or sixteen years old, and secure in the knowledge that I'd been placed on this planet to be a writer, it didn't even occur to me to wonder what sort of thing I would write. I was at the time furiously busy reading my way through the great novels of the century, the works of Steinbeck and Hemingway and Wolfe and Dos Passos and Fitzgerald and all their friends and relations, and it was ever so clear to me that I would in due course produce a Great Novel of my own.

I'd go to college first, naturally, where I might get a somewhat clearer notion of just what constituted a Great Novel. Then I'd emerge into the real world where I would Live. (I wasn't quite certain what all this capital-L Living entailed, but I figured there would be a touch of squalor in there somewhere, along with generous dollops of booze and sex.) All of this Living would ultimately distill itself into the Meaningful Experiences out of which I would eventually produce any number of Worthwhile Books.

Now there's nothing necessarily wrong with this approach. Any number of important novels are produced in this approximate fashion, and the method has the added advantage that, should you wind up writing nothing at all, you'll at least have treated yourself to plenty of booze and sex en route.

In my own case, though, I learned quickly that my self-image as a writer was stronger than my self-image as a potential great novelist. I didn't really care all that deeply about artistic achievement, nor did I aspire to wealth beyond the dreams of avarice. I wanted to write something and see it in print. I don't know that that's the noblest of motives for doing anything, but it was at the very core of my being.

Let's suppose, for a moment, that you regard yourself as similarly motivated. While you'd certainly like to write something in which you can take great personal pride, something that might win you a measure of critical recognition, something that might lead stockbrokers and accountants to vie for your custom, your primary purpose as a writer is to get something published.

If that's the case, you would probably be best advised to find a place for yourself in the field of category fiction, a term which covers the broad group of novels—generally paperback originals—which lend themselves readily to categorization as mysteries, adventure, romance, gothic, science fiction, historical saga, western, or whatever. These categories change slightly over the years, too; they go hot and cold, with one year's hot ticket next year's drug on the market.

Every once in a while a novel achieves overwhelming success, to the point where its imitators quickly come to constitute a brand-new category. Kyle Onstott's *Mandingo* went through printing after printing before other writers began to work the same vein; in due course the slave novel defined itself as a staple category of paperback fiction. Similarly, but far more rapidly, the first two steamy historical romances—Kathleen Woodiwiss's *The Flame and the Flower* and Rosemary Rogers' *Sweet Savage Love*—rolled up impressive instant sales and sparked a new category overnight.

Some writers move with no apparent effort from one category to another over the years, furnishing a steady supply of whatever the market demands. When gothics are hot they write gothics; when a publisher calls with a demand for war stories or romantic intrigue, they shift gears and maintain full production. Typically, these jacks-of-all-trades meet minimal standards in every genre they take up without really distinguishing themselves in any one area. They are always competent but never inspired.

Which, come to think of it, is not terribly surprising. Professional competence is too rare a jewel to be dismissed summarily as hack work. Nevertheless, the writer who can do every type of novel with equal facility is a writer who has not managed to zero in on a type of novel that is uniquely his own. While you may prove to be this variety of writer, and while you may be happiest covering a wide range of fictional categories, I think you would do well first to determine if there's a particular kind of novel that appeals to you more than the others.

We've established that the novel you set out to write ought to be of a type you would not find yourself unable to read had someone else written it. The converse of this argument is not necessarily true. Just because you can enjoy reading a particular sort of novel doesn't mean you'd be well advised to try writing it.

Take me, for example; there was a time when I read a great deal of science fiction. I liked most S-F stories, and I liked the good ones a lot. Furthermore, I used to hang out with several established science fiction writers. I found them a congenial bunch, fellows of infinite jest and an engagingly quirky turn of mind. I liked the way they grabbed hold of ideas and turned them into stories.

But I couldn't write science fiction. No matter how much of the stuff I read, no matter how much I enjoyed what I read, my mind simply did not yield up workable S-F ideas. I might read those stories with a fan's intense enjoyment, but what I couldn't do was get the sort of handle on what I read that left me saying to myself, "*I* could have written that. I could have come up with that idea, and I could have developed it along those lines. I might even have improved it by doing thus and so. By gum, I could have been the writer of that story."

I've enjoyed a good many historical novels over the years, and I've been deeply interested in history for as long as I can remember. There was a period of several years during which a fair percentage of my leisure-time reading consisted of works of English and Irish history. One might think

I'd do well to combine business and pleasure and turn my sights on the historical novel, trying my hand at a novel the theme and background of which might suggest itself from my reading.

I wouldn't dream of it. One of the innumerable unpleasant facts I have to face about myself is that I'm a sluggard when it comes to research. I don't enjoy it and I don't do a very good job of it. I force myself when I have to, and I've become better about this in recent years, less given to slipshod fakery, but the idea of deliberately setting out to write a book which requires a vast amount of academic research is anathema to me.

Beyond that, I'm not comfortable with the idea of writing something set in a time other than my own. I wasn't around then, so how could I presume to know how people talked? How could I expect to get their dialogue right, or to have the faintest idea what it felt like to be around in eighteenth-century Ireland, say, or Renaissance Italy? The fact that no one else knows how people talked or felt back then does nothing to put my mind at rest. I have to be able to believe in the fictive reality of what I'm doing in order to make it work.

This is not to say that I'm comfortable only when I write out of my own experience. I probably know as much about eighteenth-century Ireland as I do about contemporary Yugoslavia, yet I've blithely set several books in that country without doing more than cursory research. I've never killed anyone—yet—but I've written a great deal about murderers. I wrote a book from the point of view of a professional burglar and found the voice so natural that the book became the first of a series. I've written several books from a woman's point of view. It's a matter of identification, I suppose, of one's ability to project oneself into certain environments and situations and not into others.

More simply, it's a matter of identifying with an author. One of the things that makes fiction work is one's identification with the characters. And one of the things that makes it writable, if you will, is identification with the person who wrote it.

I can remember the first time I felt it. It was the summer after my first year at college. I picked up a paperback anthology of short stories entitled

The Jungle Kids. The author was Evan Hunter, who had recently made a name for himself with *The Blackboard Jungle*—hence the book's title, not to mention the fact of its publication. The dozen or so stories in the book all dealt with juvenile delinquents and virtually all of them had been originally published in *Manhunt*. I identified, not so much with the characters in these stories, but with Evan Hunter himself.

I was genuinely excited when I reached the end of the book. Here was someone writing and publishing well-written stories that I could respect and enjoy—and, most important, I could see myself doing what he had done. I felt it was within my abilities, and I felt plots and characters of this sort could engage and stimulate my creative imagination. And I also felt that the whole thing was eminently worth doing.

I ultimately did make my first short story sale to *Manhunt*, but that's another story. More to the point, my first novel grew directly out of a similar case of identification with the author.

I had at the time been writing and publishing crime stories for a year and felt it was time to write a novel. A senior colleague at the literary agency where I was working had suggested I try a light romance of the type Avalon was then publishing; because the rate of payment was awful, this was an easy market for the beginner to hit. I read one, and it was confessions all over again. I couldn't get through the thing and knew I'd be incapable of coming up with an idea for one, let alone writing it.

What I really wanted to do was a detective novel. I'd read hundreds, liked the form very much, and made a couple of stabs at knocking out one of my own. But for one reason or another I couldn't get a handle on a suspense novel.

During this time I had read perhaps a dozen lesbian novels. The sensitive novel of female homosexuality constituted a small but quite popular category in the '50s. I probably read the books as much for information and titillation as anything else. I wasn't personally acquainted with any lesbians at the time, nor did my knowledge of their lives go beyond what I read in those novels or witnessed on Bleecker Street in Greenwich Village.

For whatever reason, I did find the books compulsively readable, and one day I finished one and realized that I could have written it myself. Or one quite like it. Possibly, by Georgia, one a shade *better* than what I'd just read.

In the name of research, I promptly read every lesbian novel I could get my hands on. Elements of a novel of my own began percolating in my mind—fragments of a character, a scene, a setting. Then one morning I awakened with the plot ready to happen, and I sat down and typed up a two or three page outline. After a gestation period of perhaps another month I sat down and wrote the thing in two weeks flat.

It sold first time out to Fawcett, then the leading market for that sort of book, and I was a published novelist just like that. I was not an overnight success, nor did I find an immediate identity for myself as a writer of lesbian novels; curiously enough, it was years before I wrote another. But I learned a tremendous amount writing the book, as one does writing any first novel, and it was that jolting realization of I-could-do-this that got me going.

This sort of identification with the writer, this recognition of one's own capacity to write a certain type of book, is not limited to category fiction. Whatever makes you want to become a novelist, whatever sort of novelist you want to become, the process I've described is a basic starting point for finding your own first novel.

If you've decided that money is the spur that goads you and that you want to reach for the brass ring right away rather than work your way up to it, you would do well to have a broad acquaintance with the sorts of books that have made their authors rich. By regularly reading best-selling novels, and especially by concentrating on the works of those authors who consistently hit the bestseller list, you'll develop a sense of the sorts of books which tend to earn big money.

Some books make the bestseller lists by happy accident. Perhaps they are category novels which have acquired a greater than usual readership because of increasingly widespread recognition of the author's particular excellences. John D. MacDonald and Ross Macdonald are two cases in point; both continue to write the excellent hard-boiled suspense novels they've been writing for years, but their audience has swelled to the point where the books they write are bestsellers.

Other books on the list are novels of considerable literary merit which have enough breadth of appeal to make them bestsellers. E. L. Doctorow's *Ragtime* is a good example of this phenomenon, as are *The World According to Garp,* by John Irving, and *Final Payments,* by Mary Gordon. Similarly, a few highly esteemed authors hit the bestseller list routinely, not because of the type of books they write but because of the prominence they have achieved and the size of their personal following among readers. John Updike's an example. So are Gore Vidal and John Cheever.

The remainder of the bestseller list is chiefly composed of books with certain qualities common to bestsellers—and here we find ourselves on marshy terrain indeed, because I don't feel it's proper to think in terms of a bestseller class or category. Certainly there's no magic formula, and certainly these books differ enormously from one another. By familiarizing yourself with best-selling fiction, you'll get a sense of what qualities they have in common.

Perhaps more important, you'll find that you like bestsellers of one sort while disliking others. And, somewhere along the line, you'll find one or more best-selling novels that spark that identification with the author we've talked about. You'll realize you could have written a particular book, or one a good deal like it. When this happens, you will have found a direction for your writing which holds the promise of the rewards you seek while remaining compatible with your own literary inclinations.

That last point is worth a digression.

A great many people seem to believe that all it takes for a talented writer to produce a best-selling novel is a sound idea and the will to carry it out.

Writers frequently make the mistake of believing this themselves, and the results can be markedly unsuccessful.

The writers who consistently produce best-selling fiction are not writing down to their audience. They are not making deliberate compromises between the books they'd like to write and what the public wants. On the contrary, they are turning out precisely the books they were born to write, working at the top of their form, and while they may wistfully wish they were geared to write the kind of thing that wins awards and sparks doctoral theses, just as Norman Rockwell occasionally expressed regret that he didn't paint like Picasso, they have become successes by being themselves.

Bestsellers are occasionally written cynically. William Faulkner batted out *Sanctuary* with the intention of producing a potboiler that would make him rich; he remained an artist in spite of himself, and while *Sanctuary* did sell impressively it remained quintessential Faulkner. On the other hand, it's probably safe to assume that John Updike wrote *Couples* out of comparable cupidity. *Couples* did sell very well, but it's hardly vintage Updike, and the author's own detachment from it is evident throughout.

I've known several writers of category fiction who have tried to break through into the world of bestsellerdom, a natural ambition in a world where success is largely measured in dollars and cents. Some writers manage this rather neatly; they'd written category fiction as an apprenticeship, or their development carried them to a point where they are comfortable working on a broader canvas—for one reason or another, their books work. Others of us have found ourselves trying to be something we're not in order to attain a goal to which we unwisely aspire. The result, more often than not, is a book which is satisfying to neither its authors nor its readers, a financial and artistic failure. The Peter Principle seems to apply; we extend our literary horizons until we reach our level of incompetence.

I'm sorry to say that I know whereof I speak, and the knowledge was not gained painlessly. What I have learned to my cost is that I do my best work when all I am trying to do is my best work. And it is when I do this that I incidentally achieve the most critical and financial success in the bargain.

There's a moral there somewhere, and I have a hunch it shouldn't be too hard to spot.

Suppose I don't want to write category fiction? I want to write a serious mainstream novel. But I don't know what I want to write about. I don't have a setting or a plot or a character. I just know that I want to write a serious novel. How do I get started?

Maybe you're not ready yet.

Give yourself time. Read the sorts of novels you enjoy and admire, and try to spot those which afford a measure of the author-identification we've discussed. You may not want to write books which specifically resemble what you've read, but this identification process, this reading from the writer's point of view, may help your subconscious mind to begin formulating ideas for your own book.

Sooner or later, you'll begin to get ideas—out of your own background and experience, out of your imagination, out of some well of story material within yourself. This process will happen when the time is right. Until it does, there's not very much you can do.

• • •

Many years ago I heard a fellow offer this advice at a pool table: "Always take the easy shots. Leave the hard shots for the boys with rich fathers."

While this is rather less a core principle in commercial fiction than in the world of pocket billiards, the same logic applies. It's categorically easier to sell some books than others, not necessarily because it's any easier to write a good book in a particular category than another, but because a book in one genre need not be as good in order to make the grade.

Publishing follows trends, often to its own eventual detriment. When John LeCarre and Ian Fleming began to have enormous commercial success, publishers began actively seeking out other espionage fiction. The wave of reader enthusiasm was real, and other writers—Len Deighton, Adam Hall, among others—produced good books in the field, found a receptive market among publishers and readers, and had genuine success.

Then writers with less of a true penchant for the genre began writing books of their own because the market was so hungry for more, and a lot of inferior work was published even as readers who'd flocked to the field because it was trendy began to tire of it. For months it had been the easiest thing in the world to sell a spy novel, and almost overnight it became impossible. (And the core readers who'd always enjoyed the genre, after having been briefly inundated with books, were suddenly unable to find anything to read.)

Clearly, there are times when a particular book is easier or harder to sell. I wouldn't advise you to pick the latest trend and hop on board; odds are that, by the time you've finished your book, your chosen genre will be yesterday's news, and your book harder to place for being categorically out of favor.

Still, it does make a certain amount of sense to take aim at a soft target. Year in and year out, certain types of fiction are easier to sell than others, and those categories constitute natural points of entry for new writers. Fifty years ago the soft-core sex novels—we've learned nowadays to label them Midcentury Erotica—was a valuable entry-level market.

Later on, we'll examine the options afforded by self-publishing, and we'll see that it's no longer necessary to produce a book someone will want to publish, that a book can find an appreciative audience of readers whether or not it strikes a spark with a commercial publisher. But for now let's assume you want someone to publish a book, and to do so after having written you a check for an advance against royalties.

You have to write what it's in you to write; I'll say that again, although it probably ought to go without saying. Judicious sampling of the books you find on the shelves of bookstores, brick-and-mortar or online, can help you find a kind of book that you'll enjoy writing and someone will be eager to publish.

CHAPTER 3

Read...Study...Analyze

Let's suppose that you've managed to zoom in on a type of novel you think might make for comfortable writing. You don't know that you're ready to embark on a lifelong career as a writer of sweet savage romances, say, or shoot-'em-up westerns, but you feel it might be worthwhile to take a shot at writing one of them. You've found something you enjoy reading and it's also something you can see yourself writing. The talent you perceive yourself having seems likely to lend itself to this particular sort of book.

Now what do you do?

Well, it's possible you're ready to sit down and go to work at the typewriter. Maybe you've already got your book firmly in mind, plot and characters and all. If that's the case, by all means sit down and start hitting the keys. The book may or may not work, depending on the extent of your readiness, but in any event you'll learn a great deal from the experience.

It's very likely, though, that you'd do well to take another step before plunging in. This step consists of subjecting your chosen field to a detailed analysis by reading extensively and submerging yourself in what you read. The analytical process is such that you wind up with both an ingrained gut-level understanding of what constitutes a successful novel of your chosen type and a mind trained to conceive, produce and develop the ideas for such a novel.

I can't think of a better name for this process than *"market analysis,"* yet something in me recoils at the term. It's too clinical, for one thing, and it seems to imply that writing a salable novel lends itself to the Harvard Business School case-study approach. We're talking about *writing,* for Pete's sake. We're dealing with creativity. We're artists, aren't we? Market analysis is something they do in Wall Street offices, not Greenwich Village garrets.

Besides, the process I'm talking about is oriented more to the work than to the market. What we study here is the individual novel, and our concern is in discovering what makes it work, not what has induced some particular editor to publish it or some group of readers to buy it.

Okay. Whatever you call it, I want to do it. What do I do first?

Good question.

As I said, what you do is you read.

When you picked a type of book to write, one of the criteria was that it was one you were capable of reading with a certain degree of pleasure. This had better be the case, because you're going to have to do some intensive reading. Fortunately, the odds are that reading is a habit for you from the start. That's true for most people who want to write, and it's especially true for most of those who wind up successful at it. Some of us find ourselves reading less fiction as time passes, and many of us are inclined to avoid reading other people's novels while writing our own, but I rarely encounter a writer who's not a pretty enthusiastic reader by nature.

So there's a fair chance that you've been reading books in your chosen field for some time now, beginning long before you selected this field for your own novelistic endeavors. I'd had this sort of prior experience with suspense novels, for example, before I seriously attempted one of my own. On the other hand, I had not read widely in the soft-core sex novel field when the opportunity arose for me to write one. Few people had; the genre was just beginning to emerge.

Makes no difference. Either way, you have fresh reading to do. You have to read not as a normally perceptive reader, but with the special insight of a writer.

My first venture into this sort of reading came when I first began writing stories for the crime fiction magazines, but the process is pretty much the same for both short stories and novels. What I did, having made my first short story sale to *Manhunt,* was study that magazine and every other crime fiction magazine far more intensively than I have ever studied anything before or since. I bought every magazine in the field the instant it appeared on the stands. In addition, I made regular visits to back-magazine shops, where I picked up every back issue of the leading magazines that I could find. I carried check lists of these publications in my wallet to avoid buying the same issue twice, and I carted the magazines home and arranged them in orderly fashion on my shelves. At night when I got home from the office I read magazine after magazine, going through every last one of them from cover to cover.

Understand, please, that I did not learn any formulae. I don't know that such things exist. What I did learn, in a manner I cannot entirely explain, is a sense of the possible variations that could be worked upon the crime story, a sense of what worked and what didn't.

Does this mean I have to read hundreds and hundreds of novels? I'll be spending eternity in the library.

You won't have to read as many novels as I read short stories. You'll probably read hundreds of them over the years—I think it's vital to continue reading in one's field, even after one's established oneself as a writer in that field. Remember, though, a distinction we observed earlier between the short story and the novel. The short-story writer has to come up with a constant supply of ideas. The novelist, on the other hand, deals with a smaller number of ideas but must be far more concerned with their extensive development.

So you won't have to read so many novels. Eight or ten or a dozen should give you a sufficient reading background for your own first attempt. But you'll have to read them far more exhaustively than the beginning short-story writer has to read examples in his field. It's not enough simply to read these books. You'll have to take them apart and see what makes them work.

How do you go about that?

Well, let's say you've decided to take aim at the gothic novel. Chances are you've read more than a few of them in reaching this decision, but maybe not; perhaps you read one and knew in a flash it was your kind of thing. Whatever the case, you'll want to have half a dozen books on hand in order to launch this project of analyzing the gothic novel. You may elect to use your favorites among the books you've already read or make a trip to the newsstand for some new material. I'd suggest that you pick books by six different writers, choosing a mixture of established names in the field and neophytes, but that's not necessary. I've heard tell of a writer, for example, who sat down and pored over the gothic novels of Dorothy Daniels as if they were holy writ. Then he turned out a book that was described by the editor who bought it as an absolutely perfect example of second-rate Dorothy Daniels. Second-rate Dorothy Daniels is still good enough to sell, and sell it did.

I wouldn't recommend so limited an approach. While it may not be the worst way in the world to break into print, it can't do much to bring out the writer within oneself. What we're trying to achieve by this market analysis is not slavish imitation but synthesis. By digesting a genre and absorbing its parameters into one's system, one prepares oneself to write one's own books within the particular confines of that genre.

That's theoretical. Let's get down to practical matters. Having bought a half-dozen suitable gothics, what do I do?

Read them, for openers. Read them one after the other, without reading anything else in between. And don't rush this reading process. Forget any speedreading courses you may have taken. If you've gotten in the habit of skimming, break it. Slow yourself down. You want to find out more than what happens and who's the bad guy and whether or not the girl gets to keep the house at the end. You want to find out what the author's doing and how he's doing it, and you can only manage that feat by spending plenty of time with the book.

Reading slowly and deliberately is something that's come on me over the years, and I can relate it directly to my own development as a writer. Before I got into this business, and during my early years in it, I raced through books. The more I have come to read *like a writer,* the more deliberate the pace of my reading.

Once you've read all of the books at a thoughtful pace, it's time to take them apart and see how they work. First, try summing up each book in a couple of sentences, like so:

> *A young widow is hired to catalogue the antique furniture in a house on the moors in Devon. The chauffeur-handyman tries to warn her off and she knows he's up to something. She's drawn to the son and heir, whose wife is coughing her lungs out in an attic bedchamber. Turns out the son has been selling off the good furniture, replacing it with reproductions and junk, and slowly poisoning his wife. He tries to kill our heroine when she uncovers the truth but she's saved by the handyman, who's actually the disguised second son of the Earl of Dorset, and . . . .*

Well, you get the idea. I don't write gothics myself, and I see no reason why I should squander my creativity plotting this one just as an example of what a summary is. Boil each of the six novels into a paragraph. The length doesn't matter terribly much. No one else is going to read these things. The object is to reduce the sprawl of a novel to something you can grasp in a hundred words or so.

This method is useful in analyzing short fiction, too. A short-story writer would do well to write out brief summaries of dozens of short stories, paring away the writer's facility with prose and dialogue and characterization and reducing each story to its basic plot. The novelist-to-be works with a smaller number of examples and winds up studying them rather more intensively.

By this I don't mean you have to examine the plot summaries you've prepared like a paleontologist studying old dinosaur bones. Instead, you'll return to the books you've summarized and go through them again, this time outlining them chapter by chapter. For each chapter you'll write down what happens in a couple of sentences. To return to our mythical gothic, we might see something like this:

> *Chapter One—Ellen arrives at Greystokes. Liam meets her at the train and tells her the legend of the ghost in the potting shed. She*

is interviewed by Mrs. Hallburton who explains her duties and shows her to her room. She lies down on her bed and hears a woman coughing and sobbing on the floor above.

Chapter Two—Flashback. The cough triggers her recollection of her husband's death. She remembers their meeting, tender moments in their courtship, the discovery of his illness, and his final days. She recalls her determination to resume her life and the circumstances that brought her to Greystokes.

Chapter Three—Dinner the first night. She meets Tirrell Hallburton, whose wife is coughing in the room above her own. After dinner she goes to the attic to look in on Glacia, the invalid. Glacia tells her that Death is on his way to Greystokes. "Someone will die soon—take care it isn't you!" Ellen leaves, certain Glacia has a premonition of her own death....

Maybe I ought to write this thing after all. It's beginning to come to life for me in spite of myself.

I think you see how the process works. The outline may be as sketchy or as comprehensive as you want it to be—and the same rules will apply when you prepare an outline for your own novel. Because these outlines, like the outline you create for your own book, are designed to be tools. You'll use them to get a grasp on what a novel is.

Although they're often easier to write than short stories, for reasons we've already discussed at sufficient length, novels are often harder to get a grip on. So much more goes on in them that it's difficult to see their structure. Just as our summaries served to give us a clear picture of what these several novels are *about,* so will our outlines show us their structure, their component parts. Stripped to outline form, the novel is like a forest in winter; with their branches bare, the individual trees become visible where once the eye saw nothing but a mass of green.

To repeat, your outlines may be as detailed as you wish. I would suggest that you make them as complete as possible in terms of including a scene-by-scene report of what is actually taking place. There's no need in this sort of outline for explanation—why the characters do what they do, or how they feel about it—so much as there's a need to put down everything that goes on, every scene that exists as a part of the whole.

In this fashion, you'll develop a sense of the novel as a collection of scenes. God knows it's not necessary to do this in order to write a novel, or even to understand how novels are constructed, but I think it helps.

It helps in an even more obvious fashion when you set out to outline your own novel. We'll discuss this point at greater length in Chapter Six; meanwhile, suffice it to say that the best way to prepare yourself to outline your own book is by outlining someone else's book first.

Question—with all this reading and analyzing and outlining, all this mechanical swill, aren't we stifling creativity? I have a feeling I'll be trying to duplicate what's been written rather than write my own novel.

That's not how it works. But it's easy to understand the anxiety. I've heard hopeful young writers explain earnestly that they want to avoid reading fiction altogether in order to keep from being influenced by what's already been done. They use phrases like "natural creativity" a lot. What happens, more often than not, is that such writers unwittingly produce trite stories because they haven't read widely enough to know what's been done to death already. An isolated tribesman who spontaneously invents the bicycle in 1982 may be displaying enormous natural creativity, but one wouldn't expect the world to beat a path to his door.

The outlining process I've discussed doesn't stifle creativity. At least it shouldn't. I suppose a person could copy a character here and a plot line there and a setting from somewhere else, jumbling things up and putting together a novel from the chopped-up corpses of the novels he's read. But that's certainly not what we're trying to do, and it's not the best way to write something that will be commercially and artistically successful. Our object is to learn how to cast our own stories within the framework of a particular kind of novel, to stimulate our unconscious to produce plot and character ideas which lend themselves to this chosen type of novel so that it will be natural for our minds to think in these terms.

The best defense I can offer is the following exchange which appeared in an interview in the *New York Times Book Review* for December 24, 1978. The interviewer is Steve Oney; the writer interviewed is Harry Crews, the highly regarded author of *A Feast of Snakes* and several other novels noted for their imagination, originality, and technical proficiency:

> *Q. For someone who had been exposed to very little literature, how did you actually learn how to write?*
>
> *A. I guess I really learned, seriously learned, how to write just after I got out of college when I pretty much literally ate Graham Greene's "The End of the Affair." My wife and I were living in a little trailer . . . in Jacksonville, Fla., where I was teaching seventh grade . . . I wrote a novel that year, and here's how I did it. I took "The End of the Affair," and I pretty much reduced the thing to numbers. I found out how many characters were in it, how much time was in it—and that's hard to do as there is not only present time in a book but past time as well. I found out how many cities were in the book, how many rooms, where the climaxes were and how long it took Greene to get to them.*
>
> *And there were a lot of other things I reduced to numbers. I read that book until it was dog-eared and was coming apart in my hands. And then I said, "I'm going to write me a damn novel and do everything he did." I knew I was going to waste—but it wasn't a waste—a year of my time. And I knew that the end result was going to be a mechanical, unreadable novel. But I was trying to find out how in the hell you did it. So I wrote the novel, and it had to have this many rooms, this many transitions, etc. It was the bad novel I knew it would be. But by doing it I learned more about writing fiction and writing a novel and about the importance of time and place—Greene is a freak about time and place—than I*

> had from any class or anything I'd done before. I really, literally, ate that book. And that's how I learned to write.

I have no trouble believing the method Crews describes was every bit as instructive as he says it was. I don't know that I would care to write a book in this fashion, or that I would be able to discipline myself sufficiently to complete a book I knew would be unsalable by definition, but I would surely imagine that the educational potential of the process is considerable. Even without going so far as to write an imitative novel of one's own, a writer could greatly increase his understanding of what novels are and how they work by following the first stages of Crews' system—i.e., by taking an admired novel apart, reducing it to numbers, and learning how the author handles such matters as time and place and action and pace and so forth.

Getting back to the question a couple of pages back, it's evident that Crews' approach did stifle creativity in the particular novel he describes. His purpose was not creative development but technical progress—he wanted to learn what made a novel tick so he took one apart to find out, then tried putting it back together again. But you'll be studying not one but half a dozen books, books which may have the common features of their genre but which differ considerably each from the other. The book you write will in turn differ from each of them while presumably retaining those elements which make them a satisfying experience for the people who read them. That's not a matter of stifling creativity but one of finding the right frame for it and lighting it properly.

> *This outlining sounds like a WPA project. I can see doing some extensive reading, sort of soaking up the market that way, but I hate the idea of purposeless work. Is it absolutely essential to do this?*

Of course not.

I think outlining other people's novels as I've described it is as effective and expedient a way as I know to learn what a particular sort of novel is and how it works. But it's not the only way, and it's certainly no prerequisite for writing your own novel. If you find it tedious to such an extent that it seems counter-productive, by all means give it up.

You don't even have to read widely in your chosen field, as far as that goes. The only thing you absolutely *have* to do to produce a novel is sit down and write the thing. Some people profit greatly by such preparatory work as I've described. Others get along just fine without it.

I wouldn't be so sure, though, that outlining is purposeless work, or a waste of time. On the contrary, I'd be inclined to guess it saves time for most of the people who do it—time spent repairing mistakes and reworking false starts that might not have occurred had they laid the groundwork properly before starting their own novels.

But pick the approach that feels right for you as a writer. That, ultimately, is the most important thing you can do.

• • •

The intervening years haven't made me eager to amend this chapter much. Reading remains the best way I know of to internalize a sense of how fiction works, and if I were to change *gothic novel* to *time-travel zombie romance*, the foregoing would be entirely up to date.

Still, it might not be out of place to contrast the analysis I did of lesbian fiction prior to writing *Strange are the Ways of Love* (by Lesley Evans) with my more cursory analysis of Midcentury Erotica that led to *Carla* (by Sheldon Lord).

Strange are the Ways of Love was my very first novel, and I've described how, having read every lesbian novel I could find—along with Marijane Meaker's nonfiction books on the subject, written as Ann Aldrich—I woke up one morning and wrote out a chapter-by-chapter outline for my book, having apparently snatched the plot and characters out of thin air. A couple of weeks later I found time to work on the book, and managed to complete it in short order. I sent it to my agent, he sent it to an editor at the Crest Books division of Fawcett Publications, the ideal market for lesbian fiction and the publisher of Ann Bannon and Marijane Meaker. (In recent years I've become acquainted with both of these splendid women, and was not half chuffed when Ann referred to the three of us as "the last of the classic lesbian novelists.")

Carla was a different matter. While *Strange are the Ways of Love* was on an editor's desk at Crest, my agent dropped me a note. "I hope you know what a sex novel is," he said, "and how to write one." He explained that a fellow named Harry Shorten, late of Archie Comics, was starting a new firm called Midwood Tower Books, and that the erotic novels published by Beacon Books were the nearest thing to a template.

I went out and bought a couple of books by Orrie Hitt, who wrote regularly for Beacon, but I didn't have to read clear through them to realize that I knew what to do and how to do it. I wrote three chapters and a rudimentary outline, sent them to my agent, and continued writing the book while Shorten approved what I'd submitted and put through a contract.

Ten months later I'd written five or six books for Midwood and completed revisions of *Strange* for Crest. Midwood had proved so successful that another publisher—William Hamling with Nightstand Books—rushed into the field, and one of the first things he did was commission me to write a book a month for him. Sheldon Lord went on writing for Midwood—and, eventually, for Beacon as well. Andrew Shaw wrote for Nightstand. I cashed the checks.

I was in the right place at the right time, and had been yanked into an emerging market to which I was admirably suited. In a year's time I'd become a self-supporting professional novelist, and I've been one ever since.

And what research did I do in order to become Sheldon Lord and Andrew Shaw? Precious little, as you can see, having read only enough of Orrie Hitt's books to assure myself that I could do at least as well from a standing start. So how important is it to do all that reading and market analysis?

You know, there's another way to look at it. If I hadn't read all of those lesbian novels, I couldn't have written *Strange are the Ways of Love*; by internalizing their contents I got a sense of what did and didn't work, and that spawned the plot and characters that constituted the book. And, if I hadn't impressed my agent with Strange, do you suppose he'd have lined me up to write a book for Harry Shorten? All he'd seen from me were short stories, and it wasn't until that first book landed on his desk that he had any reason to believe I could turn out a novel.

CHAPTER 4

DEVELOPING PLOT IDEAS

"Where do you get your ideas?" is one of the questions writers get asked all the time. What's galling about it, in addition to its banality, is the questioner's implicit assumption that coming up with a clever idea is all there really is to the business of being a writer. Turning that idea into a book—well, that's just a matter of typing, isn't it?

But of course not. Were that the case, I'd run books through my typewriter at seventy or eighty words per minute, not four or five agonizing pages per day.

While ideas are not the *sine qua non* in the novel that they often are in the short story, they are nevertheless essential.

A handful of writers can produce books that are not specifically *about* something and make them work. It scarcely matters what *Finnegan's Wake* is about, for example. For the rest of us, a strong central idea is basic to our novels. How we are to get these ideas, and how we can best develop them into strong plots, is something with which we might well concern ourselves.

It's my own conviction that we do not *get* our ideas. They are given to us, bubbling up out of our own subconscious minds as if from some dark and murky ferment. When the conditions are right, it is neither more nor less than the natural condition of things for a writer's imagination to produce those ideas which constitute the raw material of his fiction.

I don't know that I have much control over this process of generating ideas. This is not to say that I don't *want* to control the process, or even that I don't *try* to control it. But I've gradually come to see that I can't stimulate ideas by hitting myself in the forehead with a two-by-four.

This does not mean that there's nothing the writer can do to foster the development of novelistic ideas. Note, please, my argument that the process occurs of its own accord *when the conditions are right.*

My job, when I want ideas to bubble up, is to make sure the conditions are right. Then I can let go of the controls and pick ideas like plums when they come along.

That's a little hazy. Can't we get a bit more specific? How do I adjust the conditions?

We can get a whole lot more specific. And as far as adjusting the conditions is concerned, you've already been doing that. The reading and studying and analysis we talked about in the preceding chapter has as one of its functions the development of fictional ideas. By immersing ourselves in these books and turning them inside out, we come to know them on a gut level, so that our imaginations are encouraged to toy with the kinds of plot material which will be useful to us.

There are other things we can do as well. For instance:

Pay attention. The little atoms of fact and attitude which can link up into the molecules of an idea are all over the damn place. Each of us sees and hears and reads a dozen things a day that we could feed into the idea hopper—if we were paying attention.

Back in the early sixties I was reading one of the newsmagazines when I happened on an article on sleep. I learned no end of things, all of which I promptly forgot except for one delicious nugget of information—there seem to be a certain number of cases in medical literature of human beings who do not sleep at all. They get along somehow, leading lives of permanent insomnia, but otherwise not demonstrably the worse for wear.

Fortunately, I wasn't sleeping when I read that item. I rolled it around in my brain, filed it for cocktail-party conversation, and never dreamed

I'd wind up writing seven books about a character named Evan Tanner, a free-lance secret agent whose sleep center had been destroyed during the Korean War.

A few million people probably read that article without writing a book about an insomniac. Conversely, I've undoubtedly come up against a few million facts which might have sparked a character or a setting or a plot, but didn't. What made the difference, I think, is that I happened to find this particular fact oddly provocative. My unconscious mind was eager to play with it, to add it to the murky ferment we talked about earlier. That my mind ultimately made Tanner the particular character he is may well be attributable to the particular character *I* am—as we'll observe when we look at the process of character development more closely in another chapter. That the plot in which I put Tanner took the shape it did is attributable to two things. First, I'd schooled myself and/or had been inclined by nature to develop plots that lent themselves to suspense fiction. Second, another key principle operated, to wit:

Two and two makes five. Which is to say that synergy is very much at work in the process of plot development. The whole is ever so much greater than its parts. The writer, in possession of one fact or anecdote or notion or concept or whatever, is suddenly gifted with another apparently unrelated fact or anecdote or et cetera; almost reflexively, he takes one in each hand and turns them this way and that, playing with the purposefulness of a child, trying to see if they'll fit together.

Let's get back to Tanner. A full three years after that news magazine item, I spent an evening with Lincoln W. Higgie, a numismatic journalist just back from Turkey, where he'd spent a couple of years earning a very precarious living smuggling ancient coins and Roman glass out of the country. (If he'd been caught they'd have locked him away in prison. Now this was better than a decade before *Midnight Express* taught us how much fun a Turkish prison could be, but he didn't have to wait for the film to know he didn't want to go there.)

Among the stories on which he was dining out was one about a rumor he'd heard of a cache of gold coins secreted in the front stoop of a house in Balekisir, where the Armenian community had presumably hidden its wealth at the time of the Smyrna massacres. He and some associates actually located the house as described by a survivor, broke into the stoop in the dead of night, established that the gold had been there, but also established, alas, that someone had beat them to it by a couple of decades.

Now I hadn't consciously been giving my insomniac character room in the forefront of my mind, waiting for a plot to materialize for him. But I must have been carrying him around subconsciously, because shortly after my evening with the journalist I began a book about a young man, his sleep center destroyed by shrapnel, who goes to Turkey and finds that elusive Armenian gold.

Fawcett published that book as *The Thief Who Couldn't Sleep*. For my part, I decided to write more books about Tanner, and there was a point when I could barely pick up a newspaper without running across something that would turn into plot material. Tanner was a devotee of political lost causes and national irredentist movements, and it seemed as though every other story in the first section of the daily *New York Times* was grist for my mill. By perceiving news stories this way, picking them up and seeing what I could do with them, I was following yet another principle:

Remember what you're looking for. Here's an example that happened just a couple of weeks ago. I was with a group of people, and one woman complained about a problem she was having with her upstairs neighbor. He was evidently a drunk, and was given periodically to turning his radio on at top volume and then either leaving the apartment or passing out cold on the floor. Efforts to reach him invariably failed, and the radio blared all night, keeping the woman awake and doing very little for her peace of mind.

People suggested a variety of things—that she call the police, kick the door in, report him to the landlord, and so on. "Get a flashlight," I told her, "and go down to the basement and find the fuse box and remove the fuse for his apartment. Just turn him off altogether. Pull the plug on the clown."

I don't know if she did this. That's her problem, not mine. But after the conversation shifted, I was left to think about the basic problem and let my mind wander with it. That I'd thought of the fuse box ploy was not inconsistent with my choosing burglars and such types as viewpoint characters; I'm blessed or cursed, as you prefer, with that type of mind. I thought of that, and I thought that my burglar hero, Bernie Rhodenbarr, would certainly offer the same suggestion if a friend called him in the middle of the night with that particular problem.

And then, because I've learned not to walk away from thoughts along these lines, I asked myself what Bernie would do if, for some reason or other, his friend couldn't pull the fuse or get access to the fuse box. Some fuse boxes in New York apartments are located within the individual apartment, for instance. Suppose Bernie's sidekick Carolyn Kaiser called him because of this blaring radio, and suppose Bernie was obliging enough to trot over with his burglar's tools, and suppose he did what he does best, letting himself into the offending apartment just to turn off the radio, and suppose there was a dead body spread out on the living room rug, and suppose . . . .

I may or may not use it. But a few minutes of rumination had provided me with the opening for a novel. It's not a plot. It's not enough for me to sit down and start writing. I'm not ready to write another book about Bernie just now and won't be for six or eight months. By then, if I remember who I am and what I'm looking for, I'll very likely have picked up other stray facts and thoughts and bits and pieces, and I'll have played with them and tried fitting them together, and if two and two makes five I may have a book to write.

Stay awake. I heard very early on that a writer works twenty-four hours a day, that the mind is busy sifting notions and possibilities during every waking hour and, in a less demonstrable manner, while the writer sleeps as well. I liked the sound of this from the start—it was a nice rejoinder to my then wife if she said anything about my putting in only two hours a day at the typewriter, or skipping work altogether and going to the friendly neighborhood pool hall for the afternoon. But I'm not sure I believed it.

I believe it now, but with one qualification. I believe we *can* be on the job twenty-four hours a day. I believe we can also choose not to, and those of us who make this choice severely limit ourselves.

A great many writers use alcohol and drugs, ostensibly to stimulate their creativity. This very often seems to work in the beginning; the mind, jarred out of its usual channels by this unaccustomed chemical onslaught, may respond by blazing new trails for itself. Similarly, some artists early in their careers find hangovers a creative if hardly comfortable time. The process of withdrawal from the drug evidently has a stimulating effect.

Eventually, these same writers commonly use alcohol and drugs to unwind, to turn off the spinning brain after the day's work is finished. The process is not true relaxation, of course, but anesthesia. One systematically shuts off the thinking and feeling apparatus for the night. For those who ultimately become drug- or alcohol-dependent—and a disheartening proportion of the members of our profession wind up in this category—the results are devastating. One reaches a stage wherein work is impossible without the drug or the drink, and this stage is in turn succeeded by one in which work is impossible with or without the substance. Alcoholism and drug dependency have ended too many successful careers prematurely, while they've nipped no end of promising careers in the bud.

It's hardly revolutionary to advise an alcoholic writer not to drink, anymore than it's a controversial stance to urge diabetics not to binge on deep-fried Mars bars. But I'd suggest further that heavy drinking or drug use is severely detrimental even to the writer who does *not* become alcoholic or drug-dependent, simply because it shuts off his mind.

For years I drank when my day's work was done, convinced that it helped me relax. One thing it indisputably did was take my mind off my work. This, to be sure, was one of the things I wanted it to do; I felt I ought to be able to leave the work behind when I left the typewriter.

But writing, and especially novel writing, just doesn't work that way. Writing the novel is an ongoing organic process, and we carry the book with us wherever we go. It's during the period between one day's work and the next that our minds play, both consciously and subconsciously, with the ideas that will enable us to perform creatively when we resume writing.

We may rest the mind during these times but we hurt ourselves creatively if we shut our minds off completely. Later on we'll talk about the value of daily writing. It's similarly related to the notion of keeping oneself present in one's book, day in and day out. Extended breaks in the writing interrupt this continuity, and so do those interruptions of consciousness or attentiveness or awareness caused by heavy drinking and drug use.

More recently, marijuana has been touted as a creative stimulant, presumably nonaddictive, harmless, etc. Its addictive properties and harmlessness aside, I have found that its potential for creative stimulation is largely illusory. The common marijuana experience consists of making marvelous seminal mental breakthroughs which, hard to grasp as the smoke itself, are gone the next morning. If only one could remember, if only one could hold onto those fantastic inspired insights . . . .

Well, one can. The story's been told of the fellow who kept paper and pencil at the ready, determined to write down his brilliant insights before they were lost. Somehow, though, he always drifted off before he wrote down the revelations that had come to him. Then finally he awoke one following morning, recollecting that he'd had a fantastic insight and that for once—finally!—he'd managed to write it down. He wasn't sure that it contained the absolute secret of the universe, but he knew it was dynamite.

He looked, and there on the bedside table was his pad of paper, and on it he had written, "This room smells funny."

Whether to smoke or drink or pop pills is an individual decision, as is the extent to which you may care to employ these substances. I would suggest, though, that if you do elect to drink or drug heavily, you do so between novels, not during them. And recognize that whatever excellence your work has is in spite of the substances that you're using, not because of them.

Stay hungry. Some time ago a friend of mine was on a television talk show with several other mystery writers, Mickey Spillane among them. After the program ended, Spillane announced that they'd neglected to talk about the most important topic. "We didn't say anything about money," he said.

He went on to explain that he'd spent several years on an offshore island in South Carolina, where he did nothing too much more taxing than swim and sunbathe and walk the beach for hours at a time. "Every once in a while it would come to me that it'd be fun to get started on a book," he said. "I thought I'd keep my mind in shape and I'd enjoy doing it. But I could never get a single idea for a story. I'd sit and sit, I'd walk for miles, but I couldn't get an idea.

"Then one day I got a call from my accountant to say that the money was starting to get low. Nothing serious, but I should start thinking about ways to bring in some dough. And boy, did I get ideas for books!"

Money makes the mare go. It's very often the spur for what we might prefer to think of as pure creativity. I don't believe for a moment that financial insecurity is essential to a writer's imagination. In my own case, really severe money problems have occasionally kept me from thinking of anything beyond the desperate nature of the situation, leading to a vicious circle verging on writer's block. Money doesn't have to be the spur or the genuinely rich members of our profession would not continue to write productively and well. A man like James Michener, who consistently gives away most of what he earns writing bestsellers, is certainly not driven by the desire for more cash.

But he's spurred on by something. There is a hunger at the root of all our creative work, whether it is for wealth or recognition or a sense of accomplishment or some tangible proof that we are not worthless human beings after all. To return to an earlier metaphor, we might call that hunger the yeast that starts that dark ferment working down in the unconscious.

If we can stay in touch with that hunger, the pot will keep bubbling—and ideas that engage us will continue rising to the surface.

• • •

I might add that the reception one's ideas receive has a good deal to do with the development of future ideas.

An example: my longtime friend and colleague, the late Donald E. Westlake, had a period in the mid-1960s when he kept getting ideas for short stories about relationships. (That his own relationships were in an uncertain state at the time may have had something to do with this, but never mind.) He wrote three or four stories, one right after the other, and he sent him to his agent, who admired them greatly and submitted them to markets like *Redbook* and *Cosmopolitan* and *Playboy* and the *Saturday Evening Post*. All of the editors who saw the stories professed admiration for them, but nobody liked any of them well enough to buy it, and the stories went unpublished.

And Don stopped having ideas. He didn't regret having written the stories, and he would have been perfectly happy to write more even with no guarantee of success, but the idea factory in his unconscious mind added things up and decided the hell with it. It was clear to Don that, if one or two of those stories had sold, he'd have had ideas for more. But they hadn't, and he didn't.

On the other hand, consider Walter Mosley. Shortly after the very successful 1990 publication of his first crime novel, *Devil in a Blue Dress*, Walter appeared on a panel at a mystery convention in Philadelphia. He announced that he probably didn't belong there, that this book was an anomaly, that it was actually highly unlikely that he'd write any more books within the confines of the genre.

This was certainly not a pose. He very clearly believed what he was saying. Since then, however, he's written and published a dozen more Easy Rawlins mysteries, three Fearless Jones mysteries, and five Leonid McGill mysteries—along with close to two dozen other books, most of them novels. While a cynic might simply contend that Walter has gone where the money is, I know the man too well to believe commercial considerations outweigh artistic ones for him.

The ongoing success of the Easy Rawlins books have made it almost inevitable that his unconscious would come up with a succession of ideas for additional books. They've been good ideas, engaging their author even as they've engaged an increasing audience of readers, and it would have been a great betrayal of self not to have gone on writing them.

• • •

When an idea does come along, make quite sure you don't forget it.

I would recommend carrying a notebook around as routinely as you carry your house key or wallet. Whenever an idea turns up, make a note of it. The simple act of writing down a few words will help to fix the idea in your mind so your subconscious can get hold of it.

Before you go to bed at night, make a point of glancing through the notebook. If you have the wrong attitude, this process can simply load you up with guilt over all the fiction ideas you've left undeveloped. Don't let this happen. Those scribbles and scraps in your notebook aren't things you *have* to do, and they're certainly not projects which must be undertaken right away. The notebook's a tool. It's there to make sure you don't lose sight of things that might turn out to be worth remembering; by referring to it frequently, you use it to give your memory a jog and stimulate the unconscious development of the idea over a period of time.

For some writers, a notebook comes close to being an end in itself. They approach the notebook as an art form, using it as a sort of creative journal and devoting an hour or so at the end of the day to ruminating therein. I've never been able to do this, perhaps because of a constitutional incapacity for sustained work at something without at least the possibility that what I'm doing will be publishable. Then too, it's my own feeling that the writer who puts too much energy into notebook entries is like the athlete who overtrains, like the boxer who leaves his fight in the gym.

That's just personal prejudice. Once again, writing is an utterly individual matter, and your notebook ought to be whatever you want it to be. Whatever works is what is right.

It's generally better, if rumination is your thing, to confine it to a notebook rather than to discuss your plot notion with friends. Sometimes this sort of discussion is useful, especially if the friends are writers themselves. When people in the business bat plot material around, the brainstorming process often results in clarifying and strengthening the ideas. All too often, though, talking about an idea winds up serving as an alternative to writing about it, especially if the people you talk to are not writers. I can lose enthusiasm for ideas if I talk them out at length. Perhaps the ideas I've gone stale on in this fashion are ideas that would have withered on the vine regardless, but my experience in this area has made me superstitious and secretive on the subject. I tend now to sit on my better ideas like a broody hen, letting them hatch as they will in their own good time.

• • •

All of the foregoing is perfectly valid, but it certainly makes it sound as though a notebook is an indispensable tool of mine, that I never leave home without it and jot things down in it all the time.

And it might not be a bad idea for me to do so. But the fact is that I don't, and except for brief periods of time I never have. I do what I can to welcome ideas, and I cherish them when they come along, but it's rare that I trouble to write them down. "If it's a good idea," I've been known to say, "then it'll stick around. If I forget it, then it couldn't have been all that valuable in the first place."

That sounds good, doesn't it? The only problem is I've no reason to believe it's true. My guess is that, of all the innumerable ideas that have flitted in and out of my mind, some of them might have been perfectly fine—but for the fact that I never thought of them again. Had I jotted them down where I might come across them again at an opportune moment, they might very well have led to something.

And, too, the simple act of writing them down would have put my mind on notice, and made it more likely I'd let the notion develop and flourish.

There are other processes designed to assist you in coming up with ideas. In *Write For Your Life* I explain an automatic-writing process I developed for the seminar of the same name; essentially it consists of writing nonstop for five or ten minutes, paying no attention to context or syntax, and as long as your pen is moving you're doing it right. Similarly, various forms of journal-keeping have won favor with a good many writers, and Julia Cameron has made a career out of teaching her particular approach. I would certainly encourage your investigation of these practices, while at the same time admitting that I've no interest in them for myself. It's not in my nature to write anything without being able to entertain the notion that I'm writing for eventual publication.

• • •

One thing that I've learned, occasionally to my chagrin, is that it's not enough for an idea to be a good one. It has to be a good one *for me*.

It's easy to fool oneself in this area. Just because I've thought of an idea for a novel, and just because it's the sort of idea that could be developed into a viable book, is no reason in and of itself for me to write that particular book. It may not be my type of book at all. But sometimes, overawed by the commercial potential of the project, I lose sight of this fact.

I recently had a painful lesson in this regard, and it was a long time coming. Some years ago I was reading something about Case Barbarossa, the Nazi invasion of Russia that was the beginning of the end for Hitler's Germany. I got an idea—specifically, that Hitler had been manipulated into attacking Russia by a British agent who had penetrated the Berlin government. I thought that was a neat premise to hang a novel on, and discussed it with my friend, novelist Brian Garfield, figuring it was the sort of book he could do a nice job with.

Brian was intrigued, but not quite captivated enough to do anything with the notion. Time passed, and the idea lingered in my subconscious, and two or three years later on a flight to Jamaica an idea struck me out of the blue, tying the original notion I'd dreamed up with Rudolf Hess's inexplicable flight to Scotland. A whole bunch of quirky historical elements would not fit themselves into the context of my little fiction, and the book which might result might just have the stuff of which best sellers are made.

There was only one problem. It still wasn't my kind of book. It wasn't really the kind of book I'd be terribly likely to read, let alone write. I might have recognized this, had I not had my judgment clouded by pure and simple greed. (Then too, I didn't have anything else to write, and there were no other ideas hanging fire that did much for me.)

I had a terrible time with the book, and the first draft of it, certainly, was at least as terrible as the time I had. The whole project may well turn out to be salvageable, and I may indeed wind up entering this particular book on the profit side of my ledger, but I hope I never lose sight of the fact that it was a mistake for me to write this book. If I've learned that, and if the lesson sticks, then I'll really have profited from the experience regardless of how it turns out financially.

For the beginner, a certain amount of experimentation in this regard is both inevitable and desirable. It takes a lot of writing to know with any degree of assurance what you are and are not capable of doing. Furthermore, at the start of a writing career any writing experience is valuable in and of itself. But as you grow to develop a surer sense of your individual strengths and weaknesses, you'll be better able to decide what ideas to develop, what ones to give away, and what ones to forget about altogether.

• • •

The book was *Code of Arms*, and when its editor sent me his notes, I realized the extent of my mistake, and was unwilling to waste any more time on it. My agent enlisted another writer, Harold King, to take over, and we shared a byline—and no royalties, because the book was a commercial failure. Whether it was an artistic disaster as well I'm not equipped to say. I think Hal did a creditable job with what was handed to him, but I decided writing it was bad enough, and I didn't have to read the damn thing.

• • •

Some ideas come from other people. I've had both good and bad experiences writing books based on the ideas of others. Years ago Donald E. Westlake got an idea for a suspense novel—a bride is raped on her wedding night and the bridal couple take direct revenge on the bad guys. He wrote an opening chapter, found it didn't seem to go anywhere, and he put it away and forgot about it.

A year or so after that I called him up and asked if he had any plans for the idea. When he said no, I requested permission to steal the notion—it had been percolating on a back burner of my mind ever since he first mentioned it to me. He graciously told me to go ahead, and *Deadly Honeymoon* became my first hardcover novel, a fair success in book form and ultimately the basis of a film, called *Nightmare Honeymoon* for reasons I wouldn't presume to guess.

Agents and publishers have come up with other ideas and given them to me. Sometimes I've written the books their ideas sparked, and sometimes they've turned out well.

On the other hand, I've had several experiences where ideas originated by other persons led me to books that proved ultimately unwritable, or books which gave me a great deal of trouble, or books which simply failed for one reason or another.

It can be quite difficult, for example, working from a publisher's idea. The temptation to do so can be considerable, since one is not working on speculation; the publisher, along with the idea, generally dangles a contract and an advance in front of one's eyes, and the more attractive the contract and the larger the advance, why, the better the idea is going to look. Thus you find yourself bound to an idea you might have dismissed out of hand if you'd thought it up all by yourself.

Sometimes—and I've had this experience—the publisher has only a vague idea of what he wants. In order to produce a book you'll be able to write effectively, you have to transform this idea and make it your own. If the publisher's got an open mind, that's no problem. Occasionally, however, he'll be struck by the discrepancy between what you've produced and the sublime if hazy vision with which he started. If the book's good enough in its own right you'll sell it somewhere sooner or later, but it doesn't make for the best feelings all around.

What it boils down to, then, is that you really have to be sure you like another person's idea before you use it. Remember, your own ideas bubble up from your own mind; when you work on them, that bubbling process will continue and the idea will develop. When you're working on another person's idea, you're adopting it. It has to be the sort you can love as if it were your own or you won't be able to bring your subconscious fully to bear upon it. It won't grow organically the way an idea must if it is to become a fully realized book.

How well developed does an idea have to be before you can start writing the book?

It depends.

The Thief Who Couldn't Sleep took a couple of years gestating until various plot components fitted themselves together. By the time I sat down to write the book, I had a very strong sense of the character of Tanner and a pretty good grasp of the book's plot. I didn't know everything else that was going to happen by any means, but I had the general outline of the book pretty clear in my mind.

With *Deadly Honeymoon,* I could fit the book's premise into one sentence, and that was as much of a handle as I had on the book when I sat down and wrote the first chapter. I think now that I might have written a better book if I'd known more about the various characters and had given the plot more thought before I started, but I was impatient to get on with it, and it's possible the book gained by the impatient enthusiasm that gripped its author.

One night Brian Garfield parked his car on the street in Manhattan and returned to it to find the convertible top slashed by some archfiend in human form who wanted to steal a coat from the back seat. Brian's first reaction was murderous rage. He realized he couldn't find the villain and kill him, but he could find some other villain and kill him, couldn't he? Because Brian is a writer rather than a homicidal maniac—although admittedly the two classes are not mutually exclusive—he decided to write a book about someone so motivated rather than act out his anger directly.

He might have begun work immediately upon a book about a vigilante who goes around killing people after someone slashes his convertible top—and that's not the worst premise for a book I've ever heard. But Brian gave the book plenty of time to take shape, let the character of accountant Paul Benjamin emerge from wherever our ideas grow, made the motivating experience the rape and beating of Benjamin's wife and daughter by a trio of hoodlums, with the wife dying and the daughter shocked into madness, and let the story grow from there. The result, *Death Wish,* was an artistic success as a novel and an enormous commercial triumph as a film.

Don Westlake, on the other hand, once wrote a first chapter in which a surly fellow walks across the George Washington Bridge into New York, snarling at motorists who offer him rides. Don didn't know where he was going with that one but found out as he went along. The result was the lengthy series of novels Don wrote under the pen name Richard Stark, all of them featuring Parker, a professional heist man and as unobliging a chap as he was the day he walked across the bridge.

As the years go by, which is something they do with increasing rapidity lately, I find myself giving ideas more rather than less time to take shape. I'm no longer so anxious to rush Chapter One through the typewriter if I have no idea what'll happen in Chapter Two. One learns from experience, and I've had the experience of watching far too many first chapters wither on the vine to dismiss the possibility of its happening again. I'm less inclined to worry that an idea will evaporate if I don't get it into production as quickly as possible. If I make a note of it so I won't forget it, and if I read through my notebook from time to time and make it a point to think about what I find there, the good ideas will survive and grow. The bad ones will drop out along the way, and that's fine; I don't feel compelled to add to my stack of first-chapters-of-books-destined-never-to-have-a-second-chapter.

On the other hand, the next book I intend to write is one I've been thinking about for several months now, getting more and more of a sense of the lead character, considering and rejecting any number of geographical settings, changing my mind over and over again about the nature of the plot.

I got the idea, incidentally, by the serendipitous process that yields so many ideas. I was at the library, doing research on patron saints for the sake of a bit of conversational by-play in a light mystery novel, *The Burglar Who Liked to Quote Kipling.* This led me to a passage from Aquinas that amounted to a marvelous moral justification for larceny. Then, because I was tired of saints, patron or otherwise, I started browsing magazines, something I rarely do, and came across an interview with Dennis Hopper. I felt I really ought to go home and get to work, but I felt self-indulgent that day and read the Hopper interview, and there was the idea for my next novel, just waiting there for me to find it. (I won't tell you what it is—I don't want to leave my fight in the gym.)

Anyway, I expect I'll start writing the book in a couple of months. I know the book will have benefited greatly from the time I've spent thinking about it off and on ever since I read that interview. But I'm quite certain that I won't know very much about the direction the plot will take. I'll have my first chapter pretty well worked out in my mind, and I'll know a lot about the characters, and I'll have a variety of possible directions for the book to go, but . . . .

But I won't be able to sit down and paint the thing by numbers. That's what makes it hard, no matter how much plotting time you give a book, but it's also what keeps it exciting.

• • •

"I won't tell you what it is—I don't want to leave my fight in the gym."

Yeah, right.

I wonder what idea I had, and what book I thought I was going to write. There were more than a few ideas that came to me in the late 1970s, only to lead to false starts if I indeed started them at all, and I guess this must have been one of them. An idea that grew out of a Dennis Hopper interview? Dennis Hopper? Huh?

Beats me.

You know, maybe I really ought to rethink my no-notebook policy . . . .

First, though, let me recount one of my more recent ideas, from it's out-of-the-blue origin en route to Belgium.

In May of 2014, my wife and I were in a taxi bound for New York's JFK airport. Hard Case Crime had recently published *Borderline*, a book I'd written under a pen name and lost track of after its publication in 1961. Now it had been reissued with my name on it as a hardcover book with a particularly attractive cover, and it was getting good reviews—substantially better reviews, it seemed to me, than it deserved. I was elated; not only was the book earning me a couple of bucks, but it was doing so without damaging my reputation.

"You know," I said to Lynne, "it might be fun to write a book like *Borderline*. Something fast-paced and breathless and pulpy."

"You might enjoy that," she said.

And fifteen, maybe twenty seconds later, I straightened up in my seat. "I just got an idea," I announced.

And I did. What I got was the basic premise in a couple of sentences, to wit: A woman has let the word out that she wants to hire a man to kill her husband. The police enlist a guy to get wired up and meet with her. Instead, the guy falls for her.

Just the right set-up for the kind of book I had in mind.

Now ideas come along one after another, and most of them aren't much good, and most of the few good ones peter out before too long. And this is especially true when you've been writing since the Harding Administration, and an idea has to be awfully engaging for you to try to turn it into a book.

This one was. We spent two weeks in Antwerp, Bruges, and Ghent, and in each of those picture-book cities I found myself thinking about my guy, wired for sound, behind the wheel of his beat-up Chevy Monte Carlo in the parking lot of a Wynn-Dixie somewhere in Florida. Because the idea was taking form, and I knew something about the guy, something about the setting, something about the mood.

We came home, and I booked an apartment in Philadelphia for a month, starting right after the Fourth of July. I got there by train, and four weeks later I came home, and in September of 2015 Hard Case Crime published *The Girl with the Deep Blue Eyes*.

I don't know where the idea came from, or how, or why. I'm inclined to consider it a gift, and it seems clear to me that it came to me because I was prepared to receive it. "It might be fun . . ." I said—and in no time at all I was able to announce that I had an idea.

Where do I get my ideas? Well, that's easy. I got this one in a taxi on the way to the airport.

Chapter 5

Developing Characters

The chief reason for almost any reader to go on turning the pages of almost any novel is to find out what happens next. The reason the reader *cares* what happens next is because of the author's skill at characterization. When the characters in a novel are sufficiently well drawn, and when they've been so constructed as to engage the reader's capacities for sympathy and identification, he wants to see how their lives turn out and is deeply concerned that they turn out well.

The books that I don't finish reading—and their numbers increase with the years—are generally abandoned along the way for one of two reasons. Sometimes the writer's style puts me off; because I'm a writer myself I've become increasingly aware of literary technique, much as a professional musician will notice sour notes and technical flaws that would escape my attention. Unless theme or story line or characters have a great hold upon me, I'll lose interest in an inexpertly written novel.

If the writing's competent, my interest may flag nevertheless if I find that I just don't give a damn whether the characters live or die, marry or burn, go to the Devil or come out the other side. This may happen because I just don't believe in the characters the author has created. They don't act like real people, they don't sound like real people, and they don't seem to have the emotions or thoughts of real people. Thus they're unreal as far as I'm concerned, and I say they're spinach and the hell with them.

Note, please, that my complaint is that these wooden characters don't seem like *real* people, not that they aren't *ordinary* people. Some of the most engaging characters in fiction, clutching my attention as the Wedding Guest hung on to the Ancient Mariner, have been the farthest thing from ordinary. Nothing about Sherlock Holmes is ordinary, yet the character's appeal has been such as to keep the Conan Doyle stories in print to this day, and to have Holmes resuscitated and brought back to life in several novels by contemporary authors, novels which owe their success almost entirely to public enthusiasm for Conan Doyle's eternally fascinating character.

Similarly, I've found Rex Stout's books about Nero Wolfe endlessly rereadable. There's nothing ordinary about Wolfe, and it's not only his corpulence that makes him larger than life. I don't reread the books because their plots are so compelling, certainly not the second or third time around. Nor am I dazzled by Stout's sheer writing ability; while it was considerable, I never got interested in his non-Wolfe books, either the mysteries starring other detectives or the several straight novels he wrote before creating Wolfe. No, I read him as I suspect most people do, for the sheer pleasure of watching the interplay between Nero Wolfe and Archie Goodwin, of seeing these two men react to different situations and stimuli, and of participating vicariously in the life of that legendary brownstone on West Thirty-fifth Street.

Ordinary? Scarcely that. But so real that I sometimes have to remind myself that Wolfe and Goodwin are the creations of a writer's mind, that no matter how many doorbells I ring in the West Thirties, I'll never find the right house.

That's characterization. It was the ability to create characters readers could care about, too, that made Charles Dickens a monumental popular success. While Oscar Wilde might have remarked that only a man with a heart of stone could read of the death of Little Nell without laughing, the truth of the matter is that readers did not laugh when they read that scene. They wept.

Some novels depend rather more on characterization than do others. In the novel of ideas, the characters often exist as mouthpieces for various philosophical positions; while the writer may have taken the trouble to describe them and give them diverse individual attributes, they often have little real life outside of their specific argumentative role in the novel.

Some whodunits rely on the clever intricacy of their plotting to hold the reader's attention, stinting on characterization in the process. Erle Stanley Gardner's Perry Mason mysteries can be compulsively readable, but does Mason himself ever emerge as anything more than a forceful courtroom presence and a keen legal mind? Agatha Christie supplied her Hercule Poirot with a variety of attitudes and pet expressions, but I've never found that the little Belgian added up to anything more than the sum of these quirks and phrases. He serves admirably as a vehicle for the solution of brilliant mystery puzzles but does not interest me much as a character.

On reflection, it seems to me that even in these categories—the novel of ideas, the plot-heavy whodunit—my favorite novels are those in which the author has created characters to whom I am capable of responding strongly. Arthur Koestler's *Darkness at Noon* is a brilliant novel of political and philosophical argument; I find it ever so much more effective because the lead character, Rubashov, is so absorbing a human being. And, while one of Ms. Christie's Poirot mysteries will always do to fill an idle hour, I'm a passionate fan of her Jane Marple stories, not because their plots are appreciably different from the Poirots but because Marple herself is such a fascinating character, warm and human and alive.

So characterization is important in fiction, and especially so in the novel. The argument is hardly a controversial one. With that much established, how does one go about creating characters with whom the reader can identify, characters he'll want to spend time with, characters whose fate will be a matter of concern to him?

A first principle of characterization may seem fairly obvious, but I think it's worth stating. Characters are most effective when they are so drawn that the author can identify with them, sympathize with them, care about them, and enjoy their company.

At the risk of sounding like an armchair psychoanalyst, I would suggest that all characters are to a greater or lesser extent a projection of the author's own personality. I know this is true in my own writing. While all my characters are not like me by any means, they are each and every one the people I would be were I clothed in their particular skins. In other words, when I create a character I work very much in the manner of an actor playing a role. I play that character's part, improvising his dialogue on the page, slipping into his role as I go along.

This is most obviously the case with viewpoint characters; indeed, it's commonplace for readers to make the mistake of too closely identifying an author with the attitudes and opinions of his novel's narrator. But I know that in my own writing, this identification is true too for the subordinate characters, the villains, the bit players, for everyone who puts in an appearance. I do most of the work of characterization from the inside out, playing all the parts myself, writing all the dialogue, and walking all the characters through their paces. Naturally, in any given novel there will be some characters with whom I can more readily identify than others; it's generally true those are the characters I do a better job with.

It's important, I think, to play around with the idea of a character before plunging into a book. Occasionally in the past I've rushed to get a first chapter written without taking the time to figure out who the people were, letting the characters define themselves on the page. This was the case with *Deadly Honeymoon;* I was concerned with a plot and incident and dramatic effect, and so I began writing the book with no clear picture of the bridal couple who served as the book's joint leads. I think the book might have been a good deal better had I known more about my characters before I began.

With Tanner, I had an abundance of time. After I'd first been taken with the notion of writing about a permanent insomniac, as I explained in the preceding chapter, I read something in an encyclopedia indicating that the British royal house of Stuart survived to the present time, with the current pretender some sort of Bavarian princeling. I thought this was splendid, and decided my insomniac could be plotting the restoration of the House of Stuart to the British throne.

That didn't go anywhere, but it gave me this image of Tanner as a devotee of political lost causes. I thought of him from time to time and figured out other things about his character. I decided he'd have lots of time on his hands, not having to spend eight hours a day sleeping, and I thought he could put that time to use by compulsively learning one language after another. This sort of scholarly devotion seemed to fit the occupation I decided to give him—I had him write theses and examination papers to order for students with more money than industry.

Tanner's gradual evolution over a period of a couple of years was such that, when Providence provided me with a plot, my character was all set to go. It was easy to plot the book to suit the particular character I had already created in my mind. And that character, quirky and highly individualistic, was one with whom I could identify profoundly, because for all our differences Tanner was very clearly a projection of the author. He was precisely the person I would have been had I been wearing his skin and living his life.

Another series character of mine illustrates the manner in which one can adapt and define a character to suit the requirement of author-identification.

Two things inspired the creation of Matt Scudder. First, it was an opportune time for me to do a detective series for Dell Books. Second, I'd just read *On the Pad,* Leonard Shecter's excellent book with and about Bill Phillips, the New York City cop, admittedly corrupt, who'd collected evidence for an investigative commission and who had been tried and found guilty of the murder of a call girl and her pimp. What struck me was the notion of a corrupt cop, living with and on corruption, running his own hustles, and functioning all the while as a very effective policeman, breaking cases and putting criminals in jail.

As I began working on the character, I realized that the cop I had in mind might make an absorbing character, that I might very well enjoy reading someone else's interpretation of such a character, but that he was not a character with whom I could identify sufficiently in order to write books about him myself. I'm not comfortable using viewpoint characters who function within a bureaucracy. For one reason or another, I've always felt more comfortable from the point of view of an outsider. I didn't feel at all sanguine about my ability to render a crooked cop believable, let alone sympathetic.

So I let my imagination play around with Scudder, and then I sat down at a typewriter and began writing a long memo to myself *about* the man. I decided he was something of a burnt-out case; he had been a cop, had lived with wife and children in the suburbs, and had been both a proficient detective and a man to whom small-scale corruption was a way of life. Then, while thwarting a tavern holdup while off-duty, his ricocheting bullet killed a small child. This led poor Scudder to an agonizing reappraisal of his own life and enough existential angst to drown a litter of kittens. He left his wife and kids, moved into a monastic hotel room in Manhattan, quit the police force, picked up the habit of visiting churches and lighting candles, and became a serious drinker. Occasionally he would earn money as an unofficial and unlicensed private detective, using his contacts in the NYPD and investigating cases with the special sensibilities of a hip and hard-nosed cop.

I wrote three novels and two novelettes about Scudder and took enormous satisfaction in them: I like the books as well as anything I've written. They worked, and Scudder worked, because I was able to take a generally sound character idea and transform it into a character who came to life as a projection of the author. I identified strongly with Scudder. For all the apparent difference of our lives and our selves, he and I had any number of underlying aspects in common.

> *All characters in this book are fictional, and any resemblance to persons living or dead is purely coincidental.*
> *The earth is flat.*

The above disclaimer notice, which appeared in the front of *Ronald Rabbit is a Dirty Old Man,* brought me an invitation—eagerly accepted, I might add—to join the Flat Earth Society of Canada. My purpose in including the notice was not to proselytize against the globularist heresy, as we Flat Earthers are wont to call it, but to make a point about the disclaimer notices that appear so routinely in so many novels. The statements are generally palpable nonsense; resemblance to persons living or dead is often quite intentional.

Many of the characters with whom we people our fiction are drawn from life, and how could it be otherwise? One way or another, all our writing comes from experience, and it is our experience of our fellow human beings that enables us to create characters that look and act and sound like human beings.

The average reader often seems to think that writers go about snatching people off the streets and bundling them into books with the rapacious fervor of an old-fashioned white slaver. It is as if the characters were stolen from the real world and transplanted bodily into a novel.

Once in a while it very nearly amounts to that. In the genuine *roman à clef,* where the author presumes to render real events in the guise of fiction, the characters are portrayed as much like their real life prototypes as the author can manage. Thomas Wolfe wrote in this fashion, telling his own story in *Look Homeward, Angel* and *Of Time and the River,* casting himself as Eugene Gant and his own family as the Gant family. Even so, the Gants inevitably became fictional characters; Wolfe had to invent, to devise. Even a character like Eliza Gant, modeled so faithfully upon his own mother, emerges finally as Wolfe's interpretation of the woman, as the person *he* would have been had he been her.

Furthermore, the novelist's imagination and the novelist's sense of order work changes upon characters drawn from life. In his autobiographical work, *Christopher and His Kind,* Christopher Isherwood tells of various persons with whom he was acquainted over the years, some of whom appeared previously as characters in his largely autobiographical novels. Here's how he discusses a friend and the way the man appeared in a novel:

> In *Down There on a Visit,* Francis appears as a character called Ambrose and is described as follows:
>
> > "His figure was slim and erect and there was a boyishness

> in his quick movements. But his dark-skinned face was quite shockingly lined, as if Life had mauled him with its claws. His hair fell picturesquely about his face in wavy black locks which were already streaked with grey. There was a gentle surprise in the expression of his dark brown eyes. He could become frantically nervous at an instant's notice—I saw that; with his sensitive nostrils and fine-drawn cheekbones, he had the look of a horse which may bolt without warning. And yet there was a kind of inner contemplative response in the midst of him. It made him touchingly beautiful. He could have posed for the portrait of a saint."
>
> This is true to life, more or less, except for the last three sentences, which relate only to the fictitious part of Ambrose. Photographs of Francis at that time show that he was beautiful, certainly, but that he had the face of a self-indulgent aristocrat, not a contemplative ascetic. I can't detect the inner response....

Isherwood goes on to recount several other aspects of Francis's character which he did not incorporate in the fictional Ambrose. However unmistakably the one may have been modeled upon the other, the writing process has clearly made them different personalities.

Another popular sort of novel specializes in holding up a fun-house mirror to life. This is the generally tacky type of book in which the story line is largely a matter of sheer invention, occasionally incorporating bits of rumor and scandal, and with several of the characters so obviously based on prominent persons as to make the reader regard the book almost as an unauthorized biography. Someone remarked not long ago that Frank Sinatra, for one, has been pressed into service in so many novels over the years, whether as the lead or in a cameo role, that he really deserves to collect a royalty. And any number of novels have similarly "starred" Elizabeth

Taylor, Jackie Onassis, and more other celebrities than I would care to name or number.

More often, the characters we create are drawn in part from people we have known or observed, without our in any sense attempting to recreate the person on the page. I may borrow a bit of physical description, for example, or a mannerism, or an oddity of speech. I may take an incident in the life of someone I know and use it as an item of background data in the life of one of my characters. Little touches of this sort from my own life experience get threaded into my characters much as bits of ribbon and cloth are woven into a songbird's nest—for color, to tighten things up, and because they caught my eye and seemed to belong there.

The first time I consciously transferred an aspect of a real person into a novel was when I wrote a book called *After the First Death,* a murder mystery set in the half-world of Times Square streetwalkers. I had at the time a nodding acquaintance with one such woman—and on one occasion she told me about a relationship she'd had of some duration with a married man from Scarsdale. She'd evidently been off drugs at the time, and seeing him exclusively, but after he'd cancelled a planned European trip with her and took his wife to the Caribbean instead, she ended the relationship and returned to prostitution and heroin addiction.

I don't know that the character of Jackie in my novel had much in common with the woman who told me this story. Jackie was certainly a romanticized character; if she didn't have a heart of gold, she had at the very least a soft spot in her heart of brass. Nor did I know the real-life hooker well enough to haul her off the streets and plunk her down on the printed page. But certainly the portrayal of Jackie owed a lot to my impression of her, and the story about her Scarsdale Galahad found its way almost word for word into print.

Some years later I wrote a pseudonymous novel in the manner of *Peyton Place*—sensational doings in a small town, that sort of thing. I very deliberately set the book in a particular town with which I was personally familiar, and several of the characters owed something to real people who lived in the town. For one character, I borrowed the physical description of a local actor, not intending to ape him too closely; only to find that the character I'd created had a will of his own and insisted upon speaking and behaving precisely as his real-life prototype spoke and behaved. I couldn't write the character's dialogue without hearing my friend's voice booming in my ears. Now I suppose it's possible to fight that sort of thing, but what writer in his right mind would presume to do so? The best possible thing had happened. A character had come to life. I might be inviting a lawsuit or a public thrashing by allowing him to play out his part, but I'd have been false to my art to do otherwise.

For me, the most exhilarating moment at the typewriter is when a character takes on a life of his own. It's not an easy thing to describe. But it happens. One can scarcely avoid playing God when writing a novel, creating one's own imaginary universe and arranging the destinies of the characters as one sees fit. When the magic happens, however, and a character speaks and breathes and sweats and sighs apparently of his own accord, one feels for a moment that one has created life.

It's a heady experience, and so satisfying that you'd want it to happen all the time. Unfortunately, it doesn't—at least not for me. Some of my characters live for me as I've described. Others walk around like empty suits, doing what's required of them but never coming to life. They may work well enough for the reader—craft can disguise the fact that certain characters are just walking through their roles—but not for me.

This was the case with *Code of Arms,* the war novel I talked about in the last chapter. The lead character in my first draft had a lot of interesting things about him. He was a former stunt pilot, the survivor of an unhappy love affair, an American of Irish and Jewish heritage who had enlisted in the RAF. Who could fail to make such a man interesting?

Who indeed? I could, and did. I carried the poor clown through five hundred pages of tedious manuscript and never had the feeling that he could stand up without my support. He remained a two-dimensional cardboard cutout, mouthing the lines required to fit a situation, going places and doing things, acting and reacting and doing it all like an empty suit, a brainwashed zombie.

Why didn't he come to life? I don't know. It wasn't because there was anything fundamentally unsympathetic about the sort of person he was or the acts he performed. Several minor characters in the same novel did verge on animation, including a few whom I found distinctly unpleasant, but my lead remained dead and hollow at the core. Perhaps my inability to breathe life into him owed something to my own negative feelings about the novel itself. Perhaps I couldn't get past seeing him as an instrument rather than a person.

In contrast, Bernie Rhodenbarr came to life on the very first page of the first draft of the first novel in which he made an appearance.

Previously, I'd written a couple of chapters of a Scudder novel in which a burglar's suspected of murder because he knocks off an apartment with a dead body in it. That particular burglar was a sort of gentle oaf, and Scudder was going to come to his rescue, but the book never got off the ground.

Later I decided to revive that plot notion, eliminate the detective, change the tone entirely from downbeat to sprightly, and let the burglar himself solve the crime and go on to tell the tale.

I decided to open with the initial burglary, so I sat down and typed out the following:

> *A handful of minutes after nine I hoisted my Bloomingdale's shopping bag and moved out of a doorway and into step with a tall blond fellow with a faintly equine cast to his face. He was carrying an attaché case that looked too thin to be of much use. Like a high-fashion model, you might say. His topcoat was one of those new plaid ones and his hair, a little longer than my own, had been cut a strand at a time.*

> "We meet again," I said, which was an out-and-out lie. "Turned out to be a pretty fair day after all."
>
> He smiled, perfectly willing to believe that we were neighbors who exchanged a friendly word now and then. "Little brisk this evening," he said.
>
> I agreed that it was brisk. There wasn't much he might have said that I wouldn't have gladly agreed with. He looked respectable and he was walking east on Sixty-seventh Street and that was all I required of him. I didn't want to befriend him or play handball with him or learn the name of his barber or coax him into swapping shortbread recipes. I just wanted him to help me get past a doorman.

By the time I had that much written, I knew who Bernie Rhodenbarr was. More important, he'd already begun to take on a life of his own. I didn't have to stop and think how he would phrase something; it was simply a matter of shifting gears and speaking in his voice—or, if you will, of letting go and allowing him to recite his own lines spontaneously.

I don't want to make this sound too mystical. Books don't write themselves and characters don't relieve their creators of the necessity of getting the right words on the page. But when a character does come to life in this fashion, when you find yourself knowing him from the inside out, you are then able to bring to the process of literary creation the assurance of the natural athlete.

How does one manage to make characters distinct and memorable? Is it a matter of little traits—pet expressions, a perpetually untied shoelace, a drooping eyelid? These are the little tricks of caricature, to be sure, and they are more or less effective depending on the skill with which they are managed.

In *Time to Murder and Create*, for instance, I made use of a character named Spinner Jablon. He's not onstage long; he's a stool pigeon turned blackmailer who hires Scudder to hold an envelope for him, said envelope to be opened in the event of his death, which in turn happens early in the book.

I had this to say about Spinner:

> They called him the Spinner because of a habit he had. He carried an old silver dollar as a good-luck charm, and he would haul it out of his pants pocket all the time, prop it up on a table top with his left forefinger, then cock his right middle finger and give the edge of the coin a flick. If he was talking to you, his eyes would stay on the spinning coin while he spoke, and he seemed to be directing his words as much to the dollar as to you.

This spin-a-silver-dollar bit was a handy character tag; it gave Spinner something memorable to do, made for an interesting bit of business to go on during Spinner's conversation with Scudder, and later in the book provided a way for Scudder to underscore Spinner's death—he purchases a silver dollar from a coin dealer and takes to carrying it around himself and spinning it on tabletops.

This isn't characterization. It's gimmickry, but sometimes for me that's the first step in the process of characterization. It gives me a tag, a handle, and the actual character evolves in due course through a process that seems to be largely intuitive.

The sort of handle you get on a character varies with the kind of writer you are and the particular character you're dealing with. I find I'm most likely to latch onto characters by the way they sound, the manner in which they use language. It's often through their dialogue that they become real for me, and I frequently fasten onto this while having a less concrete notion of what they look like physically. Sometimes, though, I start with a particular visual picture of a character and all the rest follows.

I still remember a line that popped into my head a few years ago after I caught a glimpse of a woman in a Los Angeles restaurant. "*She had the pinched face of someone who'd grown up on a hardscrabble hillside farm and would do anything to keep from going back.*"

I didn't write down those imperishable words but they stayed in my mind, along with not only an image of the woman I'd seen but a whole set of attitudes. I knew who the woman was and how she would sound and what her reactions would be to various phenomena. I didn't know what use I might one day make of her, whether she'd be a heroine or a villain, a protagonist or a spear carrier. So far the only use I've gotten out of her is here and now, to illustrate where characters come from and how they evolve, and it's possible that's all the use I'll ever get out of her.

If you keep a notebook, character sketches are a logical item to include. Maugham's *Writer's Notebook* makes fascinating reading because of the character sketches it contains, many of which ultimately found their way into his short stories and novels. You can jot down whatever you want—your actual observations of a real person, some bits and pieces of gimmickry you've thought up or observed and might eventually want to use for a character of your own creation, or any sort of tag or impression that might blossom into a full-blown character.

Which comes first, the plot or the character?

There's no answer for that one. A book may start with either the plot or the characters more fully grasped, but both aspects generally take shape side by side as the book itself is formed. Even in books where I think I know pretty much what's going to happen before I start writing, unplanned incidents crop up in the plotting and invariably call for the creation of new minor characters on the spot. My lead, say, goes looking for someone at a hotel. His quarry's out, but a conversation ensues with the hotel clerk, either to develop certain information or just because such a conversation would be part of the natural order of things. I can make that clerk as much or as little an individual as I want. He can be tall or short, young or old, fat or thin. He can have something or nothing much to say.

Is he doing something when my lead approaches him? Looking at a girlie magazine? Filling in a crossword puzzle in ink? Dozing? Sucking on a bottle of bourbon?

These are all decisions you make as a writer. You may make them quickly and spontaneously and intuitively. You may elect to tell a lot or a little about this sort of bit player. The success of your novel will not stand or fall upon the way you handle him, as it well may hinge on your treatment of major characters, but all characterization plays an important part in the overall impact of your fiction.

• • •

Over the years, I've continued to avoid modeling characters on real-life counterparts, with only a very few exceptions that come to mind. In *A Long Line of Dead Men*, the twelfth book about Matthew Scudder, the detective is hired by a secret club whose members have been dying at an improbable rate. One of the club's members is a radical lawyer named Raymond Gruliow, known in the tabloids as Hard-Way Ray.

I believe Gruliow came up in conversation in an earlier book, but here he plays a prominent role, and we meet him again in later books in the series.

Now there's no denying I had William M. Kunstler in mind when I first had two characters talking about Raymond Gruliow, and by the time I gave him a speaking part I saw and heard Bill Kunstler as I wrote Ray Gruliow's dialogue. While I didn't doubt that the man would recognize himself in the role, I had no reason to believe that he'd ever read the book.

I learned later that Kunstler, as a regular customer at Three Lives Bookshop, was also a regular reader of mine; I learned this one day when my phone rang. "Mr. Block? This is William Kunstler. There's a character of yours who looks and sounds a great deal like me. My seconds will call upon you in the morning."

This was followed by an invitation to his annual Halloween party, for which I was unfortunately out of town. Ray Gruliow continued to appear in Scudder novels, nor did I see any reason to cut short his fictional life and career when cancer brought Bill Kunstler's life to a close.

Chapter 6

Outlining

An outline is a tool which a writer uses to simplify the task of writing a novel and to improve the ultimate quality of that novel by giving himself more of a grasp on its overall structure.

And that's about as specifically as one can define an outline, beyond adding that it's almost invariably shorter than the book will turn out to be. What length it will run, what form it will take, how detailed it will be, and what sort of novel components it will or will not include, is and ought to be a wholly individual matter. Because the outline is prepared solely for the benefit of the writer himself, it quite properly varies from one author to another and from one novel to another. Some writers never use an outline. Others would be uncomfortable writing anything more ambitious than a shopping list without outlining it first. Some outlines, deemed very useful by their authors, run a scant page. Others, considered equally indispensable by *their* authors, run a hundred pages or more and include a detailed description of every scene that is going to take place in every chapter of the book. Neither of these extremes, nor any of the infinite gradations between the two poles, represents the right way to prepare an outline. There is no right way to do this—or, more correctly, there is no wrong way. Whatever works best for the particular writer on the particular book is demonstrably the right way.

I've written quite a few novels without employing any outline whatsoever. The advantage of eschewing outlines is quite simple. With no predetermined course, the novel is free to evolve as it goes along, with the plot growing naturally out of what has been written rather than being bound artificially to the skeletal structure of an outline like a rosebush espaliered to a trellis.

The writer who does not use an outline says that to do so would gut the book of its spontaneity and would make the writing process itself a matter of filling in the blanks of a printed form. At the root of this school of thought is the argument first propounded, I believe, by science-fiction author Theodore Sturgeon. If the writer doesn't know what's going to happen next, he argued, the reader can't possibly know what's going to happen next.

There's logic in that argument, certainly, but I'm not sure it holds up. Just because a writer worked things out as he went along is no guarantee that the book he's produced won't be obvious and predictable. Conversely, the use of an extremely detailed outline does not preclude the possibility that the book will read as though it had been written effortlessly and spontaneously by a wholly freewheeling author.

Some time ago I queried a hundred or so authors on their writing methods. A considerable number explained that they didn't outline at all, or prepared minimal outlines at most. Here's Willo Davis Roberts echoing Sturgeon's Principle:

> *I seldom outline, except insofar as I have to come up with enough to interest an editor if I want a contract before I do the book. Often I do not know how a suspense novel will turn out until I get to the last chapter, which is more fun than having the end all planned beforehand.*

Tony Hillerman takes the same position, not because it's more fun necessarily but because it's what comes naturally for him:

> *I have never been able to outline a book. I work from a basic general idea, a couple of clearly understood characters, a couple of thematic and plot ideas, and a rough conception of where I'm going with it all. I also work with a clear idea of place. I tend to write in scenes—getting one vividly in mind, then putting it quickly on paper.*

In marked contrast, consider this from Richard S. Prather, author of forty suspense novels, most of them lighthearted frothy chronicles of the doings of private eye Shell Scott:

> *I spend considerable time on plot development, typing roughly 100,000 or more words of scene fragments, gimmicks, "what if?" possibilities, alternative actions or solutions, until the overall story line satisfies me. I boil all of this down to a couple of pages, then from these prepare a detailed chapter-by-chapter synopsis, using a separate page (or more) for each of, say, twenty chapters, and expanding in those pages upon characters, motivations, scenes, action, whenever such expansion seems a natural development. When the synopsis is done, I start the first draft of the book and bang away as speedily as possible until the end.*

If I ever tried the method Prather describes, I'm sure what I produced would have all the freshness and appeal of week-old mashed potatoes; it would certainly not possess the sparkle of his Shell Scott books—which only serves to underscore the highly individual nature of outlines in particular and writing methods in general. If writing *with* an outline is for some people like filling in a printed form, writing *without* an outline is for others like playing tennis without a net—as Robert Frost said of free verse. In some instances, it's even more like walking a tightrope without a net.

It's all up to you. If you feel comfortable beginning your book without an outline—or even without all that firm an idea where it's going—by all means go ahead. If you'll feel more confident of your ability to finish the book with an outline in front of you, by all means construct and employ one. As you go along, you'll learn what works best for the particular writer you turn out to be.

And that's all that matters. No one ever bought a book because it was written with an outline, or because it wasn't.

I want to use an outline. Now what?

The first step is to find out what an outline is. And the easiest way to do that is to write one. Not of your book but of somebody else's.

In an earlier chapter, we discussed this method of preparing an outline of someone else's book as a means of understanding how novels work. The process is similarly valuable as an aid to learning what an outline is.

Some years back I decided in a weak moment that I wanted to write movies. I was bright enough to recognize that film is an infinitely different medium from prose, and reasoned that I had to familiarize myself with it before I could expect to produce anything that would fly. First thing I did was start going to movies day after day.

This was fun, and it wasn't all that bad an idea, but it didn't teach me a hell of a lot about screenwriting. I came to realize somewhere along the way that I was taking the wrong approach. I wouldn't be writing *movies*, after all. I would be writing *screenplays*. So, instead of studying the films themselves, I ought to be reading their scripts.

If it sounds like a small distinction, I suggest you give it some thought. What I wanted to write was a script, and in order to do that I had to learn what a script was, how it worked not on the screen but on the page. I had to be able to see a film as words on paper, not images on a screen, because I would be writing that script by putting words on paper.

So I read scripts, quite a few of them, and what a difference it made! In the first place, I began to understand what scripts were, how they were written, and how I could write one of my own. In the second place and at least as important, my reading of film scripts made a significant change in my perception when I looked at a film in a theater. My perspective was changed, and I'd look at the movie and mentally translate it back into the script it had come from.

This didn't make me a screenwriter. I did write a movie script, and a treatment for another movie, and in the course of doing this I learned that I wasn't really cut out to be a screenwriter and didn't really want to be one, for any of a variety of perfectly sound reasons. But I still watch films with a heightened awareness of the underlying screenplay, and I wouldn't be surprised if this has paid some dividends in my prose writing.

In the same fashion, the best preparation for writing an outline is reading outlines, not reading novels. By studying the outlines themselves you will see how an outline looks on a typed page; as important, you will develop the ability to see other novels—and, ultimately, your own novel—with x-ray eyes; i.e., you'll see through the prose and dialogue to the bare bones beneath.

How do you outline another person's novel? Whatever way you wish. Your outline of somebody else's book can be as sketchy or as detailed as you like, just as the outline you eventually work up for your own novel may be sketchy or detailed, brief or lengthy. Do whatever seems most natural to you.

Once you've familiarized yourself with outlines of other writers' novels—or once you've decided not to bother with that step—it's time to get to work on your own outline. At this point some warm-up exercises and wind sprints can be useful. Few of us would care to do as much pre-outline work as Richard S. Prather describes, with preparatory writing running to almost double the length of the finished book, but one can do as much as seems useful.

Character sketches are handy, for example. In the preceding chapter I mentioned how the evolution of my Matthew Scudder character was facilitated by the memo I wrote to myself, in which I discussed Scudder at some length, talking about his background, his habits, his current way of life, his likes and dislikes, and how he likes his eggs for breakfast. In his journals, Chekhov suggests that a writer ought to know everything he can about a character—his shoe size, the condition of his liver, lungs, clothes, habits, and intestinal track. You may not *mention* the greater portion of this in your writing, but the better you know your characters the more effectively you'll be able to write about them. I always keep learning new things about my characters as I go along; I'm still learning about Scudder and Bernie Rhodenbarr, even after several books about each of them—but the better I know them in advance, the better equipped I am for outlining and, later, for writing the novel.

It's also occasionally helpful to write an answer to the question "What is this book about?" In the early days of Hollywood, the conventional wisdom held that a story line ought to be capable of being conveyed in a single sentence. While I suspect this theory was originally propounded by illiterates who couldn't hold in their heads more than one sentence at a time, and while it unquestionably overstates the case, there's some merit to the argument. If nothing else, one feels more confident about approaching a book when one is able to say, if only to oneself, what the thing is *about*.

> Burglars Can't Be Choosers *is about a cheeky professional burglar who steals an object to order, and the cops walk in on him and catch him in the act, and there's a dead body in the apartment and he escapes and has to clear himself by solving the crime, which he does.*

That's what one novel is about, all in one sentence, cumbersome though that sentence be. Explaining what your book is to be about may take several sentences or paragraphs. It's possible, certainly, to write a book without consciously knowing in advance what it's to be about; sometimes we write the books in order to answer that very question. And it's possible to know what the book's about without spelling it out on paper. But sometimes getting it down improves one's grasp on the whole thing.

The next step is to write the outline itself, in as much or as little detail as you wish. I have frequently found it useful to make this a chapter outline, with a paragraph given to describe the action that will take place in each chapter. If you take this approach, don't be unduly concerned with just how you'll divide your narrative into chapters. When you do the actual writing, you may very well discover that the breaks come naturally in different places than the outline indicated. You'll simply ignore the division in the outline and do them whatever way seems best. This is just one way in which you'll ultimately feel free to deviate from the outline, as we'll see in due course. Writing the outline chapter by chapter, whether or not the book will correspond to this division, introduces a sense of order; I think that's why I've found it valuable.

How detailed should the outline be? Given the premise that this is an individual matter, infinitely variable from one author to another and from one book to the next, we might go on to say that there ought to be enough detail so that the story line makes sense. Outlining rarely amounts to more than putting on paper a plot that is already completely formed in your head. As you write things out, chapter by chapter, scene by scene, you'll be working out the details of the story as you go. Problems that wouldn't occur to you otherwise will present themselves.

You'll work out the solutions to some of these problems in the course of completing the outline. But you won't work out *all* of them this way, and it's important to recognize that you don't *have* to. Simply by spotting and defining a problem you have taken a step toward its solution. From then on, your unconscious mind (and your conscious mind as well, for that matter) will be able to play with the problem. While you write the early chapters, you'll have the plot and structure problems of future chapters somewhere in the back of your mind. In other words, the outlining process is part of the whole organic evolution of the book. The book grows and takes shape during it, and the book will continue to grow and shape itself as a result of it.

It's possible, I think, for an outline to be *too* detailed. And it's also possible to waste time and words in an outline explaining motives and background excessively. One thing to remember, in this sort of outline, is that you're writing this for your own benefit, not for anybody else to read. That being the case, you don't have to explain and justify things to yourself when you already have a sufficient grasp of them. Writing is liveliest when it's interesting to the person doing it. Purposeless elaboration in an outline is one way to kill your own interest in what you will later have to sit down and write.

"When *I* use a word," Humpty Dumpty said, in a rather scornful tone, "it means just what I choose it to mean—neither more nor less."

"The question is," said Alice, "Whether you *can* make words mean so many different things."

"*The question is,*" said Humpty Dumpty, "*which is to be master—that's all.*"

I don't really know that that's the question with words; it seems to me that words work best for me if I take care to employ them more or less in accordance with accepted English usage. With outlines, however, it's important that the writer be the master of the situation.

That, I think, is the chief danger of outlines—that one can feel bound by them. Remember, the book continues to grow and define itself after the outline has been written, and this process continues during the writing itself. It's important that you feel free to give your imagination its head. If you can think of a more interesting development, a sounder resolution for Chapter Six, or even a wholly different course for the book to take somewhere along the way, you have to be able to chuck the outline and do whatever's best for the book.

Some writers avoid putting their plots down on paper because an outline confines them in this fashion. I lean in this direction myself, and rarely write an outline nowadays unless I'm using it to nail down a contract. Other writers do write out an outline but then put it in a drawer and avoid referring to it during the actual writing of the book.

Robert Ludlum takes this approach. As he explained in an interview published in *Writer's Digest,*

> While working as a producer I learned to break a play down so that I developed a sense of its dimensions, where it was going, what made it work dramatically. Outlining a novel is a way to break down a book in much the same way. It gives me an understanding of the theme, the material, the main characters. I'm able to see the story in terms of beginning and middle and ending. Then, once I have a handle on the story, I don't need the outline any more. The

book itself will differ in plot specifics from the outline, but it'll be the same in thrust.

So far we have been talking about an outline strictly as an author's aid—something you write before you write the book itself, for the purpose of making the book stronger and the writing easier. Along the way, however, I've alluded a couple of times to an outline which has another purpose, that of persuading a publisher to offer a contract for a book which has not yet been written.

Writers who have established themselves professionally rarely write a complete book without having made arrangements for its publication somewhere along the line. When one is of sufficient stature, it's not even necessary to have a specific idea for a novel in order to get a publisher's signature on a contract; when one has no track record whatsoever, most publishers would prefer to have a completed manuscript in hand before making any commitment.

I would strongly advise a first novelist to finish at the very least the first draft of his book before making any attempt to sell it. Almost any publisher will look at a neophyte's chapters and outline, but he's unlikely to offer a contract on that basis. Why should he? He has no reason to assume the unproven writer has the capacity to finish the book, to sustain whatever strengths the chapters and outline display. If he is sufficiently attracted by what he sees, he may gamble to the extent of offering far less generous terms than he would for a completed manuscript.

But that's not the main reason why I would recommend writing the whole book first. More often than not, any interruption in the writing of a novel is a mistake. A loss of momentum can sometimes be fatal. If the book's going well, for heaven's sake stay with it. If it's not going well, figure out what's wrong and deal with it; bundling it off to a publisher isn't going to solve your problems. A couple of times, when I had sent chapters and outline to a publisher, I kept right on with the writing of the book while awaiting word on the portion I'd submitted. In some instances that I can recall, I had the book completed before the publisher made up his mind.

When you do reach a point in your career where it's advantageous to submit an outline, the document you will want to produce is a rather different proposition from the sort you write solely for your own benefit. Your object in this submitted outline is to convince another person—the editor or publisher—that you have a sound grasp of the book and will be able to complete a novel which will fulfill the promise of its opening chapters. A successful outline of this sort gives whoever reads it the impression that the book's already there in your mind, fully realized, just waiting for you to tap it out on the typewriter keys.

When it comes to clinching a sale, lengthy detailed outlines are best. There are two reasons for this, one logical and the other human. The logical one is that the more substance and detail you include in an outline, the more the editor is able to know about what you intend to do in the material to come, and thus the better able he is to judge whether the book you will write will be a book he would want to publish.

The other reason is rather less firmly rooted in logic. Editors are people, too—hard as I occasionally find it to admit this. If they are going to commit their firm to the purchase of a novel in progress, and if they are going to lay substantial cash on the table as an advance to bind the deal, they like to feel they are getting something tangible for their money. A fifty-page outline, comprehensive enough to be what the film industry delights in calling a "treatment," has some heft to it. You don't even have to read it to know there's something there; just weighing it in your hand will get that message across. And, by George, you can tell that the author put in some time writing it. It's infinitely different from a one-page synopsis that he could have batted out in eighteen-and-a-half minutes on a rainy afternoon. Never mind that the one-page synopsis might be as much as he'd need to have a firm grasp on the remainder of the novel—anyone would be more comfortable dealing on the basis of a fifty-page treatment.

Just how long and detailed an "outline-for-submission" must be varies greatly with circumstances. Random House contracted for my third mystery novel about burglar Bernie Rhodenbarr on the basis of a one-page letter to my editor, Barbé Hammer. In the letter I told her the book's basic premise and some of the general avenues I intended to explore. There was nothing in the letter to show that I knew how to resolve the plot complications I intended to develop, and there was considerable vagueness even in the opening premise—I said, for instance, that Bernie was going to be hired to steal a particular collector's item, from one enthusiast for another's benefit, but I didn't say what the gimcrack would be because I admittedly hadn't yet decided.

I got by with this rather cavalier approach because of the particular circumstances that were operating. Barbé knew and liked my work. Random House had already published two books about Bernie and folks there were pleased with them aesthetically and commercially. All I really had to do to get a contract was indicate that I had a sound idea for a book, that it was sufficiently "the same only different" to continue the series, and that I at least was confident of my ability to tie everything up neatly by the end of the book.

In contrast, my outline for *Code of Arms* ran a dozen or so pages and was as detailed as I could comfortably arrange. In this instance I was offering to write a book of a sort with which I had no real prior experience, and a more substantial outline was necessary not only to convince a publisher that I knew what I was setting out to do but to make *me* similarly confident. Before I began a 500-page monster of a novel, I wanted to assure myself that I wouldn't wind up somewhere around page 374 having painted myself into some plotting corner. In retrospect, I wish I'd written this particular outline two or three or four times as long; had I done so, I might have had an easier time of writing the book.

Or, even better, attempting to write a more extensive and elaborate outline might have enabled me to see that this was not the book for me to be writing—and I might have dropped the whole misbegotten project then and there.

To sum up:

An outline is a tool, the equivalent of a painter's preliminary sketches. Use it to whatever extent it is helpful. Don't be a slave to it; if the book begins to grow away from the outline, let the book chart its own course.

Above all, remember there's no one right way to do it. You can sit down with no outline whatsoever and write the whole book from first page to last. Or you can write a one-page synopsis, expand it into a chapter outline, expand *that* into a detailed chapter outline with each scene sketched in, and even expand that outline into a super-treatment with bits of dialogue included and point-of-view changes indicated. Some writers operate this way, blowing up the balloon of their novel one breath at a time, until the writing of the novel's actual first draft is just a matter of doubling the length of the final outline. If that's what works for them, then that's the right way to do it—for them.

Finally, for anyone interested in the best illustration I can recall of what an outline is and how it all works, I would recommend Donald E. Westlake's hilarious novel, *Adios, Scheherazade*. The narrator is a hapless hack who has written a sex novel a month for the past twenty-eight months and who confronts a massive writer's block when he attempts to write Opus Twenty-Nine. At one point he produces an outline for the book, an outline that's very instructive to any apprentice novelist while it finds its way to one of the funniest punchlines I ever read. I can't reproduce it here, but I earnestly commend the book to your attention.

• • •

Now why, I wonder, did I feel constrained from including the outline from *Adios, Scheherazade*? Here it is, for your edification and enjoyment:

> *So here I am, miserable, exhausted, panic-stricken, pissing away my substance on another fifteen pages of whatchamacallit that Samuel would never understand, and what am I going to do?*
>
> *What am I going to do?*

I'll tell you what I'm going to do. I am going to outline a sex novel right now, and then I am going to make myself some lunch, maybe watch some football, and then come back here and start the sex novel I have outlined. That is what I am going to do, no ifs, no ands, no buts.

Outline. Girl-on-the-make book. Call it Passion Sinner. *Do I have a book called* Passion Sinner? *I have a list of my titles here, twenty-eight lovely titles. No* Passion Sinner. *Done. Outline:*

1. Sally Maximus, having graduated from secretarial school, has decided to leave her small home town and go to New York City. With her secretarial school training she's sure she can find a good job, and she wants a little fun and excitement in her life before she settles down to being a housewife. She has done a lot of heavy petting with her boyfriend, Barry Gaiter, but she's still a virgin. The night before her departure, she and Barry go over the line. She gets too hot to stop him and they make it in the back seat of his convertible. She realizes she'd intended to devirginize herself in New York anyway, and she's glad it was good old Barry who got there first.

2. Sally boards the bus for New York and gets into conversation with Matt Sembling, an actor on his way to try for the big time in the city. They neck in the bus, and she gets hot again, and he fingers her to an orgasm. She didn't have one with Barry, and this one astonishes her.

3. In New York, Matt introduces Sally to his cousin, Anita Rorschamb, who is a copywriter in an advertising agency. She is a tall seductive brunette, a Vampira type, and she tells Sally she can stay at her place until she finds one of her own. She also brings Sally around to the advertising agency for a possible secretarial job. Sally is hired, and her boss

is Archer Frenway, who promptly rapes her in his locked office. When she cries for help, he tells her the room is soundproofed. When she says she'll tell the police he says half a dozen men in the agency will swear he was in conference with them at the time and he'll bring a suit against her for slander and libel and malicious mischief. The rape is completed, and he smiles and pats her cheek and says they'll get along fine.

4. Sally, in a state of shock, goes back to Anita's apartment. When Anita comes home that evening Sally is shivering in bed. Anita sits beside her and Sally tells her what happened. Anita says she's heard of such things, but didn't really believe it. She consoles Sally, and it gradually turns physical and Anita goes down on her and Sally comes.

5. Two weeks have passed. Sally hasn't gone back to the advertising agency, nor does she have another job. She's living in a lesbian relationship with Anita. Matt comes by to say he's gotten a job in an Off Broadway theater, and finds out what's going on. He tells Sally all men are not as heartless as Archer Frenway, and convinces her to come with him to his new apartment, in which there's a spare bedroom. He promises to make no sexual moves toward her. She goes with him, and alone in bed that night she thinks about sex straight and sex lesbian and masturbates and comes. She wonders if she can come every way but the right way.

6. Matt has a party for his Greenwich Village and Off Broadway friends. Sally is feeling somewhat better, she's been at Matt's place for two weeks, there's been no sex between them. The party becomes an orgy, which Sally observes but does not take part in.

7. Sally is backstage at the theater where Matt has a small role in an Off Broadway play. She's alone in the dressing room when Anita comes in, angry at Sally for having walked out on her. Anita starts to beat Sally up, and Rex Kilbrood, the male lead in the play, comes in and breaks it up. He consoles Sally in the dressing room, seems very attentive and compassionate and gentle, and gradually seduces her. While they're making it she suddenly realizes the whole thing has been mechanical with him, the whole seduction just a well-rehearsed play, he has no real interest in her at all. He comes, but she does not, and she cynically observes how he handles the brushoff afterwards.

8. Sally is in Matt's apartment, middle of the day. The doorbell rings and it's Archer Frenway. He is distraught, he hasn't been able to forget her, he didn't realize that day in the office that she would become so important in his mind. She sees that he wants to seduce her, more gently than the last time, and she leads him on, going through all sorts of foreplay with him, and when he's just about to score she runs into the bathroom and locks herself in and tells him he'd better leave because Matt is coming home soon. He batters at the door, but she won't let him in, and he finally leaves. It's a triumph, and a revenge, but the taste of it is sour.

9. When Matt comes home, Sally tells him about Archer's visit and what she did, and how she's afraid she's becoming as heartless as Archer himself. Matt begins to kiss her and gradually they make it, with tenderness and caring on both sides, and for the first time Sally has an orgasm with a man the primary way. She's still bathed in the glow of this, of knowing that she is normal after all, when the mail comes, with a letter from Barry saying he's coming to New York to see her. She knows she's going to have to choose between Barry and Matt.

10. Walking down the street, Sally meets a couple of sailors who engage her in conversation. They smuggle her aboard their battleship and when they are on the high seas she blows the entire Seventh Fleet until, bloated with come, she is harpooned by a passing whaler and sinks without a trace.

Now *that's* an outline. I had to type it all out, that seemed simpler than trying to scan it from my copy of *Adios, Scheherazade*, and by the time I was through it was hard for me to resist the urge to write the book. But I'm not certain the last paragraph would work . . .

It's been years since I've done any outlining, and the rare occasions I can recall have been late-in-the-game outlines, jotted down when I've found myself uncertain of my ability to complete a book in satisfactory fashion. I was within a few chapters of the ending of *The Burglar Who Painted Like Mondrian*, the fifth Bernie Rhodenbarr mystery, and couldn't find a murderer for Bernie to unmask.

A friend helped me get some perspective on my storyline, and I sketched out a scene-by-scene outline of the book's conclusion. I don't know that I made any use of this outline once it was actually written down, but the fact that it was concrete enough to appear on a page bolstered my confidence in my ability to write the rest of it.

Except for this sort of emergency first aid, I've become more comfortable in recent years writing without an outline. If I have a sufficient grasp of a book to begin it, I'm able to trust that it will grow organically. One thing will lead to another, and I'll find a way to bring it to an appropriate conclusion.

This confidence, I suspect, owes a lot to experience. I've written so many books, and have seen so many stories take form and reach an ending, that while I can't entirely take anything for granted, I can at this stage relax and trust my own creative process.

A danger with an outline, and a chief reason for me to forego their use, is that having a plot all written down on paper serves to tell the unconscious mind that the work's all done. You run the risk of seeing the completion of the book as no more than a matter of filling in the blanks. Other elements that might otherwise have occurred to you, incidents and characters and twists and turns undreamt of when you wrote your outline, are nipped in the bud.

Often, in the course of Matthew Scudder's investigations, he walks into a room to interview someone without my having the slightest idea who that person will turn out to be. In *The Devil Knows You're Dead*, backtracking a murder victim's life leads Scudder to an interview with a woman who publishes large-print editions of books, and who had employed the victim some years previously. I didn't know where the man had worked, didn't know anything about this woman until I found myself writing the scene—and had the great experience of seeing her come alive on the screen, complete with a full backstory. It was to my mind one of the best scenes in the book, and I can't imagine its having come to me if I'd been working from an outline.

Still, there are writers who continue to use outlines, feeling that their books would lack focus without this tool. To keep the outline from stifling their creativity, they use it but refuse to be constrained by it; at any point they'll deviate from it should their intuition steer them in another direction.

A further thought about the submission process:

Most agents and editors have way too much to read. It's an unfortunate truth that, while most of them found their way into the business out of a livelong love of reading, it's not long before the great bulk of their reading is more chore than pleasure.

I said earlier that agents would rather represent, and editors would rather purchase, a complete manuscript. This is still true today. But almost all of them would rather not have that complete manuscript sail over their transoms and appear on their desks. What they'd prefer for you to submit—and for many this is not a mere preference but a requirement—is a couple of chapters and an outline.

So what should you do? Write the whole book? Or send in chapters and an outline?

I suggest you do both. First, write the whole book. With or without an outline—that's up to you—write the book all the way to the end.

Then write an after-the-fact outline of the entire book from the fourth chapter on. When you submit it, along with Chapters 1–3, note in your letter that you've already written the entire book, and will be happy to send the rest of it on request.

Note, too, that this process is the same whether a particular agent or editor wants paper or electronic submissions.

CHAPTER 7

USING WHAT YOU KNOW...
AND WHAT YOU DON'T KNOW

Write about what you know.
    That's the conventional wisdom, and it seems as sensible now as it did when I first heard it back around the time when the idea of becoming a writer first occurred to me. Several writers whom I greatly admired—Thomas Wolfe for one, James T. Farrell for another—had written whole series of novels which I recognized as frankly autobiographical. Others wrote books that clearly derived from their own life experience. One dust jacket blurb after another would recount the author's background, and each of those writers seemed to have the sort of job résumé that would strike terror into the heart of a personnel manager. A writer, I quickly learned, was someone who grew up on an Indian reservation before running off with a circus. Then over a period of years he worked as an itinerant fruit picker, a gandy dancer on the railroads, a fry cook in a lumber camp, and a teacher in ghetto schools. He saw combat in an infantry division and spent a few years as a merchant seaman. He wrestled a grizzly bear and made love to an Eskimo woman—or was it the other way around?
    Never mind. In any event, it was evident to me that I had two choices. I could ramble around the world gathering up subject matter for stories and novels or I could probe the depths of my life to date, telling an eager world just what it was like to grow up in Buffalo, New York, in one of those happy families that Tolstoy has assured us are all alike.
    I recognized at a very early date that I was not temperamentally equipped to write the conventional autobiographical novel. While I

would not argue that my family and childhood contain nothing of the stuff of which novels are wrought, I was neither sufficiently perceptive nor of the right emotional bent to turn that background into fiction, though many writers have successfully done so.

Nor did I seem inclined to stride adventurously into the world, ready to take on whatever grizzly bears and grizzlier women presented themselves. I was in a hell of a hurry—not to amass experience but to get busy with the actual business of writing. As I've recounted, I wound up writing for a living at rather a tender age; I couldn't write out of my own experience because, for heaven's sake, I hadn't had any.

One way or another, this is the case with a great many of us. While a few of us actually have the adventures first and then learn how to type, that's not usually the way it goes. In actual practice most real-life adventurers never get around to writing; there's always another grizzly bear in their future, and they're too much inclined to pursue fresh experience to bother with emotion recollected in tranquility, as Wordsworth defined poetry. Even when we start out with a background of extensive life experience, adventurous or otherwise, we generally tend to use up our past in our fiction and find ourselves stranded like an overzealous general who has outrun his supply lines. It doesn't take too many books for most of us to exhaust the experiences we've piled up before we started writing. And how are we to gather fresh experience after that point? We've just been sitting in rooms, staring into space and banging away at typewriter keys, and just how shall we turn *that* experience into a novel?

The difficulty of writing out of one's experience can be vividly demonstrated in the field of genre fiction. In my own bailiwick of crime fiction, for example, I'm at a loss from the standpoint of experience. I have never been a private detective like Joe Gores, a cop like Joseph Wambaugh, or a district attorney like George V. Higgins. Neither have I worked the other side of the street and spent time in the clink like Malcolm Braly and Al Nussbaum—not yet, anyway.

All the same, I find myself using my own background and experience every time I go to work. Just as often, I find myself using what I *don't* know—putting to work a combination of research and fakery to furnish what my own background and experience cannot supply.

Let's take them in turn. How can you make your own presumably ordinary background and experience work for you? Here are a few ways to make use of what you already know.

Shape your story line to fit your personal knowledge and experience. Let's hearken back for a moment to the gothic novel we examined in outline form in an earlier chapter. Remember the premise? "A young widow is hired to catalogue the antique furniture in a house on the moors in Devon...." Perhaps you might have come up with just that plot after having done some studying of the gothic category. There's only one trouble. You don't know Louis Quinze from Weird Louie the Plumber, you don't know moors from marshmallows, and the closest you've been to Devon is St. Joe, Mo.

It might seem as though the obvious answer is to write about a weird Missouri plumber with a passion for marshmallows, but the resultant manuscript might be tricky to place with an editor of gothics. A less radical solution calls for examining your plot line and seeing how you can adapt it to fit what you've got going for you.

You say you don't know zip about antique furniture? Well, that's okay, but what *do* you know about? Rare books? Maybe your heroine has been hired to catalogue the ancestral library. Have you got some background in fine art? Maybe she was hired to clean and restore paintings, or to evaluate them or something. Is there some sort of collectible with which you have a fair degree of familiarity? Rare stamps or coins? Old porcelain? Nineteenth-century patent medicine bottles? Roman glass? Oceanic art? A good many plots are almost infinitely adaptable in this fashion, and it doesn't take too much in the way of ingenuity to discover a means of channeling such a story to fit whatever expertise you can furnish.

Use familiar settings for your material. Let's say you haven't wandered far afield from St. Joe, Mo. Or Butte or Buffalo or Bensonhurst. How are you going to write this story about the young widow on the Devonshire moors and make it authentic?

First thing you can do is decide whether or not your story really has to take place in Devon. Maybe there's a lonely house on the outskirts of St. Joseph that could serve as the setting for your story as well as any creaking windswept old manse in the West of England. Maybe there's no such place in reality, but you can build one in your imagination readily enough. Maybe you can readily figure out how people living in such a house, and warped by the strains and stresses built into your basic plot, would relate to and interact with the local people in St. Joseph, much as those moor dwellers in your original outline would relate to the townspeople in Devon. In short, maybe you can transplant all the significant elements of your plot into your own native soil.

If you can manage this, you won't be cheating; on the contrary, you'll simply be making the story that much more your own, one that derives from your own experience and reflects your own perceptions. Perhaps any of a hundred writers could turn out an acceptable book about an imagined Devon moor, but how many could write your story of an old farmhouse on the outskirts of your own town, occupied now by the descendants of the original inhabitants, the farm acreage sold off piece by piece over the years, the house itself surrounded by suburban tract houses, but still awesome and forbidding, and....

See?

On the other hand, maybe there's a reason why your book has to take place in Devon, because of some particular plot component which you regard as intrinsic to the story you want to write. Just as a writer of westerns is locked into setting his books in the Old West, you must set this book in Devon.

Fine. As we'll see shortly, there's a great deal you can do by way of research to make your setting authentic. But there's also a way in which you can exploit your own background in order to construct a setting halfway around the world.

You may not know moors from marshmallows, but if you've crossed the Central Plains you may recall the sense of infinite space, the loneliness, the uninterrupted flatness. You may have had a similar feeling in the desert.

Or you may have experienced a comparable sense of isolation in terrain that has no similarity whatsoever to the moors—the North Woods, say, or smack in the middle of a milling Times Square crowd, or sealed into your own car on a high-speed freeway. The location itself doesn't matter much. Search into your own bag of past experience, using your past like a Method actor, selecting something that will supply you not with circumstances identical to what you're writing about but with equivalent feelings.

Similarly, you can pick a house you know and plunk it down on the moors. Your research may have told you that you need a beamed Tudor dwelling, and indeed you may so describe the house in your narrative. Once you get past the beams, however, you can fill in with details of that house down the road that all the kids were scared of when you were in grade school.

Explore your background and experience as a source for story ideas. Earlier, when we talked about reading and analysis, we saw how familiarity with a genre trains the mind to come up with plot ideas suitable for that genre. Similarly, the study you do and the perception you have of yourself as a writer should result in your sifting your background for elements that will prove useful in your writing.

Once when I was in high school I came home one afternoon to find that my mother had left the place locked. I went around and crawled in through the milk chute, an accomplishment which looked to be as likely as slipping a camel through the eye of a needle, given the tiny dimensions of the milk chute and the unpleasantly plump dimensions of the embryonic author. I was to repeat this procedure on numerous occasions when the door was unlocked, for the entertainment of friends and relatives, and I can still recall squirming through that hole in the wall and landing upside down in a confusion of mops and brooms and scrub buckets; the milk chute, unused since the war, opened into a cluttered broom closet.

Nowadays I write books about a burglar. (Perhaps the seed was planted all those many years ago, when I first discovered the thrill of illicit entry.) I've written three novels to date about Bernie Rhodenbarr without making use of that milk-chute entrance, but I recalled it a week or so ago, and this time I saw it from the stance of one who writes about burglary. I immediately saw any number of ways such a bit of business could fit into a novel about a burglar, and I let my mind play with the possibilities, and I filed them all away in the cluttered broom closet I call a mind; someday I'll quite probably get some use out of it.

In the same fashion, ongoing experience becomes grist for the mill. I can't seem to enter a building without pondering how Bernie would enter it illegally. When I visit a museum I see not merely objects of artistic and historical significance, but things for him to steal. On a recent trip to London, a visit to the Sir John Soane's Museum in Lincoln's Inn Fields turned up a display of the photograph of a pistol which Soane purchased in the belief that it had belonged to Napoleon. It was actually an utter fake and the whole story about its provenance a pawnbroker's fabrication; however, only the photo was on display because the actual pistol, fake or no, had been stolen from the museum in 1969.

I think I'd like that story even if I wrote nothing but stories about kittens and bunny rabbits for preschoolers. Given the kind of writing I do, I immediately thought of six different ways to work that item into fiction. I may never use it at all, but my writer's eye and my writer's imagination have taken a museum exhibit and turned it into the raw material out of which fiction may someday be fashioned.

Cultivating this habit becomes increasingly important the more time you spend in this business. Consider the paradox of the full-time professional writer: He writes out of his experience, using up his past, and the greater his success the less likely he is to store up useful new experiences. I don't get a hell of a lot of fresh input sitting at a desk with a typewriter for company. And, while I derive enormous essential stimulation from the company of other writers, I don't often get source material from them.

Happily, my inclinations are such that I spend a great deal of time away from my desk. My circle of friends includes people of all sorts, and their conversation puts me in worlds I'd never explore otherwise. Just the other day a policeman friend of mine told three or four stories that will very likely turn up in my work sooner or later; more important, his company sharpens and deepens my sense of what a cop's life is like.

Some years ago a friend told me of an evening his father, then the manager of a Miami Beach hotel, had spent in the company of John D. MacDonald. As a long-time fan of MacDonald, I was very interested in knowing what he was like and what he'd had to say.

"Well, he didn't have much to say at all," my friend reported. "He got my father talking, and evidently he's the world's best listener. By the time the evening was done, my father didn't know too much about John D. MacDonald, but MacDonald sure learned a lot about hotel management and the life history of Seymour Dresner."

And that's how it works. A lot of us enjoy holding court, sitting back and talking expansively about our work. It's hearty fare for the ego, to be sure. But if instead we make a real effort to draw out other people's stories, we'll be using the time to good advantage, providing ourselves in due course with stories of our own.

• • •

When I became friends with Evan Hunter, I discovered how good he was at talking to people—or, more to the point, *listening* to them. A cab ride elicited the driver's life history. I'd have ignored the cabby altogether; Evan drew him out, and who knows what might have eventually found its way into a book?

As for that milk chute, somewhere along the way it turned up in one of the later Burglar books. It seems to me Bernie recalled a childhood experience similar to my own, and subsequently reprised that mode of entry as an adult criminal.

• • •

The use of conversation just described is another example of the manner in which the writer is always working, even if he doesn't know for certain what he's working on or what he'll ultimately wind up doing with it. Every conversation, every book read, every new place visited, is a part of the endless and all-encompassing business of nonspecific research.

Which in turn leads us—and I hope you're paying attention to the facility with which I'm making these transitions—which leads us, then, to the business of specific research. We've seen a few of the ways to use what we know. How do we cover ourselves when it comes to something we don't know?

Let's go back to our hypothetical gothic novel, our widow's tale of furniture appraisal on the moors of Devon. Having examined some of the ways we could change that story to fit our own areas of knowledge and experience, let's suppose that for one reason or another we've considered them and ruled them out. Because of particular plot elements we like too much to sacrifice, we're locked to the antique furniture business and the Devon location.

The obvious answer is research. Before you start to write, you have to learn enough about Devon and the antique trade to allow you to feel confident writing about them.

You do not have to become an expert. I'm italicizing this because it's worth stressing. Research is invaluable, but it's important that you keep it in proportion. You are not writing *The Encyclopedia of Antique Furniture*. Neither are you writing *A Traveller's Comprehensive Guide to Devon and Cornwall*. You may well consult both of these books, and any number of others, but you're not going to be tested on their contents.

On the whole, I don't doubt for a moment that too much research is better than too little. Sometimes, though, research becomes a very seductive way to avoid writing.

Ages ago, before I began the first novel I've mentioned earlier, I decided that a historical novel set during the 1916 Easter Rising in Dublin would be a good first book for me to write. I knew nothing about Ireland in general or the Rising in particular, so I read several books on the subject. These made it clear to me that I lacked the necessary background. I decided it was important to begin at the beginning, and I decided further that I couldn't properly grasp Irish history without a thorough knowledge of English history, whereupon I set about amassing an impressive library of books on the subject. You might well ask what Professor Oman's six-volume history of Britain before the Norman Conquest had to do with the purported subject of my novel; I can reply now, in retrospect, that I evidently found reading history a more congenial prospect than writing that novel, and that I found buying books an even more attractive occupation than reading them.

Over the years I did do considerable reading in English and Irish history, for recreational purposes rather than research, and I don't doubt that it enriched my writing in various subtle ways. But I never did write that Irish novel and I doubt I ever shall. I didn't really want to write it in the first place and used research as a way out.

• • •

While it's hard to improve on reading medieval English history to prepare for writing about 1916 Ireland, I know a woman who came close. For a few months in 1984 I conducted a writing workshop under the auspices of Mystery Writers of America. One of our number was fully prepared to fly to Jerusalem so that she'd have a working knowledge of the place before she went to work. Now that might have made sense had she been planning a lengthy novel, but ours was a short-story workshop and she had in mind a suspense short story set almost incidentally in that city. I suggested that she could pick up all the street names and local color she required without leaving New York, and she came to realize that her focus on research was simply a way to postpone the awful moment when she had to sit down and write something.

• • •

George Washington Hill, the legendary tobacco company president, used to say that half the money he spent on advertising was a flat-out waste. "The trouble is," he added, "there's no way of telling which half it is."

Research is a lot like that. For the mythical book we've been discussing, you would want to browse extensively in books on antique furniture, nibbling here and there, trying to get a sense of the antique business while deciding what type of furniture to deal with in the novel and picking up here and there some specific facts and labels and bits of jargon to give your writing the flavor of authenticity.

Some general reading along these lines, perhaps coupled with a few visits to antique shops and auction galleries, ought to precede the full-scale plotting of your novel, whether such plotting will involve a formal written outline or not. In this way the perspective of your research will very likely enrich the actual plot of the book. Then, having plotted the book in detail, you can return for the pinpoint research, picking up the specific fact that you now know to be necessary for the book.

This is what I did with *The Burglar Who Liked to Quote Kipling*. In the original proposal for the book, I supplied a vague outline, explaining that Bernie Rhodenbarr, now operating a bookstore as a cover occupation, is engaged to steal an unidentified whatsit from one collector for another. During the idea's gestation period, I decided to make the stolen item a book of some sort, figuring this would go nicely with Bernie's cover as bookstore proprietor.

Because I envisioned the man who hired him as a pukka sahib type, the thought came to me of making the elusive volume one of Rudyard Kipling's. I accordingly availed myself of an armload of rare book catalogues to find out where Kipling stood in the antiquarian book market. I also got hold of a biography of the author and read it.

My research and my vaunted writer's imagination worked hand in hand. I figured out that the particular book in question would be the sole surviving copy of a privately printed edition which Kipling saw fit to destroy; my copy would be one he'd already presented to his great good friend, writer H. Rider Haggard. I plotted the book accordingly, then went back to the research desk to learn more about Kipling now that I knew what I was looking for. I read a collection of his poems. I sifted some anecdotal material.

Then I started writing the book. And, intermittently, I stopped for some specific spot-research when points came up during the writing that required it.

I could have done more research. I could have read everything Rudyard

Kipling wrote instead of limiting myself to the poetry collection and the *Just So Stories*. I can't see that it would have hurt the book had I known more, because there's always the possibility I would have stumbled on something that would have enriched my novel.

By the same token, I could have managed to write this book with considerably *less* research than I did. I could have invented an item of rare Kiplingana without taking pains to root it in the facts of his life. It would have been *good enough* with less research, I suspect, but it would not have been as good a book as it is now (whatever its overall merits may be).

How much or how little research any area demands is very definitely a subjective judgment. If the Kipling book played a less central role in the mystery, I'd have been wasting time to delve into the subject so deeply. If it played a greater role—if, say, the whole puzzle hinged on various events in the great man's life—then more extensive research might well have been indicated.

If you substitute antique furniture for Rudyard Kipling in what I've just recounted, you'll see how the same principles would apply in our gothic novel. And if you'll substitute whatever unfamiliar subject matter plays a role in your own novel, you'll be able to see to what extent research is required.

What about geographical research? How much do you have to know about a place in order to set a novel there?

Once again, the amount of research advisable is both subjective and relative. Feasibility is a consideration here. I spent an afternoon in Forest Hills Gardens walking around the neighborhood where Bernie was to steal *The Deliverance of Fort Bucklow,* but Forest Hills Gardens is only a fifty-cent subway ride from my door. If I were writing that gothic novel we've been talking about—and I'm beginning to feel as though I am—I could hardly afford to go winging off to Devon for the sake of local color.

On the other hand, if I felt this gothic had enough going for it so that it might transcend its genre and be a candidate for "bestsellerdom," then it might indeed be worth a trip to Devon to give it that added dimension. But if my plot's nothing more than a good honest sow's ear, in no way transmutable into silk-purse status, I don't want to spend as much on research as I can legitimately expect to earn on the finished book.

When I wrote the Tanner books, my hero commonly visited eight or ten countries in a single novel, zipping sleeplessly if not tirelessly all over the globe. Equipped with a decent atlas and a library of travel guides, it's not all that difficult to do an acceptable job of faking a location. A few details and deft touches in the right places can do more to make your book *appear* authentic than you might manage via months of expensive and painstaking on-the-spot research.

I don't want to suggest that such research would be detrimental to a book, just that it's often too costly in time and money to be undertaken. It's worth noting, too, that in certain instances a smattering of ignorance can be useful. In the Tanner books, I'm quite sure my Balkan settings bore little relationship to reality. Then again, I'm equally certain the overwhelming majority of my readers weren't aware of the discrepancy between my version of Yugoslavia and the real one. I was free to make Yugoslavia as I wished it to be for the purpose of the story I wanted to tell, as if I were a science-fiction writer shaping an uncharted planet to my fictive purpose.

I don't know how comfortable I'd be working this way now; I've become a more meticulous writer, sacrificing brash self-confidence in the process. I know, too, that the cavalier attitude I showed would have been a mistake if I had been writing for a market composed of readers who knew Yugoslavia firsthand. One thing a reader will not abide is glaring evidence that the writer doesn't know what he's talking about.

The work of James Hadley Chase is a good example of this. Chase writes hard-boiled suspense novels set in the United States, and while he may have visited here briefly he certainly never spent substantial time on these shores. His American locations never ring true and his American slang is wildly off the mark, the American equivalent of having a duchess drop her "aitches" like a Cockney costermonger. Because of this, his novels have never sold terribly well in the U.S. and most of them are not published over here.

But this doesn't hurt him in England. Some of his readers may realize that the United States of James Hadley Chase bears about as much resemblance to reality as the Africa of Edgar Rice Burroughs, but the false notes don't constantly hit them between the eyes—and they're reading the books for action and suspense, not for their travelogue value. So Chase continues to sell very well over there, year in and year out.

Is Chase a poorer writer because the United States of his fiction differs so greatly from the real United States? I don't think so. It's worth remembering, I think, that fakery is the very heart and soul of fiction. Unless your writing is pure autobiography in the guise of a novel, you will continually find yourself practicing the dark arts of the illusionist and the trade of the counterfeiter. All our stories are nothing but a pack of lies. Research is one of the tools we use to veil this deception from our readers, but this is not to say that the purpose of research is to make our stories real. It's to make them *look* real, and there's a big difference.

Sometimes a few little details will turn the trick, doing far more to provide the illusion of reality than a mind-numbing assortment of empty facts and figures. Sometimes a phony detail works as well as a real one. Bernie Rhodenbarr talks admiringly of the Rabson lock, making me sound quite the expert; there is no Rabson lock—I borrowed the name from Rex Stout's novels. Archie Goodwin always has things to say about the Rabson lock.

Sometimes these little "authentic touches" can happen quite by accident. When I read galleys of *Two For Tanner,* I was startled when a CIA agent in Bangkok pointed out "drops and meeting places and fronts—a travel agency, a tobbo shop, a cocktail lounge, a restaurant...."

A tobbo shop?

What on earth was a tobbo shop?

I checked my manuscript. I'd written "a tobacco shop" and a creative linotypist had vastly improved on it. I decided a tobbo shop would be the perfect CIA front, adding a cracker-jack bit of local color.

So I left it like that.

And now I look forward to the day when I spot in someone else's fiction a reference to the notorious tobbo shops of Thailand. And who's to say that the day will never come when some enterprising Thai opens a tobbo shop of his own? Stranger things have happened.

A very important part of research consists of making use of acquaintances and friends. You'll learn more about what it's like to be a sandhog or a scrap dealer or a bond salesman by hanging out with one than by reading books on the subject. Friends with an expert's knowledge of an area can frequently help you work out bits of plot business; if you present them with a problem, they may be able to think of a solution which would never occur to you.

I've found people even more useful after the book is written. They can read the manuscript and may spot the sort of howlers that, once in print, will draw you no end of angry letters from outraged readers. I don't know much about guns, for instance, and I doubt I ever will; the subject is of limited fascination to me. But I've learned to check points occasionally with a friend of mine who's a gun enthusiast; otherwise the mailman gets tired of bringing me letters from indignant gun nuts.

I wouldn't worry too much over imposing upon acquaintances in this fashion. People like to help writers in their own areas of expertise. I suppose it's ego food. Then too, it gives them a brief role in the writing world, a world which appears to those outside of it to be somehow touched with glamour and romance. I don't know what they think is glamorous about it, but I do know that an astonishing percentage of people go out of their way to help writers, and it makes sense to take advantage of this help when you can use it.

• • •

Research is a very different matter in the age of the computer. It's so easy nowadays to find out almost anything in hardly any time at all that I can find out more without leaving my desk than I used to dig up spending a whole day at the library.

In order to dig deeply into a subject, there's no substitute for sitting down with a stack of books, or conversing at length with an expert. But often one doesn't want to know everything; one simply wants to know enough.

Two words: Google. Wikipedia.

Obviously, neither existed when I initially wrote *Writing the Novel*, or when I wrote any of the books discussed in its pages. Now it's hard to imagine writing *anything* without having access to the Internet and all its resources. I'm working right now in a small office generously made available to me by two friends in the film business, and the first thing I asked on the first day I sat down at my desk was what the password was for the Wi-Fi network. I knew there'd be one, because my friends are as Internet-dependent as I am. And a good thing, because if I can't get online, why come here at all?

There's a free downloadable app called *Freedom* that's had a vogue among writers; you program it for fifteen minutes or an hour, as much time as you want, and during that time it prevents you from getting online. The idea is that you engage *Freedom* to prevent yourself from wasting time.

I downloaded it once, tried it, and decided the hell with it. It worked fine, but I had to override it periodically when I needed to know some specific fact—a state capital, a book's publication date, the proper spelling of some proper name, any of the innumerable facts one needs to know in order to avoid a textual mistake. Yes, I could go ahead and risk the mistake and fix it later on, but why not get it right from the onset?

When I holed up in Philadelphia to write *The Girl with the Deep Blue Eyes*, I was stymied one morning when the Wi-Fi connection went temporarily kerblooey. I wanted to set my story in a fictional county, and needed a name for it. Gallatin Country seemed perfect to me, but was there already a Gallatin County?

I was online throughout the writing of the book—checking maps, working out logistics. My hero spent a lot of downtime watching classic noir films on television, and Wikipedia supplied cast lists and plot summaries. I hadn't known he'd be doing this, so I couldn't have prepared myself and brought a book along, but I didn't need one. My computer gave me access to everything I needed to know.

Aside from the peril of using research as a way to postpone actual writing, it shouldn't be possible to know too much. The greater your body of knowledge, the better equipped you are to select just the right kernels of fact, just the right background trimming, to make a book feel authentic.

Yet sometimes a little knowledge—or a lot of knowledge—is indeed a dangerous thing, and the danger lies in falling in love with what you've learned. "This is a great fact," you tell yourself, "and so what if all it does is slow down the story? I've got to share my new knowledge with my readers!"

The result can be a book that smells of the lamp. Some years ago, a friend of mine told me what a great time he'd had researching his new book, and he needn't have said a word; reading it, I kept encountering facts he'd uncovered and couldn't bear to keep to himself. They got in the way of the story and gave it the tone of a college term paper.

Some writers employ researchers, and swear that key plot elements would never have come to them without the background material and data the researcher was able to provide. And that may well be, and I know Elmore Leonard considered his researcher invaluable, and made extensive use of him for years.

But I nevertheless recall *Killshot*, in which the hero's pursuit of the villain takes him at one point to a stint on an iron ore boat on the Mississippi River. Next thing you know the guy is on the phone with his wife, telling her all of these fascinating details about ore boats and what kind of men work on them and the nature of a typical day on the river. I found it interesting enough, though nowhere near as interesting as did Leonard and his researcher, and it was all to clear to me what that scene was doing there. Leonard couldn't bear to waste what his researcher had handed him, so there it was, whether it belonged there or not.

Elmore Leonard was a wonderful writer, and was justly renowned for a style which he characterized as "leaving out the parts people skip." Well, most of the time . . .

CHAPTER 8

Getting Started

Every novel has a beginning, a middle, and an ending.

I picked up this nugget of information when I first studied writing in college, and I've heard it restated no end of times since then. I pass it on to you because I've never been able to challenge the essential truth of the statement.

I've been trying to think of one solitary instance over the past twenty years when it's helped me to know that a novel has a beginning, a middle and an ending. And I can't come up with a one. I learned at about the same time that in 1938 the state of Wyoming produced one-third of a pound of dry edible beans for every man, woman and child in the nation, and that fact too has lingered in my mind for all these many years, and it hasn't done me a whole hell of a lot of good either. But I pass it on, too, for whatever it's worth.

A beginning, a middle and an ending?

Let's start with the beginning.

Openings are important. In a more leisurely world—a couple of centuries ago, say—the novelist had things pretty much to himself. There was no competition from radio and television, nor were there very many other novelists around. The form was new. Furthermore, life as a whole moved at a gentler pace. There were no cars, let alone moon rockets. One took one's time, and one expected others to take their time—in life or in print.

Accordingly, a novel could move off sedately from a standing start.

A long first chapter might be given over to a thoroughgoing summary of events which we are told took place *before* our story gets underway. It is not uncommon to encounter a Georgian or Victorian novel in which the first chapter constitutes little more than an extended family tree; the story's protagonist doesn't even land in the cradle until Chapter Two.

Things are different now. Novels, crowded together like subway riders at rush hour, stand on tiptoe shouting "Read me! Read me!" They compete with each other and with the myriad other leisure-time activities clamoring for public favor. The reader, however prepared he may be for a long leisurely perusal, is not of a mind to spend a first chapter pruning a family tree. He expects a book to catch his interest right away; if it doesn't, it's the easiest thing in the world for him to reach for another.

"The first chapter sells the book," Mickey Spillane says. "And the last chapter sells the next book."

Spillane, I'm told, also claims to write a book's final chapter first. His entire book is geared to build up to the impact of the finale, he theorizes, so he can best achieve a powerful climax by writing that last scene first, then writing the rest of the book as prelude. I can see the logic in this, but we'll go with the premise for now that you're going to write your book more or less in order, beginning with page one. If nothing else, it makes numbering the pages ever so much simpler.

To return to the point, the first chapter does indeed sell the book. If it is to do so successfully, the reader must be caught up in the story as quickly as possible. Things must be going on in which he can become immediately involved. If you can open with action, physical or otherwise, so much the better.

Beginners frequently have trouble managing this. I know I did. My first chapters tended to introduce characters. I would have them arriving in town, or moving into a new apartment, or otherwise embarking on a new chapter in their lives even as I embarked upon the first chapter of a new book. They would meet people and have exploratory conversations. What kind of a way is that to grab the reader's attention in a grip of steel?

There's a trick I'm going to share with you. I learned it almost twenty years ago and I've never forgotten it, and it's yours for $9.95. If I were you and that were all I got for the price of this book, I don't think I'd have cause to complain. So pay attention.

Don't begin at the beginning.

Let me tell you how I first came to hear those five precious words. I had written a mystery novel, the second to be published under my own name; Gold Medal issued it under the eminently forgettable title of *Death Pulls a Doublecross*. The book was a reasonably straightforward detective story in the Chandler-Macdonald mode featuring one Ed London, an amiable private eye who drank a lot of brandy and smoked a pipe incessantly and otherwise had no distinguishing traits. I don't recall that he was hit on the head during the book, nor did he fall down a flight of stairs. Those were the only two clichés I managed to avoid.

My original version of the book opened with London being visited by his rat of a brother-in-law, whose mistress has recently been slain in such a way as to leave the brother-in-law holding the bag, or the baby, or the bathwater, or whatever. In the second chapter London wraps the young lady's remains in an oriental rug, takes her to Central Park, unrolls the rug and leaves her to heaven. Then he sets about solving the case.

I showed the book to Henry Morrison, who was then my agent. He read it all the way through without gagging, then called me to discuss it.

"Switch your first two chapters around," he said.

"Huh?" I said.

"Put your second chapter first," he said patiently. "And put your first chapter second. You'll have to run them through the typewriter so the transitions work smoothly but the rewriting should be minimal. The idea is to start in the middle of the action, with London carting the corpse around, and then go back and explain what he's doing and just what he's got in mind."

"Oh," I said. And glanced up quickly to see if a lightbulb had taken form above my head. I guess it only happens that way in comic strips.

Now this change, which was a cinch to make, didn't turn *Death Pulls a Doublecross* into an Edgar candidate. All the perfumes of Arabia wouldn't have turned the trick. But it did improve the book immeasurably. By beginning with Chapter Two, I opened the book with the action in progress. There was movement. Something was happening. The reader had no idea who Ed London was or why this young lady was wrapped in her Bokhara like cheese in a blintz, but he had plenty of time later to dope out the whys and wherefores. After he'd been hooked by the action.

(The reader may have further wondered where Ed London got the muscles to manhandle a rug with a corpse rolled in it; oriental rugs are pretty heavy, even without bodies in them. This whole question never occurred to me until years later.)

Ever since Death pulled that doublecross, I've used this opening gambit more often than not. All seven Tanner books employed this device. In some of them I wrote a single chapter before doubling back to explain the book's premise, while in others I let the story line run on for two or three chapters before flashing back and explaining who these people were and what they were doing and why. In the Tanner books, a secondary purpose was served by this technique. The opening chapter or chapters generally left Tanner up against the wall—suspended in a bamboo cage in northern Thailand in *Two For Tanner,* and informed that he's to be executed at sunrise; on a train in Czechoslovakia in *The Canceled Czech,* with a cop asking him for his papers; and literally buried alive in Modonoland in *Me Tanner, You Jane.* This tension was maintained and even heightened by forcing the reader to pause for a flashback; the effect was that of a cliffhanger in an old-fashioned serial.

This business of beginning after the beginning is a natural for novels of suspense and adventure and action. But it works as well in the sort of novel in which characters do not get tossed off Czech trains or buried alive or shot at sunrise. If your story is one of a young man's loss of innocence in the big city, you don't have to begin with him arriving in town. You can choose instead to open with a scene involving him and a girl he's taken up with some weeks after his arrival. They're at a party, or in bed, or having a fight, or whatever—you're writing this, not me. Then in the next chapter you can fill in whatever background has to be filled in. The point, remember, is to involve the reader, to make him care what happens next. You do this by showing your characters in action, in conflict, in motion, not sitting on a park bench musing about the meaning of life.

Innumerable examples of mainstream fiction of the highest order are structured along these lines. They open with a scene designed to get things off to a good start. Indeed, I've read a slew of novels in which the first chapter poses a crisis, the ensuing thirty chapters recount the hero's entire life up to the moment of that crisis, and the final chapter resolves it. Jerome Weidman's *The Enemy Camp* is a vivid example of this approach. By and large this strikes me as too much of a good thing; if the problem is such that it can be stated and resolved in two chapters, why must we wade through a hundred thousand words of background between the statement and the resolution?

Is it always a mistake to begin at the beginning?

Of course not. Always is a word we're trying to stay away from, remember? There are very few absolutes in this business of novel writing, and the First-Things-Second Principle is definitely not one of them. It's extremely useful, and it's always worth considering, but there are times when the best way to start a novel is the most natural way—i.e., at the beginning.

Here are some examples from my own work:

Deadly Honeymoon features a newlywed couple. On their wedding night thugs kill a man at a nearby lakeside cabin. Almost as an afterthought, the bad guys beat up the husband and rape the bride. Our leads do not report this to the cops but hunt down the villains themselves. Here I felt the rape scene was of paramount importance, supplying the motive for everything that follows and making the vigilante activity acceptable and even laudable. Furthermore, there's more action and involvement in that rape scene than in the rather plodding chapters which follow, in which Dave and Jill set about the nuts-and-bolts work of tracking the killers. To open with them making phone calls and checking city directories and then flash back to the rape scene would be spectacularly senseless.

Such Men Are Dangerous—written under the pen name of Paul Kavanagh—concerns a burnt-out ex-Green Beret on the verge of a breakdown who hies himself off to an island in the Florida Keys and lives a hermit's existence. Then a CIA type drops in and involves him in a caper. This would have been a natural for the First-Things-Second approach, but I was more interested in establishing the lead's character at the beginning since I saw that as the most important single element in the book. Moreover, I wanted to show the character going through the process of personality disintegration before he found his way to the Keys, then show the contrast achieved through some months of solitude and self-sufficiency.

The Sins of the Fathers, the first of three books about Matthew Scudder, begins with his being hired by the father of a murder victim. The action which follows is gradual and I felt the book would build more effectively if events were dealt with in chronological order. The two succeeding Scudder books, however, open First-Things-Second.

There are two schools of thought about the opening of a novel. One holds that the important thing is to get it written, the other that the important thing is to get it right. Both of them are quite valid, of course; the distinction is one of emphasis, and it will vary with the writer and with the particular novel.

In my own case, a book is never entirely real for me until I begin putting words on paper. The words of an outline or treatment somehow don't count. I have to be doing the actual writing, pulling finished pages of prose and dialogue from my typewriter. The pages may not be finished in any true sense; I may throw them out, or rewrite them any number of times, before the book is in final form. But they have the look of finished pages, and when they begin to accumulate to the left of my machine, I know I'm really engaged in the curious process of writing a book.

Because of this, I probably start some books prematurely, before they're as well thought out as they might be. My first drafts of my first several chapters are frequently a part of this thinking-out process. It's in the course of writing them that I find out a lot of essential information about my characters and the plot in which they're caught up.

This happened in *The Burglar Who Liked to Quote Kipling*.

Having already written two books about Bernie Rhodenbarr, I probably didn't have to type out fifty pages of first draft in order to make his acquaintance. Nor was I running blind as far as plot was concerned; I already had a pretty clear view of the plot for at least the first hundred pages when I sat down to write page one.

Even so, fifty pages in I decided I didn't like what I'd done. The pace felt wrong to me. There were some characters I wanted to drop, some scenes I wanted to compress. There was a relationship between Bernie and his sidekick Carolyn Kaiser which I knew more about for having written the fifty pages; as a result I wanted to do them over so I could redefine it in the early pages. There were some things I knew about the plot that I hadn't known when I started, and I wanted to lay the groundwork for them in my opening.

On the other hand, I wrote a book called *After The First Death* knowing a great deal about the opening and not too much about what would happen later on. The premise is simple enough: a man has spent time in prison for killing a prostitute during an alcoholic blackout. He wins his release via one of those landmark decisions of the early '60s—Miranda, Escobedo, Gideon, one of those cases. The book opens First-Things-Second style, with Alex waking slowly, coming out of blackout in a Times Square hotel room, seeing a dead woman on the floor in a pool of blood and rocked with the thought that he'd done it again. In the second chapter he decides not to turn himself in, as he did the first time, but becomes a fugitive from justice. Then we're at last told who he is and what it is that he seems to have done again, and then, the flashback completed, he searches his memory and gets a tiny flash of the moment just before he went into blackout, enough of a flash to convince him that he didn't kill the hooker after all and that he has to find out who did. The rest of the book concerns his attempts to do so.

I didn't know who the killer was when I started the book. I didn't even have a clue who the various suspects would be. All I really knew was how I wanted the book to open. That scene was vivid in my mind, and during the writing of it I got enough of an idea who the lead was to write the second chapter. After that point I largely plotted the book as I went along. For all of that, I never did have to rewrite the first two chapters. They were sufficiently well realized to hold up fine despite the fact that I wrote them without knowing what would follow them.

By and large, though, first chapters are more apt to need rewriting than subsequent chapters, at least in my own novels. When this proves to be the case, I have the choice of rewriting my opening immediately or pushing on with the book and redoing the opening after I've completed the first draft.

Again, the decision is individual and arbitrary. Do you get it written first or do you first get it right? I've come to the conclusion that I'm more comfortable with a book if I rewrite this sort of thing as I go along; otherwise my concentration on Chapter Fifteen, say, is diffused by the nagging awareness that Chapters One through Three have to make another trip through the typewriter. We'll discuss this general dilemma again in a chapter on revision, but it seems worth a brief mention here because beginning sections are so often apt to be out of synch with the rest of the book.

Knowing that an opening may very well need to be rewritten can make you sloppy. For this reason, I always proceed on the premise that what I'm writing is what will one day be set in type, word for imperishable word.

But that's just my approach. For another writer, that sort of sloppiness might be worth encouraging; he might be infinitely less inhibited typing an unabashedly rudimentary first draft on yellow second sheets than if he felt his words were being carved on stone tablets.

The important thing, as I've said before, is neither to get it written nor to get it right. The important thing is to do what works.

• • •

As noted, novels were apt to take their time getting off the ground a century or more ago. In this regard, consider Sherlock Holmes debut in *A Study in Scarlet*. In the novel's extended first chapter, virtually nothing takes place. The scene is set for us at 221B Baker Street, but nothing may be said to happen. Now this was by no means unusual in novels of the period, but what strokes me as particularly noteworthy here is that the novel first appeared as a serial in a magazine. Thus, once the stage had been very deliberately set, the reader got to wait a full month to find out whether anything at all would ever occur.

As I've said, I rarely outline, and often begin a book without knowing very much about what's going to happen. More often than not it all works out, and the book finds its way to a satisfactory conclusion.

But there's one experience I had that might be worth noting in this chapter on beginnings.

Quite a few years ago I got an idea for a Matthew Scudder novel. More specifically, I got an idea for the book's ending. I was able to see the climactic scene in considerable detail, and I knew how it might best proceed to the denouement.

I knew what I had in mind was good, and I decided to think about it until I had more of the story in mind. But the more I thought about it, the more vividly the ending played itself out in my mind. Patches of dialogue wrote themselves, and bits of action stood out in sharp relief. I think I could have sat down then and there and written the book's final chapters, and they'd have been fine chapters indeed, but they needed fifteen or twenty chapters in front of them, and I didn't have a clue what they might be.

Now I'm comfortable when all I know of a book is how it begins, because I can take a shot at it. I can sit down and start typing, and by the time I get to the end of the first chapter it's likely that I'll know what to put in the second chapter, and so on. As E.L. Doctorow famously observed, writing a novel is like driving at night; you can only see as far as the headlights reach, but you can get clear across the country that way.

If you know how to start.

But what the hell are you supposed to do when all you know is the ending? You can't just write it down and see where it came from. It doesn't work that way.

No, my task was to find the story to which I'd already been given an ending. And I tried, and some months after I got the idea I was in residence at the Virginia Center for the Creative Arts—a writers colony—and I went to work.

A couple of weeks later I had almost 200 pages written, at which point it became distressingly clear to me that I'd gotten off on the wrong track. I had two weeks left at VCCA, but I knew I couldn't spend them on this book, which would have to be abandoned for the time being and restarted at some later date.

I made the best of those two weeks, spending the days writing short stories. Two of them sold to *Playboy*, including one called "Answers to Soldier," which introduced a hired killer named Keller who went on to star in five books.

Some months later, I found the right approach to the Scudder novel. My false start had allowed me to begin to get the handle on the story that wanted to be told. When I did write it, I was able to use only half a page of the 30,000+ words I'd written in Virginia. But if I hadn't written those unusable words, I don't think I'd have found my way to the story.

And I'd have to say the game was worth the candle. The novel, published as *A Dance at the Slaughterhouse,* was well received by readers and reviewers, and won an Edgar Allan Poe award. So I can't really regret the unorthodox manner in which the story revealed itself to me.

Still, I'd just as soon not have to go through all that again, nor would I recommend it to anyone. Whether you begin your novel at its chronological beginning, or skip ahead a little ways and return to it in a flashback, I'd say you're better off knowing how your book starts before you start it.

CHAPTER 9

Getting It Written

Writing a novel is hard work.

Now writing anything well is work, whether it's an epic trilogy or the last line of a limerick for a deodorant contest. But when it comes to the novel you have to work long and hard even to produce a bad one. This may help explain why there are so many more bad amateur poets around than there are bad amateur novelists. Writing a good poem may be as difficult as writing a good novel. It may even be harder. But any clown with a sharp pencil can write out a dozen lines of verse and call them a poem. Not just any clown can fill 200 pages with prose and call it a novel. Only the more determined clowns can get the job done.

"I could never be a writer," countless acquaintances have told me, "because I just don't have the necessary self-discipline. I'd keep finding other things to do. I'd never get around to working on the book. I wouldn't get anything accomplished."

Let's not kid ourselves. It does take self-discipline. On the dullest day imaginable, I can always find something to do besides writing. I have innumerable choices. I can read, I can watch television, I can pick up the phone and call somebody, I can hit the refrigerator—or I can decide instead to sit at a typewriter, pick words out of the air, put them in order, and spread them on the page.

Unless I can consistently choose to work, I'm not going to get books written.

Self-discipline takes a variety of forms. In this regard we might consider two of the most prolific novelists the world has ever known, Georges Simenon and John Creasey. Each wrote several hundred books, and each achieved considerable prominence in the field of crime fiction.

John Creasey wrote every day. He worked seven days a week, fifty-two weeks a year, producing approximately 2,000 words each morning before breakfast. His routine never varied; at home or abroad, tired or bursting with energy, he got up, brushed his teeth, and started writing. He admitted his behavior was compulsive, explaining that he couldn't relax and enjoy the rest of the day unless he'd first tended to his writing chores. If you write 2,000 words a day, you are going to turn out close to a dozen books a year, and Creasey did just that for most of his lifetime.

Georges Simenon's approach was altogether different. You may have seen a television documentary on his writing habits; it has had considerable exposure over the educational channels. Typically, he would pack a bag and a typewriter and travel to one European city or another where he would check into a hotel. There he would work in the most intense manner imaginable, immersing himself utterly in his work, avoiding human contact for the duration, and producing a finished manuscript in ten or twelve days. The book finished, he would return home and resume his everyday life, letting the plot gradually develop for his next novel, and ultimately heading off to another city and repeating the process once again.

My own writing methods have changed constantly over the past twenty years, forever shaping themselves to fit my state of mind, time of life, and various special circumstances. In the early years, the Simenon approach had a tremendous appeal for me. I can still see something to be said for the idea of completing a book in as short a total span of time as possible; that way one remains very much in the book during the term of its production, and one's involvement can be very intense indeed.

I have on occasion written books in as little as three days; I've written a couple that took only seven or eight days that are probably as good as anything I've done. I can't argue that I made a mistake writing those books as rapidly as I did. Nor am I at all inclined to attempt to do that sort of thing now.

Nowadays I try to write not twenty or thirty pages in a day's time but five or six or seven. Age may very well be a factor, but I rather doubt that it's the only one, or even the major one. It's at least as significant, I think, that I've become a more careful writer and a more flexible one. When I was a brash and cocky young scribbler I was blessed with a very useful sort of tunnel vision; i.e., I could just see one way to do something in a book, and so I lowered my head and charged right in and did it. Now my vision has widened. I'm apt to be more aware of possibilities, of the multiplicity of options available to me as a writer. I'm able to see any number of ways to structure a scene. A slower pace helps me choose among them, selecting the one I'm most comfortable with.

Years ago I was apt to work late at night, and that's something else I don't do any more. I'm sure part of the appeal of the midnight oil lay in the image that went with it—the lonely toiler, fortifying himself with endless cups of coffee, smoking endless cigarettes, and fighting the good fight while the rest of the world slept. There was also a practical element involved; with the rest of my family (like the rest of the world) asleep, I could work without interruption, a consummation devoutly to be wished if ever there was one.

Then too, at that stage in my life I appeared to be more of a night person. I felt the wise thing to do with mornings was to sleep through them, and that a sunrise was a marvelous thing to look at immediately before going to bed.

Ah, well, the only constant is change, and now I almost always make work the thing I do at the beginning of the day, not the end. My work is done most frequently in the morning, immediately after breakfast. When I try to work considerably later in the day, I find my mind's not up to it. I'm fresher first thing in the morning, when I've had six or eight hours of sleep to clear the garbage out of my head.

A majority of professional writers seem to have found this to be true. Quite a few report that they used to work in the evening, or late at night, but that they gradually found themselves becoming morning writers. Others work at night still, and find it's the only time they can work. Others work any old time, whenever they can get it together.

There's no magic answer, and there are certainly more exceptions than there are rules, so I would not dream of advocating that anyone abandon a system that seems to be working just fine. However, for someone trying to decide at what point of the day to schedule writing time, I would very strongly recommend working first thing in the morning, especially for those writers with nonwriting jobs. It's easier to write, and to write well, after a night's sleep than after a hard day's work. It's also a sounder policy to write after morning coffee than after the post-rat race martini.

More important than what hours you spend at the typewriter are how often you choose to spend them. If there's one thing I'm convinced of, on the basis of my own experience and the experience of others, it is the desirability of steady production. There are exceptions—there are always exceptions—but as a rule the people who make a success of novel writing work regularly and consistently. They may take time off between books, or between drafts of a book, but when they're working they damn well work—five or six or even seven days a week until it's done.

There are two reasons why this is important. Obviously, the more steadily you work the sooner you'll be done with this monumental task. If you write two pages a day, a two hundred-page book is going to take you one hundred days. If you write every day, you'll complete that book in a little over three months. If you only average three writing days a week, the same book will take the better part of a year.

More important, I believe, is that steady day-in-day-out work on a book keeps you *in* the book from start to finish, and keeps the book very much in your mind during those hours you're at the typewriter and during those hours you're doing something else—playing, reading, sleeping. You and the book become part of one another for the duration. Your unconscious mind can bring its resources to bear upon plot problems as they present themselves. You don't have to stop at the beginning of the day's work to read over what you've already written and try to remember what you had in mind when you left off last week.

"A novelist," Herbert Gold says, "has to think/dream his story every day. Poets and story writers can go for the inspired midnight with quill dipped in ink-filled skull." And Joseph Hansen adds, "I have made a number of young novelists angry by saying that writing is something you do when you get up in the morning, like eating breakfast or brushing your teeth. And it is. Or it had better be."

After you've determined when to write and how often to write, there's something else you have to work out. That's how much you'll write each day, or how many hours you'll spend doing it.

Some writers put in a certain number of hours each working day. I've never worked that way, and research leads me to believe that most pros pace themselves more by the amount they produce than the time it takes to produce it.

I'm certainly more comfortable making a contract with myself to produce five pages of copy, than to spend three hours at the typewriter. For one thing, the amount of time I spend working doesn't seem particularly relevant. Nobody's paying me by the hour, and nobody's checking to see if I punched the old time clock at the appointed hour. The idea of spending a set number of hours working may help to allay one's conscience, but I don't think it has much to do with the business of writing.

Some days the writing flows and I can do my five pages in one glorious hour. When that happens, I'm free to do as I wish with the rest of the day. I've learned to stop writing then and there, because my mind's tired after five pages, whether it took me one hour or three hours to get them written.

Other days, the writing pours like January molasses. Maybe I'll take five hours to do as many usable pages. Those days aren't much fun, but I've learned to keep at it for as long as it takes, because for all the agony of their composition, those pages are apt to read just as smoothly as the ones that came with no effort. If I threw in the sponge after three hours, those pages wouldn't get written.

I had much the same system at the beginning of my career, when I wrote soft-core sex novels in two weeks' time, five days on, a weekend off, then five days to finish the book. Then I wrote twenty pages a day where now I write five, but the basic principle was the same.

The number of pages you shoot for is for you to decide. My pace changes depending on the book I'm writing. Some novels seem to demand a more intense level of concentration, and a smaller number of pages will tire me. Others, for whatever reason, move at a faster natural pace.

You may find that one page a day is as much as you can easily manage. That's fine. Work six days a week and you'll produce a book in a year. You may find that it's no strain for you to turn out ten or twenty or thirty pages at a stretch. That's fine, too—enjoy yourself. My questionnaire responses suggest that a preponderance of pros do four or five pages a day, but that doesn't mean you'll be less than professional by shooting for a higher or lower number. They settled on that figure because they found out it seemed to be right for them, just as you'll find out what's the right pace for your own novel.

One thing you might try to avoid, in this connection, is attempting to extend your productivity. This sort of overload principle works fine in weightlifting, where one's ability to manage more weight increases as one lifts more weight, but it doesn't work that way in writing. It's tempting to try to do a little more each day than we did the day before, and I still find myself intermittently struggling to resist this particular temptation, even after lo these many years. If I can do five pages today, why can't I do six tomorrow? And seven the day after? For that matter, if I really catch fire and do seven today, that proves I can definitely do a minimum of seven tomorrow. Doesn't it?

No, it doesn't.

What does happen, in point of fact, is that this sort of overload generally leads to exhaustion. Then I can rationalize taking a couple days off—after all, I'm ahead of schedule, aren't I?—and the next thing I know I'm not producing consistently at all. I'm writing in fits and starts, stealing days off and then trying to make up for them by doubling up on my work. The book suffers, the manuscript takes longer than it would have taken otherwise, and once again the tortoise nips the hare at the finish line.

The motto is "Easy does it." Find your right pace, make sure it's one that's not going to be a strain, and then stick with it. If you do have a day when you write an extra page or two, don't waste time thinking about it. Regard it as a freak occurrence, nothing to be deplored but nothing you should make an effort to repeat. When the next day dawns, resume your regular pace and go on writing the book one day at a time.

For years I proofread my manuscripts after they were finished. I hated doing this. When I wrote "The End" in the middle of the last page I felt like a marathon runner crossing the finish line. I wanted to lie down, not jog back over the route and see if I'd dropped my keys somewhere along the way.

As a result, I tended to give my scripts a rather slipshod proofing. That wasn't disastrous—I tend to turn out a reasonably clean script anyway—but after a number of years I found a way to avoid being confronted with that unpleasant postwriting chore, and it paid unanticipated dividends. So I'll share it with you.

I proofread the book as I go along. Not a page at a time, certainly, but either a chapter at a time or a day's work at a time. I perform this little chore either at the end of the day's work or before beginning work the following day.

The effect of this ongoing proofreading is threefold. First, it keeps me very much in the book, especially if I do the job immediately before beginning the next day's work. In the course of proofreading, I'm picking up where I left off and getting my mind set for resuming the narrative.

Second, I do a much more thorough job of proofing when I have a molehill to deal with instead of a mountain. I'm able to take the time to notice changes I want to make. I can spot stylistic irregularities and change them then and there.

Third, I'm more comfortable with what I've done because those pages stacked to the left of my typewriter are in more finished form. True, I may wind up rewriting the whole damned thing—but that's immaterial at this stage. As far as I'm concerned while I'm writing, those neatly stacked pages are what the linotype operator is going to set type from.

Another stray word about proofreading, while we're on the subject. While I'm writing, I tend to xxxxxx out mistyped words and failed phrases. I obliterate these xxxxxx'd out passages with a thick marking pen when I proofread. To expedite matters, I go through the pages once just dealing with the xxxxxx'd out portions; then I can concentrate more deliberately on the actual text when I go through it a second time with a fine-tipped pen.

Seems to me you're making a pretty broad assumption. You seem to take it for granted that all I have to do is put my body in front of my typewriter and everything will follow. What about the days when my mind's a blank?

There are a couple of ways to answer that question. For openers, I'd have to say that the most important step I can take to assure that I'll get work done today is to plant my behind in my desk chair and face the typewriter. While it may not be absolutely true that if you bring the body the mind will follow, the reverse is indisputable; if I don't show up for work I'm not going to get work done. Period.

When in spite of this my mind doesn't seem to be doing its job, it usually means one of two things. Either I'm paralyzed by an inability to figure out What Happens Next, or my mental attitude is keeping my fingers off the keys, making me dissatisfied with my sentences even as I try to form them in my mind.

The first problem, being unable to decide What Happens Next, is one that turns out to be projection a good nine-tenths of the time. Most frequently I know what's going to happen in the five pages I intend to write today; I'm paralyzed because I'm worrying about what's going to happen tomorrow, or the day after, or sometime in early April.

That way lies madness. The better I'm able to focus only on what I'm going to write today, the better equipped I find myself to do a good job with today's writing.

And tomorrow generally takes care of itself. Understand, I'm not denigrating the value of true and proper planning. That's why outlining can be so useful, whether your outline is formal or unwritten. And planning continues to be useful on a day by day basis. I often find myself looking up from a magazine of an evening and letting my mind ruminate upon some plot problem a few days in the book's future.

But when I'm writing, I do best if I concern myself only with that day's writing. Because that's all I'm in a position to deal with at the time. I can no more write tomorrow's pages today than I can breathe tomorrow's air today. The fact that I don't know what I'm going to write tomorrow doesn't matter much today. I don't have to know until tomorrow. And, when tomorrow comes, I'll probably have the answer when I need it. It'll grow out of what I manage to write today and whatever processes my unconscious mind sets in motion between now and then.

Sometimes, however, I know what's going to happen next, both today and tomorrow. What stops me in my tracks is that the words just don't seem to come out right. Nothing seems to work and I begin to have dark suspicions of organic brain damage.

That brings us to our second problem: There are days when all you can do is go to the movies. But there aren't really very many days like that. What I've learned to do on those headful-of-cotton-candy mornings is to sit down and write my daily quota of pages anyway.

I make a bargain with myself. I give myself full permission to decide after the fact that the five pages read as though they were typed by an orangutan. If I hate them the following morning, I can throw them out with a clear conscience. But in the meantime I'm going to sit down and get them written, for better or for worse.

You'd be surprised how often I wind up with five pages of perfectly acceptable copy this way. I may yank a lot of sheets out of the typewriter en route, crumpling them up, hurling them at the wastebasket, and shattering the air with colorful imprecations. But I generally get five pages written that prove to be, if not divinely inspired, nevertheless as good as my prose is apt to get. And, on those genuinely rare occasions when I throw out the five pages on the morning after, I've nonetheless gained from the ordeal; the struggle will have jarred something loose, and I can approach with a clear vision the task that had been so impossibly muddled the day before.

Here's where it's so important that your daily quota is not too great a burden. For my part, I can always manage to squeeze five pages out of my typewriter. It's a manageable burden. If I set my goals higher, I might have no trouble fulfilling them on good days, but on bad ones I'd be awed by having to produce ten or twelve pages. So I'd do none at all, and instead of making progress I'd sacrifice momentum.

Now and then a book grinds to a halt not because of projection or muddleheadedness but because something has Gone Wrong. We'll deal with that in the next chapter.

• • •

But before we do, I should probably discuss the way my own writing methods have changed since I wrote the foregoing.

Since 1987, I've almost always gone away to work. This is not to say that I don't put in time in my home office, writing blog posts and articles and short stories, keeping in touch with the world in the oh-so-social media, responding to a surprising amount of the emails that turn up in my inbox, and (oh, go ahead, admit it) playing innumerable games of computer solitaire.

But when it's time for me to write a book, I get out of Dodge.

This had been an occasional practice of mine since my earliest years as a writer. When I had trouble with a book, I'd pack it and a typewriter and a change of underwear and go find some other venue, most often a hotel room in another city, in which to write.

In the summer of 1987, wanting to write the sixth book in the Burglar series and by no means confident I could do so, I booked my first stay at a writers colony. I was living in Florida at the time, and a week before I was set to drive to Virginia, I had this out-of-the-blue vision of people walking eastward across the United States.

Over the next couple of days, my mind filled with more plot elements, and it became evident that I couldn't spend the next month writing anything other than this book, which clearly was demanding to be written. It was going to be a sprawling multiple-viewpoint book, but perhaps I could get some work done on a first draft.

I drove to Virginia, was assigned a room to sleep in and another to work in, unpacked and went to sleep. In the morning I went to my studio and wrote twenty pages, and I did precisely that for twenty-three days, and it really was like Doctorow's metaphor of night driving; each morning I knew what to write that day, and at the end of 23 days I had 460 typewritten pages, and I packed up and went home.

(I should point out that the book, published by Tor as *Random Walk*, was a massive commercial failure. As much as it insisted on being written, it was evidently less concerned about being read. But that's beside the point. As far as I was concerned, it was a great success, and I still remember fondly and with awe the experience of writing it.)

That sold me on the idea of writers colonies, and on various occasions over the past thirty years I've returned to the Virginia Center for the Creative Arts or to Ragdale, in Lake Forest, Illinois. I haven't been to either colony for quite a while, having reached an age when it just feels a little too much like summer camp for verbal kiddies, but I'm grateful for the residencies I've had there, and recommend them (and others of their ilk) wholeheartedly.

More often in recent years I've made my own personal colony. I wrote a novel (*Hit and Run*) in a rented apartment in New Orleans, and returned to turn another novel into a screenplay. I wrote books in a borrowed apartment in Key West and a budget hotel in San Francisco's Tenderloin district. In a crosscultural extravaganza, I checked into the Listowel Arms, in Co. Kerry, to write *Tanner on Ice*—set in Burma. More recently, I wrote *The Burglar who Counted the Spoons* on a five-week Holland America cruise of the North Atlantic, and *The Girl with the Deep Blue Eyes* in an airbnb rental in Philadelphia.

And so on.

The point is that this seems to work best for me. Typically, on the first morning that I wake up in my temporary abode, I sit down and go to work. I won't leave my desk until I've produced a quantity of work that I find acceptable. While in the typewriter era it was natural to think in terms of pages, the computer makes it simpler and unquestionably more accurate to think in terms of word count. (Way more accurate. "How many words on a page?" is right up there with "How long is a piece of string?" in the Big Book of Unanswerable Questions.)

Whatever quantity I settle on that first day—generally somewhere between 2000 and 4000 words—becomes my quota for that particular book. I won't quit for the day until I reach it, nor will I exceed it by much. Most of the time I'll work seven days a week, although sometimes I might take a day off.

So you no longer recommend writing four or five pages a day?

Sure I do—except that I'd be more inclined now to suggest that you make it 1000 to 1500 words a day. That works best for most writers, and it worked well enough for me for a long time. But over the years I've become more like Simenon and less like Creasey, more inclined to work intensely and in seclusion for short periods of time than to put in regular work sessions all year long.

Either way, the point is to stay at it and get the work done. And either way it's work. I'm exhausted after a productive day at the keyboard, tired and wired to the max, and it's hard to believe that something so enervating burns so few calories. It doesn't seem fair.

Chapter 10

Snags, Dead Ends and False Trails

Sometimes a book just plain runs into a wall. It moves merrily along, lulling you into a false sense of security—is there any other kind?—and then a wheel comes off and there you are, knowing only that it's your fault and that there ought to be something you can do about it.

If I had a magic answer, I would not be writing this book. Not because I'd be unwilling to share such divinely-inspired insight with you. Nothing would give me more pleasure. But I'd be too busy finishing up the dozen or more books of mine that ran into walls over the years, and that have languished unfinished in drawers and cardboard boxes ever since.

I'm not talking about those false starts where I knocked out one or two chapters of a book, then gave it up as a bad job. Those were just ideas I ran up the flagpole; when nobody saluted I hauled 'em down without a second thought. No, I'm talking about books that I stayed with for fifty or a hundred or a hundred fifty pages before something went curiously wrong, with them or with their author, and nothing more ever happened with them.

In some instances, this has happened to me because of my propensity for writing books without having a terribly clear idea where I'm going. I'm sure that if I always worked from a reasonably detailed outline I would run into dead ends far less frequently. On the other hand, my willingness to take a well-realized opening sequence and follow it to see where it leads has enabled me to write several of my most successful novels. If a trunkful of false starts is part of the price I've had to pay along the way, I can't argue that it hasn't been worth it.

All the same, it's never fun investing substantial time and effort, not to mention mental and emotional involvement, in a never-to-be-finished book. Schubert's "Unfinished Symphony" is part of every symphony orchestra's repertoire, and *The Mystery of Edwin Drood* has remained in print since Dickens left it unfinished at his death, but this doesn't mean any of my stillborn literary offspring will ever get anywhere. While regretting them is a waste of time, I'd certainly like to have as few of those abortive efforts as possible in my future.

One thing I've come to recognize is that I tend to run into a wall at a certain point in almost all of my books. I've been given to understand that marathon runners experience this sort of exhaustion somewhere around the twenty-mile mark when their glycogen stores run out. They keep going anyway and generally finish the race on their feet.

Most of my suspense novels run a shade over two hundred pages in manuscript, which probably comes to something like sixty thousand words. More often than not, these books hit the wall somewhere around page 120. It's around that point that I find myself losing confidence in the book—or, more precisely, in my ability to make it work. The plot seems to be either too simple and straightforward to hold the reader's interest or too complicated to be neatly resolved. I find myself worrying that there's not enough action, that the lead's situation is not sufficiently desperate, that the book has been struck boring while my attention was directed elsewhere.

I have come to realize that this conviction is largely illusory. I don't know what causes this misperception of mine, but I would suspect it reflects attitudes of my own that have nothing much to do with the book. In any event, I know from experience that there's very likely nothing wrong with the book, and that if I push on and get over the hump I'll probably have a relatively easy time with the final third of the manuscript, and that the book itself will be fine.

If I put it aside, however, and wait for something wonderful to happen, I'll very likely never get back to it.

It may not work this way for everyone, but I've learned to my cost that it works this way for me. The temptation to take a break from a novel when it runs out of gas is overwhelming. It seems so logical that such a break will have a favorable effect; phrases like "recharging one's batteries" come readily to mind. The wish, I'm afraid, is father to the thought; struggling with a difficult book is unpleasant, and one very naturally wishes to be doing something else—anything else!—instead. But such a move is generally undertaken at the cost of completing the book.

I hardly ever go back to the books I abandon. Maybe that's as well, maybe they're better off rusting out on the side of the road, but I don't think so. It seems to me that some of the ones I let go of had just run into that wall around page 120; if I'd stayed with them they'd have worked out fine. By taking a break from them I sacrificed all the momentum I'd built up. In addition, I let my grasp of the characters and settings loosen up. The book drew away from my consciousness and from my unconscious as well.

Understand, please, that I'm not referring to an occasional break of a day or two. That may be useful for me when I've been working too hard for too long and I need to relax. But when I put a book aside for a week or a month, when I deliberately elect to shelve it while I work on something else, I'm really laying it aside forever.

This said, the fact remains that many books do hit snags, run into dead ends, or wander off down false trails. Having established that the thing to do is press on with them, the question arises as to how best to manage this.

Frequently the trouble is plot. If you outline as I generally do, with a more comprehensive picture of the early portion of the book and blind faith that the latter chapters will take care of themselves, the problem is often one of planning what will occur next. In mysteries, where the unfolding of action occurs simultaneously with the gradual discovery of what's really been happening, this business of figuring out what's going on is doubly problematic.

But people who outline carefully can have the same sort of plot trouble. For them—or for me, with those books in which I use a detailed outline—the problem comes when the book grows apart from its outline. Perhaps a certain character has taken shape in such a way as to make what's scheduled to happen no longer viable. We spoke earlier of the need for flexibility, stressing that you have to be willing to adapt your outline to allow for the organic growth of your novel. When this happens, you're in the same place as the person writing without an outline to start with. You have to figure out what happens next.

The image that comes to mind when I think of this sort of snag is that of a log jam. I've generally got enough ideas in my mind but they're snarled up like floating timber in a river, pinning each other down, getting in each other's way. If I could just shake things loose the book would flow downstream with no trouble at all.

The best way I've found to jar thoughts loose is to talk to myself at the typewriter, babbling away at myself without regard to style or sense, producing something that's a combination of stream-of-consciousness, letter to self, and outline of the remainder of the book. I usually throw these things away when they've ceased to be useful—I've never seen the point in saving remnants for posterity, figuring it's unlikely enough that posterity will be interested in my books, let alone my literary fingernail clippings. With my most recent book, however, I ran headlong into what looked at the time to be a serious plotting problem. I resolved it by chattering to myself at the typewriter, and I haven't yet discarded the gibberish I produced, having realized at the time that it might come in handy to illustrate a point in this present volume. Here, then, is how I talked to myself during a difficult stage of *The Burglar Who Liked to Quote Kipling:*

> All right, where's the book going? Bernie stole the book from Arkwright on Whelkin's orders. Then went to meet Whelkin at Porlock's apartment. She drugged him, and when he woke he was framed for her murder. Meanwhile, a Sikh tried to get the book from Bernie and went off with the wrong book.
>
> Okay. Say the Sikh worked for the Maharajah of Jaipur. Madeleine Porlock was being kept by somebody, stole the book and sold it to Arkwright. Suppose Porlock was sleeping with Arkwright, kept

by him. Bernie could know this from fur labels in her closet. She and Whelkin knew each other—that's why she wore the wig to the bookstore—and she managed to learn that Whelkin was going to try to steal the book via Bernie.

Suppose Arkwright wanted the book to swing an import-export deal with a Saudi Arabian big shot who collects anti-Semitic material. The book would be a sweetener. Arkwright's enough of a collector to have gotten into a book discussion with the Saudi.

Suppose there were a couple of dozens of these books. Whelkin got hold of the cache in England and faked the Haggard inscription on all of them, selling them one at a time to rich book collectors with the proviso that they keep it a secret. He's sold a copy to Arkwright. Then he finds out Arkwright is going to show his copy to the Saudi. He has to get the Arkwright copy back or the Saudi will know there's been fraud committed.

Who killed Porlock?

Could be Whelkin. Say Whelkin worked through Porlock to get Arkwright to buy the book. Porlock was trying to recover the book herself to sell it elsewhere. Whelkin entered the apartment after she drugged Bernie and killed her, framing Bernie for it.

Or suppose it was Arkwright? When he found the book missing he suspected Porlock engineered the theft. He figured she played him for a sucker and shot her and left the gun in Bernie's hand to get rid of the disloyal mistress and the actual burglar in one swoop. Bernie could half-recognize the gun from having seen it in Arkwright's den.

What about the Sikh? He works for somebody, the Saudi or the Maharajah, who cares?, and he learned that Bernie had stolen the book....

This process of talking out loud goes on for another couple of hundred words, with more possibilities brought up and discussed and set out for inspection. Then I wrote an outline of the next three chapters to be written, and then, unblocked and a little bit clearer, I sat down and wrote them.

That wasn't the end of my problems with *The Burglar Who Liked To Quote Kipling*. The plot was a complicated affair and it continued to work itself out as it went along, and twice more I rolled a sheet of paper into the typewriter and did some thinking on the keys. Both times I managed in this fashion to shake something loose and I was able to continue plotting and writing the book, carrying it through to completion. I not only finished a book that at one point looked unworkable, but I wound up producing a novel I'm pleased with.

If instead I had put it on the shelf to sort itself out, I'm certain it would still be there, gathering dust and serving as the source of monumental guilt. Snags and dead ends don't sort themselves out, I've come to believe. They get sorted out, and it takes work, and you have to do it yourself.

You don't have to do this sort of thing on paper. Some writers find it useful to talk this sort of a problem into a tape recorder. Later they play back the tape and find out what they've got in mind. Others work things out by discussing things with a friend. Not every friend will do for this process, and you have to experiment to determine which of your acquaintances serves you best as a sounding board. Some people—well-meaning, certainly, and often creative themselves—serve only to stifle your imagination. Others prove enormously helpful, perhaps because they're capable of listening so attentively. The person you select may be an agent or an editor. It may as easily be someone unconnected with the business, someone who doesn't even read much. You can try different people to see who does you some good, bearing in mind the distinct possibility that this is a process you can only handle on your own.

Sometimes my difficulty in writing Chapter Eleven is directly attributable to the way I wrote Chapter Ten. If I take a wrong turn in a book, that can fence me in further down the line.

The answer's clear enough. You drop back fifteen yards and punt. In other words, I go back to the point where things took that wrong turn and start rewriting from there.

The problem lies in knowing when that's what's hanging you up. Happily enough, the solution sometimes works even when this isn't the real problem. Maybe you're blocked because of atmospheric conditions, or phases of the moon, or what you had for dinner last night. Even so, redoing a chapter you've already written may start the juices flowing and unblock you all the same.

When John D. MacDonald goes stale, he props open somebody else's book and starts copy typing. After a few paragraphs or pages, he finds himself changing a word here and a phrase there, improving what he's copying. Pretty soon he's ready to get back to work on something of his own.

Perhaps you'll find this approach useful should you go stale in the course of writing your novel. There are a few other suggestions that may or may not prove helpful.

Read what you've written. Suppose you've had to spend a week or two away from the manuscript, not because you've been avoiding it but because something else came up. The danger here is not just loss of momentum but that the book slips out of mind. Take your time and read it over before plunging back into it. You may even want to read it more than once. Remember that, important as it is for us to stay in the now while we write a book, a portion of our mind deals with the past and the future—i.e., what we've already written and what we'll be writing next. Reading the manuscript recharges those batteries.

Retype the last few pages. This is a good way to get back into the rhythm of your writing, whether you've been away from it for a short or long period of time. I've heard of writers who make it a practice to begin each day's work by retyping the last page they wrote the day before. The habit may have started when they left off in the middle of the page and wanted to start in on a clean page; it endured when they found it helped them recapture the flow of the previous day's writing.

Break in the middle of a sentence. I've read this advice in various forms over the years. Some people advocate stopping at the bottom of the fifth page of the day, say, even if it's smack in the middle of a hyphenated word. Others are less compulsive about where you stop but merely suggest that it be at a point where you know precisely what sentence you're going to write next.

The theory here is that you'll have an easier time picking the book up the next day because you already know what your first sentence or two will be. I offer this suggestion because it evidently works for some people, but I'm not going to tout it too strongly because I've really made some grim mornings for myself this way.

Imagine, for instance, sitting down to the typewriter and seeing this looking back at you. "She looked up at me, bright-eyed, and her smile was like...."

Like *what*, for the love of God? I obviously had a simile in mind when I wrote what I wrote, and I'll never come up with a new simile and believe it to be as good as the lost one, and in the meantime I may spend half an hour scratching my head and trying to recall what I was thinking of. If I've got a good sentence in mind, the best thing I can do with it is commit it to paper before I lose it. So my own advice would be more along the lines of this:

Find a logical place to break off. At the end of a chapter, or the end of a scene, or the end of a paragraph, or at the very least at the end of a sentence. Not only does this avoid the sort of minor aggravation described above, but I believe it helps focus the attention of the subconscious mind upon the new chapter or scene or whatever to be tackled next.

You've abandoned books—quite a few of them, from the sound of it. And you've already said there's a strong possibility that my first novel won't prove publishable, that its main function may be as a learning experience. Suppose I reach a point where I'm sure it's not going to succeed. Wouldn't I be justified in abandoning it?

No.

Oh, you *can* abandon the book. For that matter, you didn't have to start writing it in the first place.

But once you do undertake to write a first novel, I strongly urge you to finish it. Whether or not you lose faith in it along the way. Whether or not you're convinced it stinks. No matter what, stay with it a day at a time and see it through to completion. If its chief function is to be educational, rest assured that you'll learn infinitely more by finishing a first novel than by casting it aside.

I'd suggest further that you complete a first draft from beginning to end before getting involved with substantial revision. There's one exception—if you want to go back and start over after you've done forty or fifty pages, feel free to do so. But after you've passed the fifty-page mark, I would recommend that you push onward to the end before giving any thought to rewriting.

I have a reason for this stance. I've observed that most of the people who start first novels never finish them, and I've come to believe that actually seeing a book through to the finish line is the most important thing you can do in your first essay at the novel. This to my mind is what separates the sheep from the goats and the ribbon from the clerks: the determination to stay with a book until it's done, for better or for worse.

If you abandon a first novel, the chances of your ever writing and completing a second novel are rather slim. If you pause in the course of a first novel for substantial revision, the chances of your finishing the book are lessened. Finishing a novel isn't a cinch, even if you've done it a dozen times already. When you're making your initial attempt, I would suggest that other considerations be kept in the background. In this case, the first thing is to get it written. Later on you can worry more about getting it right.

• • •

Some further thoughts:

If you get stuck, keep it to yourself. On several occasions over the years, I took a manuscript I'd gone stale on and showed it to my then-agent, the late Knox Burger. In every case he would respond by questioning the book's premise, or finding the characters uninteresting or unsympathetic, or simply stating that he certainly couldn't see a way to save it. And I, with a mixture of disappointment and relief, would feel justified in abandoning the damn thing.

Eventually I realized what I was doing: I was passing the buck to Knox, confident that he'd give me permission to quit. Knowing what I was doing meant I really couldn't do it anymore, and I stopped making that particular mistake.

On the other hand . . .

If you get stuck, show it to somebody. When I was writing *The Burglar Who Painted Like Mondrian*, the fifth Bernie Rhodenbarr mystery, I reached a point where I couldn't find a way to solve it. Because the Burglar books are deductive mysteries, with a puzzle to be solved by the protagonist in the course of which he unmasks a killer, they require a reasonably intricate plot; since I don't outline them, this can leave Bernie confronting a puzzle for which there is no solution. I'm told that lab rats who've been taught to solve mazes, and who are subsequently placed in an insoluble maze, respond eventually by sitting in a corner and eating their own feet. I'm not sure if this is true, but I'm inclined to believe it, and I think I know just how they feel.

I mentioned the problem to a friend of mine, Laurence Anne Coe, who at the time was involved in theatrical production. She pointed out that her work consisted in part of helping people fix what wasn't working, and offered to read my work in progress. While I don't recall her coming up with a solution, the discussion I had with her triggered something, and I was able to complete the book successfully.

Writer's Block? There's an app for that. Well, no, there's not, although I'm not convinced there won't be by the time you read this. But what there is, I'm pleased to report, is a book for it. It's *Break Writer's Block Now!* and my friend Jerrold Mundis is its author. He's also its ebook publisher, and you can find it offered at a very reasonable price at all ebook sales platforms.

St. Martin's Press published the book in hardcover in 1991. It went out of print within a few years, at which time Jerry bought the remainder but lacked storage space for them. He sold them to me, and for years now I've been selling the book, most recently in my eBay store.

Chapter 11

Matters of Style

In stating as fully as I could how things really were, it was often very difficult and I wrote awkwardly and the awkwardness is what they called my style. All mistakes and awkwardnesses are easy to see, and they called it style.
   —Ernest Hemingway

I've often wondered, when contemplating the passage quoted above, whether or not the author wasn't being a trifle disingenuous. We certainly regard Hemingway as a highly stylized writer. Passages from his works, taken out of context, are unmistakably his, and the Hemingway style is as inviting a target for the parodist as is the Bogart lisp for an impressionist. It's hard to believe a man could develop a style at once so individualized and so influential without having the slightest suspicion of what he was doing.

Be that as it may, I have no quarrel with the implied message—i.e., that the best way to develop a style is to make every effort to write as naturally and honestly as possible. It is not intentionally mannered writing that adds up to style, or richly poetic paragraphs, or the frenetic pursuit of novel prose rhythms. The writer's own style emerges when he makes no deliberate attempt to have any style at all. Through his efforts to create characters, describe settings, and tell a story, elements of his literary personality will fashion his style, imposing an individual stamp on his material.

There are a handful of writers we read as much for style as for content. John Updike is one example who comes quickly to mind. The manner in which he expresses himself is often interesting in and of itself. It is occasionally said of a particularly effective actor that one would gladly pay money to hear him read the telephone directory. Similarly, there are readers who would gladly *read* the phone book—if someone like Updike had written it.

The flip side of this sort of style is that it sometimes gets in the way of content in the sense that it blunts the impact of the narrative. Remember, fiction works upon us largely because we are able to choose to believe in its reality. Hence we care about the characters and how their problems are resolved. Just as a poor style gets in our way, making us constantly aware that we are reading a work of the imagination, so does an overly elaborate and refined style set up roadblocks to the voluntary suspension of our disbelief. From this standpoint, one may argue that the very best style is that which looks for all the world like no style at all.

Style, along with the various technical matters that come under that heading, is difficult for me to write about, very possibly because my own approach has always been instinctive rather than methodical. From my earliest beginnings as a writer, it was always a relatively easy matter for me to write smoothly. My prose rhythms and dialogue were good. Just as there are natural athletes, so was I—from the standpoint of technique, at least—a natural writer.

This gave me a considerable advantage in breaking into print. I can see now that a lot of my early pulp stories had rather little to recommend them in terms of plot and characterization, but the fact that they were relatively well-written in comparison to the efforts of other tyros got me sales I wouldn't have had otherwise. But a smooth style in and of itself is no guarantee of true success. For years I was accustomed to a particular message in letters of rejection. "The author writes well," my agent would be advised. "This book didn't work for us, but we'd be very interested in seeing something else he's written." That sort of response is encouraging the first few times you receive it. When it becomes a common refrain, all it sparks is frustration.

I know several writers who were similarly gifted stylistically and who report similar early experiences. Over the years we've worked to develop our abilities at plotting and characterization, though for some of us the disparity is still in evidence. In my own case, it hasn't been all that long since an editor last explained how much he liked my writing—but that he didn't like my book.

Other writers have the opposite problem. A friend of mine has an extraordinary natural sense of story, coupled with an enthusiasm for his plots and characters which communicates itself in the drive of his narrative. From a technical standpoint, however, he's almost numbingly maladroit. His first novel was rewritten several times prior to publication, and received extensive textual editing from his publisher; even so, it remained a crude book. He has improved considerably since then, but to this day, ten books later, he is still very much the heavy-handed writer. Nevertheless, his books are almost invariably best sellers because of the particular strengths they do possess.

My point here is that someone like my friend, who has had to teach himself so much about the nuts-and-bolts side of writing, might well be better equipped than I to discuss the subject. It's harder to discourse effectively upon something when one's approach to it has always been intuitive.

That said, perhaps we can have a look at a handful of subjects which fit under the general umbrella of style. Perhaps you'll find something here of some value, whether you yourself are a natural literary athlete or whether you have to work very hard to make it look easy.

Grammar, Diction and Usage

A fiction writer doesn't have to be the strictest grammarian around. He can get by without a clear understanding of the subjunctive. Indeed, the sort of slavish devotion to the rules of grammar that might gladden the heart of an old-fashioned English teacher can get in the way of the novelist, giving his prose a stilted quality and leading his characters to talk not as people speak but as they ought to.

In my own case, I'm aware that I make certain grammatical errors, some of them deliberate, others through sheer ignorance. I have a copy of Fowler's *Modern English Usage*, a book I unhesitatingly recommend, and yet months pass without my referring to it. When I'm hammering away at the typewriter keys, trying to get a scene written and to get it right, I'm not remotely inclined to interrupt the flow for the sake of what Churchill called "the sort of errant pedantry up with which I will not put."

In first-person writing, I would maintain that the writer is fully justified in breaking grammatical rules and regulations at will. How the narrator expresses himself, the words he uses and the way he puts them together, is part of the manner in which his character is defined. I will argue further that a first-person narrator may follow a particular precept on one page and violate it on another. If our characters are to be lifelike, we can hardly demand absolute consistency of them.

The same principle applies, and rather more obviously, in dialogue. Most people don't express themselves the way English teachers wish they would, and it's part of the novelist's license to make their speech as grammatical or ungrammatical as suits his purpose.

You'd think this would go without saying. I've far too often had my characters' grammar corrected by overzealous copy editors to believe that *anything* in this area goes without saying.

Copy editors are even more of a nuisance when it comes to punctuation. Various rules for punctuation have grown up over the years, but it's a moot point whether they apply to fiction, where punctuation may be properly regarded as a device the writer can use to obtain the effect he desires. You can choose to write this sentence:

She was angry, and not a little frightened.

Or you can write it this way:

She was angry and not a little frightened.

The decision, I maintain, is personal. The presence or absence of a comma in this sentence determines the rhythm of its reading, and that's a choice the author is fully entitled to make. It will hinge on the rhythm of the sentences which precede and follow it, on the author's natural style, on the effect he's trying to achieve, and on such intangibles as the weather and the astrological aspects. It should not hinge on what someone with a red pencil was taught in English Comp 101.

I get rather emotional on this subject. For years copy editors have gone through my manuscripts, arbitrarily deleting commas of mine and inserting commas of their own. I don't put up with this sort of thing anymore. Brian Garfield, similarly infuriated, has taken to writing before-the-fact memos to copy editors, explaining that he's been in this line for a few years now and knows the rules of punctuation sufficiently well to break them at will.

And yet, and yet....

I remember, back in school, a student's inquiring of a teacher as to whether spelling errors would lower one's grade on a particular examination.

"That depends," the teacher explained. "If you spell cat with two t's, I might let it pass. If you spell it D-O-G, it's a mistake."

Some writers approach grammar and usage and punctuation like the kid who spelled cat D-O-G. I've been trying lately to read what is either a memoir of Hollywood or a novel in the form of a memoir—the publisher's blurb leaves the question open—and the author's cavalier disregard for matters of usage makes the book sporadically unreadable, for all that's interesting in the material.

Consider this sentence, a personal favorite of mine: *They didn't even say "Presbyterian Church"—they called it "the First Pres," that's how the texture of even as innocuous as watered-down Protestantism was watered down.*

Now the trouble with that sentence is that you can read it three times trying to figure out what it means and you won't get anywhere. I can't even figure out how to fix it. The whole book is full of stuff like this, and it's enough to give you a headache.

A reputable publisher issued this one, and I can only assume the author had strong feelings about the integrity of her prose. Otherwise a copy editor would have made any number of changes, most of which could only have been for the better. When a writer's style is at the expense of clarity, when the prose obscures the meaning, something's wrong.

Dialogue

When you're looking for something to read at a library or bookstore, do you ever flip through books to see how much dialogue they have? I do, and I gather I'm not alone.

There's a reason. Dialogue, more than anything else, increases a book's readability. Readers have an easier and more enjoyable time with those books in which the characters do a lot of talking to one another than those in which the author spends all his time telling what's happening. Nothing conveys the nature of a character more effectively than overhearing that character's conversation. Nothing draws a reader into a story line better than listening to a couple of characters talking it over.

A good ear for dialogue, like a sense of prose rhythms, can be a gift. *Ear* is the right word here, I believe, because I think it's the ability one has to hear what's distinctive in people's speech that expresses itself in the ability to create vivid dialogue in print. (Likewise, I think it's the ear that enables some people to mimic regional accents better than others; the acuity with which you perceive these things largely determines your ability to reproduce them.)

I think a writer can improve his ear by learning to keep it open—i.e., by making a conscious effort to listen not only to what people say but to the way they say it.

It's worth noting that the best dialogue does not consist of the verbatim reproduction of the way people talk. Most people, you'll notice, speak in fits and starts, in phrases and half-sentences, with "uh" and "er" and "you know" tossed in like commas. "I was, see, like the other day I was goin' to the store, see, and uh, and like I was, you know, like, walkin' down the street, and...."

People do talk this way, but who the hell would want to read it? It's tedious. This doesn't mean that you can't have a character express himself in this fashion, but that you would do so not by holding a tape recorder in front of him but by *suggesting* his conversational manner: "Like the other day I was goin' to the store, see, and I was like walkin' down the street . . . ."

A little goes a long way. Same thing with phonetic spelling of dialogue. There was a great vogue for that sort of thing a while back, when regional fiction was in its heyday, and there are still people who are crazy about it. Most people find it off-putting. There's no question that it slows things down for the reader; he has to translate everything before going on.

Here again, the answer lies in suggestion, in picking a couple of key words and using them to illustrate the character's unorthodox speech patterns. You might indicate a West Indian accent by spelling man *M-O-N*, for example, or a Puerto Rican inflection by rendering don't *doan* or affixing an *E* to the front of a word like *study*. A light sprinkling of this sort of thing reminds the reader that the speaker has a particular accent; he'll then be able to supply the rest of the accent, hearing it in his mind as he reads the character's dialogue, even though the rest of the words are spelled in the traditional manner.

Remember, less is better, and when in doubt, forget it.

Richard Price handles dialogue brilliantly. His first book, *The Wanderers,* traces the lives of members of a Bronx street gang. Their speech patterns are faithfully rendered and add greatly to the book's impact. Recently, though, I happened on a back issue of a literary quarterly in which a chapter of *The Wanderers* appeared prior to the book's publication. In that version, Price made extensive use of phonetic spelling, and while other elements of the story were identical, the spelling put me off. Evidently the book's editor reacted similarly. Whether Price or his editor made the actual changes is immaterial. The book gained greatly by them.

Good dialogue differs from real-life dialogue in another respect. It's written out. The reader gets the words without the inflection. If you just put down the words, the result can be ambiguous. You can italicize a word to show that it's being *stressed* by the speaker, or you can include the occasional notation that a given sentence was said lightly or seriously or heavily or archly or whateverly, but sometimes you have to restructure a sentence so that the reader will not have trouble getting your meaning.

Another thing you have to do in dialogue is compress things. People generally have more time for conversation in real life than in books. You have to speed things up in the actual dialogue, cutting out a certain amount of the normal volleying, and you also have to do a certain amount of summing up. In my Scudder novels, for example, Scudder receives the bulk of his information by going around and talking to people, and the reader overhears much of this in the form of dialogue. But from time to time Scudder will break off reporting exactly what was said in dialogue form and simply give the gist of a conversation in a sentence or two.

When this isn't done, when a book's all dialogue, it feels puffy and padded. It moves fast and it's easy to read, but it's ultimately unsatisfying. One's left with the feeling that nothing has happened at great length.

Past versus Present Tense

The great majority of fiction is written in the past tense. The effect is that one is being told a story which has taken place. Even if the story is set in future time, as in most science fiction, either the narrator or the disembodied voice recounting the story is presumably speaking at a later time than the action occurred.

There is an alternative to this which is achieved through the use of what is known as the historical present tense. Those who prefer this tense argue that it makes the story a more immediate experience for the reader; it is going on as he reads it.

They are also apt to take the position that it is more contemporary, less old-fashioned. There is, as it happens, nothing particularly new about the historical present. Offhand, I can recall that the Marquis de Sade used it in his novels in the eighteenth century, and it may for all I know go back halfway to Homer. In our own time, there is something distinctly cinematic about writing in the present tense. It has a screenplay feel to it.

There's rather more to the use of the historical present than a simple change of tense. This becomes clear when you take a patch of prose written in the past tense and change it to the present. It will very likely be stiff and awkward, unnatural. In order for the historical present to be effective, the whole narrative attitude changes in subtle ways.

Whether or not to employ the historical present is entirely a matter of choice. In genre fiction I would consider it a poor idea, if only because category novels are hardly ever written in present tense. I wouldn't care for the job of trying to sell a gothic or a western, say, written in the historical present, though I do not doubt for a moment that such a novel could be written effectively and might even find its way into print.

My own personal bias against the historical present is a very strong one, so much so that, when I'm browsing paperback racks looking for something to read, I'm inclined to pass up books written in present tense. The one time I tried to write a novel in the present tense I found myself incapable of sustaining the voice past a couple of pages. But that's my personal reaction, and has nothing much to do with the relative merits of the two tenses.

• • •

My distaste for present-tense fiction hasn't changed over the years, but I've got a little more perspective on what I dislike about it.

It became clearer for me when I read *A Son of the Middle Border*, Hamlin Garland's memoir of a 19th Century boyhood in the American Midwest. In the book, Garland moved back and forth between the tenses. He wrote mostly in the past tense, but switched to the present tense to recall an incident in detail.

This worked very well, and it took me a while to figure out why. Writing in the past tense is precise and factual, and the reader believes those declarative sentences because they are presented as historical fact. When I write, say, "John Carver walked down Crestwood Avenue, and his arms were swinging at his sides," how can you doubt my word? I said it, and part of the compact between writer and reader is that you'll believe what I tell you.

And if I were to write instead, "John Carver walks down Crestwood Avenue, and his arms are swinging at his sides," well, it's not a fact so much as it's a picture being drawn for you. It's the way you'd write it in a screen treatment, so that the reader might picture it. And it works; you do in fact picture it, but it's not something that has happened. It's something that is happening, jotted down in pencil rather than carved in stone.

That made the present tense ideal for Garland when he wanted you to visualize a scene that was vivid in his memory. But when he wanted to tell you what happened, he moved into the past tense, and that was the better choice.

I've used the present tense on a couple of occasions in recent years, and only for certain scenes. In two of the later books in the Matthew Scudder series, *Hope to Die* and *All the Flowers Are Dying*, I departed from my usual practice of recounting all scenes in Scudder's first-person narration. Instead I chose to tell part of the story from the point of view of the villain, and I wanted it to be very clear that this was not Scudder talking. I wrote those scenes in the third person, and in the present tense, and set them in italics. And, I should say, I found it difficult to *stay* in the present tense, as past-tense narration comes much more naturally to me.

Literary fiction by writers fresh out of MFA programs seems very often to be written in the present tense. It seems to me that most of them eventually outgrow it.

• • •

First versus Third Person

Correspondingly, I've noticed in my paperback rack browsing that I'm distinctly biased in favor of books written in the first person. Perhaps this is not surprising in view of the fact that a majority of my own novels have been first-person narratives.

The conventional advice to beginning writers of fiction is to abjure the first person. It's allegedly full of pitfalls for the tyro, serves as a distancing mechanism between the reader and the story, limits the scope of the narrative, and causes dental caries in children and skin tumors in laboratory mice.

For my part, I find I'm more likely to enjoy a novel by an unfamiliar writer if it's written in the first than the third person because the writing itself is more likely to have a natural flow to it. The first-person voice is, after all, the one we all grow up using. First-person novels have an immediacy to them that helps close the gap between writer and reader. It's as if the writer, clothed in the flesh of his narrator, is holding me by the elbow and telling me the story.

Some novels, to be sure, cannot be written in the first person. It's only an option when your novel is to be told from a single point of view, and it becomes a sensible choice in direct proportion to your ability to identify with that particular character. If your lead's larger than life—the President of the United States, a glamorous movie star, Al Capone, or whoever—the third person might be a wiser choice; you might be more comfortable writing the character from the outside, and the reader might be more comfortable reading about him that way.

Single versus Multiple Viewpoint

It's probably easiest, in a first novel, to show everything through the eyes of a single lead character—whether the voice you choose is first or third person. Single viewpoint keeps a novel on a true course. It limits options and cuts down the opportunity for diffusion of the force of the narrative.

This does not mean that it's perforce the right choice for your novel. Some books depend upon a broad scope for a measure of their strength. The story you choose to tell will very often dictate whether it is to be told from one or several points of view.

Whether you select single or multiple viewpoint for your novel, you would probably do well to avoid changing point of view within a scene, switching back and forth from one character's mind to another's. In a book in which the author maintains a consistent overview, never really getting inside the skins of his characters but describing all their actions from without, it may be permissible to move around the room within a scene, telling what the various characters in turn are thinking or feeling. But when you make this sort of viewpoint switch within a scene in a book where characters are shown from within, the result is apt to be confusion—the reader can't remember who's thinking what—and a slowdown in the book's pace. I was most recently made aware of this while reading *True Confessions,* John Gregory Dunne's generally successful novel of clerical and police political machinations.

An advantage of multiple viewpoint lies in the fact that the author is not stuck with a single character for the duration of the book. When a scene winds to a close, and when there's nothing further to be said about the viewpoint character for the time being, you simply skip two spaces and pick up one of the other principals.

In any novel of this sort, it makes good sense to keep your number of principal characters down to a manageable figure. When you pass the half dozen mark, it becomes a little more difficult for the reader to remember what's going on and who's doing what and why. You can, however, have any number of additional *minor* viewpoint characters, from whose vantage point an occasional scene or two is portrayed. This can add a sense of richness to a novel without diluting the reader's attention to the main characters.

More important than learning a multitude of rules on the subject of viewpoint is that you be aware of the question of the point of view in your own reading. Your perceptions of the way other writers handle viewpoint changes, your sense of what works and what doesn't, will teach you more about the subject than you can learn by reading *about* it.

I doubt that many readers are aware of point of view. They're interested in characters and story. It's possible, too, that I tend to pay more attention to consistency in this area than I need to.

Some years ago, for example, I wrote *The Triumph of Evil* under the pen name of Paul Kavanagh. The entire novel, written in the third person, was told from the point of view of Miles Dorn, assassin and agent provocateur. The entire novel, that is, with the exception of a single chapter which dealt with an assassination at which Dorn was not physically present. He was over a thousand miles away at the time, and it seemed essential to me that the scene be viewed from close up.

After considerable soul-searching, I shrugged heroically and wrote the scene from the point of view of the young man used as a pawn by Dorn. I felt this was a jarring inconsistency but couldn't think of a better way to deal with it.

As far as I know, no one was ever bothered by this inconsistency, or even aware of it. No editor or writer who read the book mentioned it. Rereading the section preparatory to writing this chapter, it seemed to me unlikely that I would have noticed it myself—had I not been the book's author. We who write these books are inevitably more aware of their essential structure than are the people who read them.

Don Westlake employs an interesting original framework for his Richard Stark novels about Parker, and I wonder if many of his faithful readers are aware of it. In almost every Parker novel, the first two quarters of the book are told exclusively from Parker's point of view. The third quarter is told from the individual points of view of all of the other principal characters. Then, in the fourth section, once again Parker is the viewpoint character throughout.

I think this serves Westlake superbly. But I doubt that very many Parker fans pay much mind to the almost symphonic structure of these books. I suspect they're interested in the plot and the characters, and they want to find out how the heist turns out and who winds up alive and dead when it's over. I don't think they care how the author does it.

It's useful for us as writers to care, and to pay attention. But an excessive preoccupation may be more liability than asset. The main thing is always the story.

Transitions

When I first started writing, I had a certain amount of difficulty getting from one scene to the next. I also had trouble getting my characters on and off stage, or in and out of the room.

This difficulty was most pronounced in first-person novels. If I had a character in conversation at a bar one night, and then I had something for him to do the next morning, I wasn't sure how to get him through the intervening hours. I figured I had to explain where he went and what he did at all times.

I found out that's not necessary. I could let the bar conversation run its course. Then I could skip an extra space, and then I could write, "At ten the next morning I showed up at Waldron's office. I was wearing my blue pinstripe and his secretary seemed to like the looks of it."

They learned some years ago in the film business that the best transitions are nice clean abrupt ones. Remember the slow dissolves you used to see in movies? Remember how they would indicate the passage of time by showing different shots of a clock, or pages flipping on some dumb calendar? They don't do that any more, and that's largely because they realized that they don't have to. Contemporary audiences are hip enough to put two and two together.

So can readers. I learned a lot about transitions by reading Mickey Spillane. In the early Mike Hammer books, he hardly ever explained how Hammer got from one place to another, or wasted time setting scenes up elaborately. There were no slow dissolves in those books. They were all fast cuts, with each scene beginning right on the heels of the one before it. Since the books had enormous appeal to a generally unsophisticated audience, I would assume few readers had trouble following the action line, for all the abruptness of the transitions.

Temporal transitions—jumps back and forth in time—can be handled most expeditiously simply by crediting the reader with the intelligence to figure out what you're doing without over-explaining yourself. In this area, too, I suspect the techniques of the visual media, including not only the cinema but especially television commercials with their intricate crosscutting in a thirty- or sixty-second span, have contributed greatly to the sophistication of the public.

I can recall seeing *Two For The Road,* a film with Audrey Hepburn and Albert Finney, sometime in the late '60s. Director Stanley Donen salted the film with flashbacks, providing no special indication of the temporal changes, simply cutting from one present-time sequence to one in past time. I was as interested in the audience as in the film. Some older viewers, I noticed, were utterly confounded; their frame of reference was too rigidly linear for them to know what the hell was going on. But the majority of the audience, including all of its younger members, seemed perfectly at ease.

For a particularly well-crafted example of a novel in which several temporal phases of a story are simultaneously related, you might have a look at *Some Unknown Person*, by Sandra Scoppettone. The book is based on the life and death of Starr Faithfull, the star-crossed girl-about-town who served as a model for Gloria Wandrous in John O'Hara's *BUtterfield 8*. Scoppettone interweaves her lead character's early years, the life story of a man instrumental in her death, the events leading up to her death, the last days years later of the aforementioned man, and several other aspects of the story, cutting back and forth through time in a most instructive fashion.

• • •

Some years ago, an interviewer asked Robert B. Parker why he thought his books about a private eye named Spenser were so popular with readers. "I dunno," Bob said. "I think people like the way they sound."

Indeed, and how could they not? Spenser's voice, as written by Parker, is immediately engaging. One wants to continue to hear it.

This comes under the heading of style, I suppose, but there's another word for it, and that's *voice*. I'm not sure how to define exactly what an author's voice is, but it's something more specific than style. One can deliberately create a style, but one can only allow one's voice to come through.

Many of us start writing in the hope of sounding like other writers whom we admire. That may be a good enough place to begin, but the ultimate goal, it seems to me, must be to learn how to sound like oneself.

Toward that end, and in order to improve one's style and the overall quality of one's prose and dialogue, a very effective acid test consists in reading one's work aloud. It's possible to write unwittingly sentences that are awkward and unwieldy on the page, and one may scan them without seeing anything wrong with them. Read them aloud and their essential clunkiness is apt to reveal itself.

I should add that I have never used this method myself, but not because I doubt its value. My response to my own work, as I type the words and later when I look at what I've written, is as much auditory as visual. I hear what I'm writing—which helps explain why the typographical errors I tend to make consist chiefly of ill-chosen homonyms. I'll type *their* for *there* or *they're,* and even on occasion *know* for *no.* My ear doesn't hear anything wrong—and neither, I might add, does my Spell-Check function . . .

Chapter 12

Length

In *Threesome,* one of Jill Emerson's characters wants to know how long a chapter ought to be. As long as Abraham Lincoln's legs, another character assures her. (Lincoln, you may recall, informed a heckler that a man's legs ought to be long enough to extend from his body to the ground.)

A chapter, then, should be long enough to reach from the one before it to the one that follows it. In other words, there is no fit and proper length for a chapter.

When I wrote midcentury erotica, I tended to be compulsive about chapter length. Originally my books were two hundred pages long, and were written in the form of ten twenty-page chapters. Then, when my publisher complained that they were running a wee bit short, I upped the length to 205 pages, alternating twenty-one page chapters with twenty-page chapters and stopping when I had written five of each. In retrospect, I can see readily enough that this rigidity was pointless insofar as the reader was concerned. I'm positive my average fan, busy turning the pages with one hand and panting over the lurid innuendo, barely realized that the book was divided into chapters in the first place. In his mind, it was more conveniently divided into hot parts and dull stretches.

Now that the books I write no longer contain hot parts, I'm a good deal more flexible in dividing the dull stretches into chapters. In a series of four novels written about (and ostensibly by) Chip Harrison, I furnished each book with one chapter a single sentence in length. *"The gun jammed,"* for instance, was an entire chapter in *No Score; "Chip, I'm pregnant"* was a similarly complete chapter in *Chip Harrison Scores Again.* The two other books each contained an equally terse chapter. I did this sort of thing for the fun of it, not for any particular effect.

· · ·

Some things don't change. In 2013's *The Burglar Who Counted the Spoons*, there's a chapter that contains not a single word. Just three asterisks.

· · ·

If I'm less compulsive about chapter length nowadays, I still tend to keep the chapters of a particular book roughly the same length. An occasional chapter shorter than its fellows provides a sort of staccato effect that is not without dramatic value. When you break for a chapter you're slamming a door on the action. The reader has to pause and think for a moment, if only for the length of time it takes him to turn the page.

Some books aren't divided into chapters at all. The author just skips an extra space between scenes and lets it go at that. An advantage of chapter breaks—that they provide a convenient place for the reader to stop—is also their disadvantage, in that the reader may elect not to pick the book up again. Some writers avoid chapter breaks because they don't want to encourage the reader to pause in the course of their heart-pounding narrative. One might argue in reply that a story that's all that gripping will hold its readers through a chapter break. In my own reading, I've found that chapterization tends to keep me reading. I tell myself I can stop in a few minutes, at the end of the next chapter, and I keep telling myself that until I've finished the book.

One function of chapters is that they reduce the book in the writer's own eyes to manageable dimensions. If your prior experience is with short stories, you may find it easier to imagine yourself writing a three or four or five thousand-word chapter than a full-length novel. By parceling your book into such bite-sized portions the task of writing it may seem within your abilities. A chapter can be grasped all at once as a book frequently cannot, and of course when you've written twenty or thirty chapters of this sort, you'll have produced a novel.

Another use of chapters is for viewpoint shifts—which is not to say that every change in point of view calls for a new chapter. In *Not Comin' Home To You,* written under the Paul Kavanagh pen name, the viewpoint shifts back and forth between the two leads, who see the emerging story very differently. Breaking chapters for these viewpoint shifts prepares the reader better than simple double spacing.

Finally, it's worth noting that the manner in which you do or don't divide your novel into chapters is not something that will have any discernible effect upon a publisher's decision to accept or reject your book. It's not too likely he'll care one way or the other, but if he does it's the easiest sort of change for him to suggest, and the easiest change for you to make. For this reason, whether you use chapters and how long you make them is a minor point at most and one you should arrange to suit yourself while you write the book.

• • •

In recent years, I've found myself writing shorter chapters. I got the idea from James Patterson, who argued persuasively that the reader is more likely to keep going to the end of a short chapter, and then to start the next one when he can see it's not all that long—and so on, all the way through the book. While one may or may not delight in Mr. Patterson as a novelist, it's hard to deny that he's a brilliant marketer, and knows considerably more about the subject than most of the world's publishers. In this instance, I think he's right—and my chapters are accordingly briefer these days.

• • •

The length of your chapters may not be important. The length of your novel is.

From a purely aesthetic standpoint, a novel's like a chapter. It should be long enough to get from the beginning to the end. But length is rather more rigidly determined on the basis of various commercial considerations which a novelist neglects at his peril.

As far as category fiction is concerned, length is largely predetermined.

If you want to write a light romance for Harlequin, let's say, you'll probably have noticed that all the Harlequin romances on the newsstands run the same number of pages and have the same number of words on a page. If the books all run fifty-five thousand words and you submit an eighty thousand-word manuscript, the likelihood of their accepting your novel is considerably diminished.

Not all length requirements in category novels are equally strict. Most houses might try a longer-than-usual gothic mystery or western if they felt its strengths were such as to offset the disadvantage of its unusual length. But you're swimming against the tide when you try this sort of thing. It's hard to sell a first novel without increasing the difficulty by failing to conform to market requirements in this area.

If your book's too long, an editor may still like it enough to suggest cuts. If it's too short, you've really got a problem. With a handful of very obvious exceptions, really short books really don't sell. It may not be impossible to write a novel in less than fifty thousand words, but it's evidently very tricky to convince the reader that he's getting his money's worth. Nor is an editor as likely to feel comfortable suggesting ways to beef up a book as he may feel suggesting deletions.

How do you make sure your book's the right length? We'll assume that your market study has led you to select an ideal length. You want to write a mystery, say, and a study of the type of mystery you intend to write indicates that the most successful books tend to run in the neighborhood of sixty-five to seventy thousand words. You've calculated that, given the way you set your margins and other quirks of style, you'll need to write 225 pages to come in at the optimum length.

Outlining's a help in giving you a sense of the relationship between your plot and your predetermined length. It makes it easier for you to see how much should happen within the first fifty or hundred pages in order for things to be working out on schedule. Even without an outline, it's frequently possible to sense as you go along whether you're running long or short.

If you're running short, you have several choices. You can reexamine your plot and see if there's a way to add scenes and complications to it that will give the book more bulk. You can decide that the problem is not in the plot but in the writing, and can accordingly write your scenes so that they run longer, furnishing rather more in the way of dialogue and description. Finally, you can just press on to the end in the manner that seems most comfortable, figuring you'll add substance one way or another in your second draft.

Your choices are essentially the same if you find your book running long, but here you'd probably be best advised to pick the last option and let the first draft run its course at whatever wordage seems natural. A great many writers do this as a matter of course and produce their best work in this fashion.

Robert Ludlum, for example, almost invariably trims his first draft by a third when he rewrites it. Sidney Sheldon has said that he puts everything he can think of into his first draft, giving his imagination free rein; he commonly cuts more than half of what he has written.

I'm not happy working this way. As I've said, I do my best work when I'm operating under the assumption that what I'm writing is going to be set in type as soon as I've got the last page written. (One writer, Noel Loomis, was a skilled linotypist, and could compose faster on that machine than on a typewriter; he wrote his westerns on a linotype, pulled galley proofs from the chases of set type, and submitted galleys to his publishers. I'd do that myself if I could.)

I can see, though, a great advantage in writing long and cutting afterward. If you work that way, your first draft contains all the possibilities your creative imagination hands you. Then, when you rewrite, you're able to skim the cream.

There's another advantage in writing long. If your book simply works best at a greater length than you had in mind for it, it may have greater commercial value than you planned.

There's a paradox here that requires a word of explanation. On the one hand, the average thriller runs somewhere around sixty or seventy thousand words, and a book that runs substantially longer than that is going to present problems to a publisher of category fiction.

On the other hand, those occasional thrillers that turn up on the best seller list are generally a hundred to a hundred fifty thousand words long. The same length that would preclude their sale as paperback originals serves to swing them right up onto the hardcover sales counter.

The conventional explanation holds that longer books have more to them, that they have greater depth and stronger story values, that they are more to be taken seriously on account of their length. Because of these factors, such books are said to transcend their categories and appeal to readers who do not ordinarily read that type of novel.

Very often this is demonstrably true. Brian Garfield's *Hard Times* is an epic novel of the Old West, with only its setting to link it with standard westerns. Any best seller list will yield similar examples.

Even so, other books turn up on the lists with nothing remarkable about them but their bulk. I read one recently, a detective novel by a writer who has produced some best-selling thrillers over the years. Unlike his other books, this had nothing special going for it; it was a standard straight-line detective plot told from a single point of view and overblown to a hundred fifty thousand words. It was a poorer book for its length, but a better seller because of it.

What it comes down to, I'm afraid, is that readers of best sellers—which is to say the majority of readers in this country—prefer long books. This is their right, certainly, and it is only sensible for the writer who wants to sell to this best seller audience to provide them with what they're looking for.

It almost seems to be true that there's no such thing as a book that's too long to be commercially viable. For years publishers resisted overlong first novels, saying that higher production costs made such books even more unprofitable than trimmer first novels. Nowadays the trend is in the other direction. If a first novel is sufficiently substantial—and of course if it satisfies other commercial considerations as well—then it can be promoted and ballyhooed and even *sold*.

James Clavell's novel *Shogun* had a long run as a best seller a couple of years back. While it was an engrossing reading experience for me all the way through, I could not avoid applying to it Dr. Johnson's observation regarding *Paradise Lost*—i.e., no one ever wished it were longer. For all its 1,400 pages, and for all that more readers started it than finished it, the book was a literary and commercial success. Not too many years ago a publisher might have hesitated to bring out quite so long a novel, especially one set in medieval Japan. Clavell's track record helped, certainly, but equally helpful I suspect was the growing recognition that great length helps more books than it hinders.

Does this mean you should aim from the beginning at long books?

No, not necessarily. It may mean that you shouldn't try to hit the best seller list with a short book, any more than you should try to peddle a quarter of a million words as a paperback.

But your first object, remember, is to write your own kind of book. You'll learn, from your own reading and as you begin writing, what sort of book suits you best. I've come to see that I myself am most comfortable writing relatively lean, spare volumes. This no doubt limits my potential from a commercial standpoint, but I'd be limiting myself rather more severely were I to force myself to write books that suited me less for purely commercial motives.

That said, it's worth noting that a great many writers find themselves producing longer books as time goes by. This does not mean that they are attempting to respond to the dictates of the marketplace. While that may be a factor, it's at least as likely that this extension of their range has simply come about naturally. An intimidating length becomes less intimidating after one has written a batch of short novels.

I could go on. But this chapter, like Abraham Lincoln's legs, is plenty long enough as it is.

And that's the long and short of it.

• • •

The most important consideration in this regard is the book itself. At the end of the day, it should be neither longer nor shorter than its ideal length.

In 1981, I began work on the fifth book about Matthew Scudder. The first three, published in the mid-1970s as paperback originals, were short—perhaps 60,000 words each. The fourth, *A Stab in the Dark*, was a little longer; it was written on spec, and published in hardcover by Arbor House.

The fifth, though, was a more ambitious effort. It had several stories to tell. The first, naturally enough, was the fairly complex case Scudder takes on; he's hired by a pimp to investigate the murder of a call girl.

He's also just had an alcoholic grand mal seizure, and has to confront the mounting evidence of his own alcoholism, and find a way to come to terms with it. He struggles to stay sober, walks into and out of AA meetings.

Finally, the book has as a central theme the frailty of human life, in New York specifically. As he contends with his case and with his alcoholism, he is forever noting newspaper and television reports of violent deaths, all echoing and underscoring the book's title, which itself derives from a line of dialogue. Scudder's cop friend Joe Durkin, recalling an old TV series (Sterling Silliphant's *Naked City*), insists that what you have in New York is not eight million stories but eight million ways to die.

As I wrote the book, it soon became clear that I was not going to wrap it up in 65-70,000 words. That was probably the optimum commercial length for a category mystery, and the book I was writing—a private detective's first-person narrative, and a volume in an ongoing series—was unquestionably that.

There was no padding in what I was writing. Every scene had a purpose. I decided I'd write it as it wanted to be written, and would let it find its own length, and when I'd finished it ran to something like 120,000 words. It was twice as long as any of the first three books in the series.

I was concerned that the book might be too long to work optimally for a reader. 120,000 words is, after all, a lot to listen to, all in the voice of a single character. And I was concerned that my publisher, Don Fine at Arbor House, might want the book reduced to a more commercially viable specimen of category fiction.

Neither Don Fine or my editor, Arnold Ehrlich, ever said a word about the length, or asked me to cut a syllable. And the book was well received by critics and the reading public, and appears on a lot of Best Mystery lists.

I don't know whether it was artistic integrity or plain cussed stubbornness that made me write the book as long as I did. Whatever it was, I'm grateful for it.

It's been remarked that writers have tended to turn in longer manuscripts in recent years, and credit or blame for this has been directed at the computer. It is presumably easier to natter on and on and on when one is using a computer.

Well, maybe. I know that the books I've written since I switched from a Smith-Corona to a Mac have put on a few pounds.

But consider this: In 1998, I took myself off to Listowel, a town in County Kerry in the west of Ireland, to write what would be the eighth Evan Tanner novel, and the first in something like 28 years. The seven preceding Tanner books all ran around 60,000 words, and I assumed the eighth would run about the same.

It came in at around 80,000 words.

Well, blame it on the computer, right? Uh, maybe not. See, I was not comfortable taking a computer to a small town in Ireland. Suppose something went wrong with it? Suppose the hotel's electricity didn't support it? Nowadays I take my MacBook Air everywhere, but the world was a little different back then.

So I went to Listowel with a handful of ballpoint pens and a couple of legal pads, and I wrote the entire book by hand.

Can't blame technology, can I? Can't hold the computer accountable for my increasing verbosity. The simplest explanation is the most likely one, and here it is: I've simply grown more garrulous with age.

Another thought on length: In a foreword to *Here's O'Hara*, a collection of John O'Hara's short fiction written over a considerable span of years, editor Albert Erskine observes that the stories written early in the author's career tended to be quite short, while the most recent stories tended to be longer than average. Erskine notes, too, that the longer stories seem to him to be superior to the shorter stories.

He goes on to say that he would not for a moment argue that the later stories are better because they are longer; rather, he contends that they are longer because they are better. In other words, O'Hara has become a better writer over time, and now brings more talent and perception to a story, and takes more words to tell a fuller and richer tale.

CHAPTER 13

Rewriting

I rewrite constantly. For every page that gets printed there must be five that go into the wastebasket. One of the hardest aspects of writing is accepting this squandering of labor, but it is essential. I doubt if there is one page in a thousand, throughout the whole of literature, that wouldn't have been improved by the author's redoing it.
—Russell H. Greenan

Professional writers vary considerably in their approach to rewriting. Some would endorse the observation quoted above while others would dismiss it as nonsense. Some regard rewriting as the genuinely enjoyable side of their occupation, the stage in which one sees the book taking its final form. Others hate rewriting but do it anyway. Some do one complete draft after another until the book satisfies them. Others polish each page before moving on to the next one. Some write five or more drafts of a book before they feel they've got it right. Others submit their first drafts.

I don't believe there's any right or wrong way to approach rewriting, not with so many pros having so much success with so many widely divergent methods. As with so many aspects of writing, each writer must determine what works best in his own particular case—what method produces the best work and makes him most comfortable.

I myself have always been the sort of writer who loathes revision. Looking back over the years, I can see a couple of factors which tend to explain this attitude. I was always more concerned with the accomplishment than the act; I was interested less in writing, you might say, than in having written. Once I finished writing a short story or a novel I wanted to consider myself done with it for all time. Indeed, the minute I typed "The End" I wanted to be able to take a deep breath, walk around the corner, and see my work in print at the newsstand. The last thing I desired at such a moment was to sit down, take an even deeper breath, and commence feeding the whole thing through the typewriter a second time.

Because I was a naturally smooth stylist, as I mentioned a couple of chapters back, I could get away with submitting first drafts. They didn't look rough. And, because I had a sort of fictive tunnel vision, I was unlikely to see more than one way that a book could be written.

When I was writing the soft-core sex novels, economic considerations largely ruled out rewriting. Who could afford it? Who had time for it? When you're turning out somewhere between twelve and twenty books a year, you may cheerfully agree with Greenan's point and still never rewrite a line. So what if every last one of your pages could be improved by making another trip through your typewriter? There's no time to polish each page to perfection, and no incentive, either. The readers won't notice the difference. The publisher probably won't notice either, and wouldn't care if he did.

There's even an argument *against* revision, and it may have applied to those early sex novels. Jack Kerouac advanced it when he spoke of his writing as "spontaneous bop prosody," equating his manner of composition to a jazz musician's creative improvisation. More cynically, the lead character in Barry N. Malzberg's *Herovit's World,* a hack science-fiction writer enormously contemptuous of his own work, argues that rewriting would rob his crap of the only thing it has going for it, its freshness. Once you start rewriting, Herovit holds, you're not able to stop. With each draft the fundamental banality and worthlessness of the material becomes more evident even as its vitality and spontaneity are drained from it. All you wind up doing is what William Goldman, discussing the agony of rewriting an inadequate play prior to its opening, called "washing garbage."

I never washed my garbage in those days. Thinking back, I'm astonished at the sangfroid with which I presumed to forego revision altogether. I scarcely ever retyped a page.

There was one time I well remember when, checking the pages at the end of the day's work, I discovered that I'd written pages 31 through 45 but had somehow jumped in my page numbering from 38 to 40. Rather than renumber the pages, I simply sat down and wrote page 39 to fit. Since page 38 ended in the middle of a sentence, a sentence which then resumed on page 40, it took a little fancy footwork to slide page 39 in there, but the brash self-assurance of youth was evidently up to that sort of challenge.

Jacqueline Susann used to tell talk show audiences how she rewrote every book four or five times, using yellow paper for one draft, green for a second, pink for a third, blue for a fourth, and finally producing finished copy on white bond. I don't seem to recall the point of this rainbow approach to revision, nor am I sure I believe Susann actually did this; anyone as accomplished as she at self-promotion might well have been capable of embroidery.

But that hardly matters. What's relevant, I think, is that Susann knew her audience. The public evidently likes the idea of reading books over which writers have labored endlessly. Perhaps readers find it galling to shell out upwards of $8.95 for a book that flowed from its author's typewriter like water from a cleft rock. The stuff's supposed to *read* as though it came naturally and effortlessly, but one wants to be assured that a soul-satisfying amount of hard work went into it.

That's nice to know when Dick Cavett holds your book up and asks you how you did it, but in the meantime you're naturally more concerned with producing the best possible novel than with figuring out how best to push it on the tube. Is revision necessary? And what's the proper approach to it?

For me, the best approach involves a sort of doublethink. If I take it for granted while writing a book that I'm going to have to sit down and do it over, I'm encouraging myself to be sloppy. I don't have to find the right word or phrase. I don't have to think a scene through and decide which way I want to tackle it. I can just slap any old thing on the page, telling myself that the important thing is to get words on paper, that I can always clean up my act in the rewrite.

Now this may be precisely what you require in order to conquer your inhibitions at the typewriter. Earlier I mentioned a couple of writers who produce lengthy first drafts, throwing in everything that occurs to them, then pruning ruthlessly in their second drafts.

I find, though, that unless I regard what I'm writing as final copy, I don't take it seriously enough to give it my best shot. For this reason I proofread as I go along, do my first drafts on damnably expensive high-rag-content white bond, and get each page right before I go on to the next one. I don't necessarily rewrite as I go along, but neither do I leave anything standing if it bothers me. Sometimes I'll have twenty or thirty crumpled pages in or around my wastebasket by the time I've produced my daily five pages of finished copy. Other times I won't have to throw out a single page, but even then I'll be doing what you might call rewriting-in-advance in that I'll try sentences and paragraphs a few different ways in my mind before committing them to the page.

In the chapter on starting your novel, I mentioned that I frequently rewrite the opening chapters of a book. Aside from that, I usually push on all the way through to the end without any substantial rewriting other than the polish-as-you-go business just described. Now and then, however, upon proofreading yesterday's work prior to beginning today's production, I'll find something bothersome in the last couple of pages. This may happen because the unconscious mind, laboring during the night with what's to be written next, will have come up with something that calls for changes in the section immediately preceding it. It may happen, too, because I was tired when I reached the end of yesterday's work, and the results of fatigue are evident in the light of dawn. When this occurs, I'll naturally redo the offending pages; this serves the dual purpose of getting me into the swing of my narrative even as I'm improving yesterday's work.

Some writers elaborate on this method, rewriting their whole manuscript as they go along. They begin each day by rewriting *in toto* the first draft they produced the day before, then go on to churn out fresh first-draft copy which they will in turn revise the following morning, and so on a day at a time until the book is finished.

There's a lot to be said for this method. If your first drafts are stylistically choppy enough to require revision as a matter of course, and if the idea of being faced with a top-to-bottom rewrite all in one chunk is unattractive, this sort of pay-as-you-go revision policy has much to recommend it. Among other things, you don't encourage yourself to be slipshod in your first draft, since your day of reckoning isn't that far in the future.

This won't work, incidentally, if you produce the sort of first drafts that require substantial structural revision, with lots of cutting and splicing.

A couple of pages back I described my present approach to writing and rewriting as a sort of doublethink. By this I mean that, although I work with the intention of producing final copy the first time around, I keep myself open to the possibility that a full second draft will be required. If I determine that this is the case, the fact that my first draft is neatly typed on crisp white bond paper doesn't alter the fact that I have to redo it from top to bottom.

When I wrote *Burglars Can't Be Choosers,* I stopped one chapter from the end and rewrote the whole thing. I suppose I could have written the final chapter of the first draft before starting the rewrite, but I didn't see the point; I knew that my final chapter would be affected by the revisions I'd make in earlier chapters, so that I'd only wind up redoing it entirely later on.

Burglars Can't Be Choosers got a complete rewrite for a couple of reasons. One stemmed from the fact that I didn't know the identity of the murderer until I was almost three-quarters of the way through the book. The solution I hit on necessitated a certain amount of changes along the way. I wanted to push on to the end—or almost to the end, as it turned out—before making them, but they did have to be made in order for the book to hold up.

In addition, I was dissatisfied with the pace of the novel. While most of the scenes worked well enough, I felt there was too much wasted time in the story line. A rereading convinced me that I could eliminate a day from the plot, tightening things up a good deal in the process.

I could have tried making these changes by cutting and pasting, redoing selected pages here and there. I considered this but couldn't avoid the conclusion that the book would profit considerably from a complete rewrite. While it seemed to me that some portions of the book didn't require any changes beyond an occasional sentence here and there, I decided to retype everything.

By doing this, I made an incalculable number of changes. It's virtually impossible for me to retype a page of my own work without changing something. Sometimes it was clear to me that these changes constituted a substantial improvement, although this improvement might not have been apparent to most of the book's audience. In other cases it's moot whether the changes I made were for better or worse; I occasionally had the feeling I was changing phrasing solely as a respite from the boredom of pure copy typing.

I would never have rewritten *Burglars Can't Be Choosers* for stylistic reasons alone. The book was written smoothly enough the first time around, and if I hadn't had to make structural changes I would have submitted my first draft as it stood. In retrospect, I'm glad I was forced to rewrite it; it's a better book for the extra work it received.

It's possible you'll produce a first draft which looks to be submittable without a major rewrite. You may find, however, that the manuscript needs to be retyped before you send it off.

If so, I have a suggestion. Unless you absolutely can't stand the idea, do the final typescript yourself.

You can probably guess the reason from my discussion of the revision of *Burglars Can't Be Choosers*. No matter how much editing you do in pen or pencil, no matter how thoroughly you rework your material before having it typed, you'll find more little changes to make when you actually hammer away at the keys yourself.

A friend of mind used to do this. Then she started to get higher advances and her books began earning more subsidiary income, and she decided she could afford the luxury of hiring somebody to type her final drafts for her. She works very hard over them, making innumerable pencil corrections before bundling them off to the typist, but her style's not as polished in her latest books because she's not doing her own typing. She's omitting what was always a set stage in her personal process of revision, and while her books are still well written, I think they used to be smoother.

Earlier, in the chapter on snags and dead ends, I advised against setting a book aside when you run into trouble with it. Although it may seem like a good idea, it rarely lets you develop a fresh slant on your novel. The books I abandon in midstream invariably float off out of my life and are never seen again.

When you finish a first draft, however, I think you should give yourself breathing space before plunging into a rewrite. There's a reason for this beyond the very real fact that you're likely to be tired and deserving of a break.

The writer who has just completed a book cannot usually be sufficiently objective about it to appraise it properly with an eye toward revision. In my own case, it's hard enough to be objective about my work ten years after it's been published, let alone when the pages are still warm and the ink still wet. At that stage I'm not only too close to the book, I'm still *inside* it. A break of a couple of weeks lets me unwind, and when I sit down and read the thing from start to finish I just might have a certain amount of perspective on it.

During this cooling-off period, you might want to have someone else read the book—but only if you've got someone around whose judgment you trust. If a negative reaction might paralyze you, don't take any chances. Wait until you've done your rewriting before you show the book to anybody.

Now's the time to have the book read by a knowledgeable acquaintance if you're concerned about your lack of expertise in a certain area. Suppose the book has a background in coin collecting, for instance. You've done a ton of research on the subject but you're no numismatist and you can't be certain you've got the lingo right. Maybe you've committed the sort of glaring error that'll get you snotty letters from your readers.

Show the book to someone with the right background, explaining your uncertainty to him and asking him to read it with that consideration in mind. Make it clear to him that you want him to spot errors, that you're not showing him the book in the hope that he'll praise it. (It's necessary to state this out front, because most people assume that most authors want not criticism but praise. And most of the time, incidentally, they're absolutely right.) When he tells you what's wrong and how to fix it, you can incorporate the information you get from him in your rewrite. If he tells you everything's fine and your book is numismatically accurate, you can stop worrying about that aspect of it while you rewrite.

And, if he offers a lot of nonnumismatic criticisms of your story and characters and writing style, you can thank him politely and pay him no more attention in this respect than you see fit. Remember, you showed him the book because of his knowledge about rare coins, not because you figured him as the most perceptive editor since Maxwell Perkins.

Which leads us, neatly enough, into another area of the question of rewriting. So far we've dealt with the matter of the revision work that you do or don't perform before submitting the manuscript. Of another sort altogether are those changes you make at the suggestion of an agent or publisher.

Most new writers will change almost anything to get a book published, and that's probably as it should be. Just as the first law of nature is quite properly self-preservation, so is the first commandment of the first novelist to get published if it is at all possible. If you can accomplish this simply by revising your manuscript as an editor suggests, you would probably be foolish to do otherwise.

Hopeful writers have a fairly common fantasy in this area. It usually involves a hard-boiled editor trying to seduce them into making crass commercial changes to the book's artistic detriment. The author either makes the changes only to discover the hollowness of great financial success at the cost of his soul, or he stands up for what he believes, tells the editor to go climb a tree, and (a) finds a more understanding publisher through whose efforts his book brings him wealth and glory beyond his wildest imaginings or (b) drinks himself to death in righteous indignation.

It all makes alluring fantasy, but it's not too well grounded in reality. An agent or editor suggests changes because he thinks the changes will improve the book, not because he's anxious to louse it up. His point of view may be in part the result of his commercial orientation, and if that's not somewhat true he's probably limited in his effectiveness in the business. But I've never known an editor to ask for a change that he didn't believe would result in a stronger book.

Beliefs, however, are not facts. Agents and editors are wrong often enough. And in the world of fiction, rightness and wrongness are often subjective matters.

To get to the point, what do you do when an editor wants changes with which you disagree? Do you bite the bullet and make the changes? Do you stand up for what you believe in? Come to think of it, how do you *know* what you believe in?

How much significance can you attach to your own feelings? After all, all you did was write the thing.

It's a tricky question, and you can spend years in this business and still have occasional trouble answering it. One thing that's certain is that the decision is yours to make. It's your book, it's going to have your name on it, and only you can decide how strongly you feel about what's between the covers. If you refuse to make certain changes, you may be saying "no" to publication, and another opportunity for publication may not ever come along. You can't assume no one else will ever take the book, but you may have to acknowledge the possibility, especially with a first novel.

Generally speaking, writers gain confidence with increased experience. I made some changes at an editor's suggestion in my own first book, the lesbian novel I discussed earlier. One of those changes was a bad idea and I disliked making it, but it didn't really occur to me to demur. I was twenty years old, delirious at the thought of having a book published, and awestruck at the two-thousand-dollar advance they were handing me. I know now that I could have talked my way clear of the one change I really hated making, but I didn't even try.

That was minor. A friend of mine cut a long novel drastically some years ago at the suggestion of a respected editor. He felt at the time that the book would be weaker, both commercially and artistically, as a result of the cuts; however, he also felt the editor's opinion was worth more than his. Perhaps it might have been in most cases but in this one it manifestly was not. He now regrets making those cuts. With the experience he now has under his belt, and with the track record he has since amassed as a successful commercial novelist, he would be far more likely to resist making similar changes.

Experience, the very factor that supplies confidence and self-assurance, can also deepen one's humility and enable one to recognize and admit flaws in one's work. In my own case, I know I've become more open to suggestions regarding revision than I was a number of years ago, although I'm apt to be unyielding when I'm convinced my position is right.

I'm sure I was inclined to take a stand against revision on some prior occasions because of simple laziness. I didn't want to do the work, so my mind obligingly supplied reasons why the indicated changes were not a good idea. I still have a tendency to think this way, but I'm more inclined to see it now for what it is, and thus have trouble mistaking it for artistic integrity.

Your own decision, then, is your own decision. You'll have to make it yourself when the time comes. It may help you to know that almost all novels require some work after they've caught an editor's eye, and a great many of them require considerable rewriting. While John O'Hara might snarl that the only way to improve a story after you've written it is by telling an editor to go to hell, you probably won't want to be quite that quick to suggest travel plans to the editor who asks you to make changes. And a look at O'Hara's correspondence shows that he wasn't either—not until he was so well established that he could afford to be.

But this is all cart-before-horse stuff, isn't it? First you have to find a publisher who's interested enough to want changes in the first place.

Which, conveniently enough, brings us to our next chapter.

• • •

Rewriting becomes rather a different matter in the age of the computer. It's unchanged in its essence, in that one is still faced with the task of modifying one's own words, trying to improve on what one prefers to regard as perfection. But, while it may be no easier to bring oneself to do it, once one does it's easier than it used to be.

Reading over my words from 1978, I can only shake my head at all that retyping, all those crumpled pages in the wastebasket. Nowadays one highlights a wayward phrase and types its replacement, and Bob's your uncle. Second thoughts? Hit Command+z (or whatever works on your PC) and your original is back there in front of you.

As far as I can recall, I've only done one top-to-bottom rewrite since *Burglars Can't Be Choosers*. (That would have been *Ariel*, a difficult novel written at the specific suggestion of a publisher, who changed his mind when he saw it. Time passed, and a new agent showed it to Don Fine at Arbor House, and Don's suggestions plus some thoughts of my own led to another trip through the typewriter.)

But I do more rewriting than I did in years past, because it's so easy to do. There are no pages to retype, no sentences crossed out, no illegible notes in the margins. When I read what I've written, any word or phrase that doesn't work can be dealt with quickly and easily, and without leaving fingerprints or bloodstains. If a plot change in Chapter Eight demands a corresponding change in Chapter Two, it's equally simple and painless.

One of the first books I wrote on a computer was the sixth Bernie Rhodenbarr mystery, *The Burglar who Traded Ted Williams.* As I neared the end, I realized I didn't care for the surname of one of the principal characters. You wouldn't believe what a pain in the neck it used to be to make a change like that. Read, searching for the *Thompson.* Ink it out with a felt-tip pen. Print *Tompkins* above the thick black line. And on and on and on, and you'd still wind up with an ugly manuscript, very likely with an unaltered *Thompson* here and there, but what else could you do? Retype the whole bloody thing?

What you might do instead—well, what *I* might do—is decide *Thompson* was quite good enough, and leave it.

But I'd written this latest book on a computer! At the time I had a different file for each chapter—I think someone told me it was safer that way, or easier to work with—so I had to open each chapter in turn, do a *Search and Replace All* operation, and, just like that, all my Thompsons were Tompkins. In later books, after I'd learned that a single file would do just fine for a complete book, I could change a character's name or a street address or, well, just about anything with a couple of keystrokes.

All of this is good, and one more reason I can't imagine writing other than with a computer. Still, there's the very real danger that one can become compulsive about rewriting. It's simple and it's easy and you don't fill your wastebasket to overflowing, so why not keep polishing every sentence over and over? Why not make it perfect?

And, see, as long as you're busy rewriting what you've written, you don't have to bite the bullet and finish it, or submit it and risk rejection, or publish it and risk being hated and despised forever by your parents/friends/lover/cat.

It might be worth noting that some writers are temporarily disposed to polish their work, while others are similarly inclined to get on with it. And a perfect illustration of this distinction is the friendship of two supremely talented writers, Stanley Ellin and Evan Hunter.

Stan Ellin spent much of his career as a writer of short stories, and early on he wrote them slowly and deliberately—and, I should say, brilliantly. He would probably have agreed with the Russell Greenan quote that opens this chapter; a perfectionist, Ellin would not go on to the second page until the first page was as good as he could make it, and sometimes reworked his opening paragraph twenty or more times. Then he'd rewrite page two until he was satisfied, and so on, until the story was finished.

Evan Hunter, on the other hand, was a naturally fast writer, capable of writing first drafts as smooth and well-crafted as anybody else's fifth draft. The two men, each an admirer of the other's work, became friends, whereupon Evan decided that Stan had the answer, and that his own hurried pace was keeping him from the heights of literary stardom.

So he decided to slow himself down. And, after a couple of weeks, he called Stan in triumph. "I've got myself down to eight pages a day," he announced.

One can only imagine the response of Stan Ellin, for whom eight pages would have been a very good week's work.

Chapter 14

Getting Published

Writing on a computer is very different from writing with a typewriter. Online research is very different from a trip to a library. Still, the essence of writing is much the same irrespective of the tools involved; you have to figure out what you want to say and how to say it, and that's the same challenge whether the words you choose appear on clay tablets, sheets of bond paper, or a computer screen.

And the same goes for research. However and wherever you do it, what you're doing is unearthing the data you need to inform your fiction.

The world of publishing and bookselling, however, has changed almost beyond recognition since the first edition of this book was published. Nor has this process of change ground to a halt. The change goes on—and on and on—and it's quite clear that nobody knows what the future holds. (Nobody ever does, the phrase *foreseeable future* has always been oxymoronic, but these days it's a rare person in publishing who claims to know what it'll be like six months from now, let alone in ten years' time.)

I'd thought to scrap this chapter altogether, and write an entirely new one to reflect the way things are now. On reflection, I've decided to do here as I've done in the preceding chapters, reproducing the original text and adding to it what seems useful. I suspect there may be rather more of those additions in this chapter than previously.

• • •

Once you've written your novel, you're probably going to want to get it published.

It's a curious fact about this whole business of writing that the preceding sentence almost goes without saying. The great majority of us write with the absolute intention of publishing what we have written.

This isn't generally true with other artistic pursuits. The man who paints as a hobby doesn't necessarily aspire to gallery showings. The woman who plays the cello once a week in an amateur string quartet doesn't call herself a failure because she's not on her way to Carnegie Hall.

The writer's different. For a writer, publication is seen as part of the process that begins with an idea. His manuscript, unlike an artist's finished canvas, is not in final form; his novel will only be in that condition when it has been set in type, printed, and bound.

This is unfortunate. While writing is unquestionably a profession, it is also a hobby, and functions very nicely in that capacity. Of those who write, I suspect it will always be the case that a relatively small percentage will be able to produce salable, publishable work, while the greater majority will be writing essentially for their own amusement. There's nothing wrong with this; about the same ratio obtains in all artistic occupations. What's tragic is that the amateur writer is so likely to consider himself a failure because of his inability to publish.

• • •

I suspect many writers, amateur and professional, will go on considering ourselves failures to one extent or another. That seems to be a part of the human condition. But one undeniable change in our world is that anyone can be published. We'll look more closely at this fact later on, but at the moment it seems important to state it, and even put it in italics: *Anyone can be published.*

Okay, back to 1978 . . .

• • •

I elaborated on these thoughts a while ago in a *Writer's Digest* column on Sunday writers, suggesting that we needn't publish in order to consider ourselves successful writers. A heartening number of readers wrote to say they'd drawn encouragement from my observations. Suffice it to say now that I feel anyone who manages to complete the task of writing a novel ought to consider himself a success whatever its merits or publishability. If you've written a novel, you're already a winner. Whether you try to publish it, whether you succeed or fail in your efforts, you've run a marathon and finished on your feet.

Congratulations.

That said, let's suppose you've decided to make a few tries for the brass ring before stuffing your manuscript in a trunk. What are your chances of success? And what can you do to improve them?

Let's not kid ourselves. It's not going to be ice cream and cake all the way. Like a dime-novel hero, you're going to need luck and pluck—and plenty of both.

I might be tempted to offer the bromidic message that every novel will get published sooner or later if it's good enough and if you work hard enough at the business of offering it to publishers. It's the conventional wisdom, and it's the sort of thing one likes to hear and would prefer to say.

I'm beginning to doubt that it's true.

A case in point: In 1977 a fellow named Chuck Ross set out to establish the difficulties faced by new novelists. He submitted a novel to fourteen publishers and thirteen literary agents.

And the novel he submitted wasn't one of his own but a freshly-typed copy of Jerzy Kosinski's *Steps,* the National Book Award winner for 1969.

No one recognized the manuscript, although one editor compared the author's style to Kosinski. Neither did any publisher want to issue the book or any agent offer to represent it. Admittedly, Kosinski's novel is an experimental work, and not the sort of item that has best seller written all over it when it comes in the guise of an unknown writer's work. The experiment doesn't prove that agents and publishers are all idiots, or that the emperor has no clothes, or anything of the sort.

But it should give you an idea of what you're up against.

And just what am I up against? The wall? Is it safe to say that the new writer is facing impossible odds, that I'd be better off putting my book in a dresser drawer, or not writing it in the first place? Should I take up Sunday painting instead? Start taking cello lessons?

You can do any or all of those things if you want. I told you before that nobody ever said you had to write a novel. Nobody's saying now that you have to publish one, or try to publish one. It's your novel, for heaven's sake. You can circulate copies among your friends, lock it away in a safe deposit box, or use it to insulate your attic. You can submit it to fourteen publishers and thirteen agents, and then, satisfied that you've made the effort, you can put it in the outhouse next to the Monkey Ward catalog, so that it won't be wasted.

Or you can bundle it off to a fifteenth publisher or a fourteenth agent.

If you want something badly enough, Fredric Brown pointed out in *The Screaming Mimi,* you'll get it. If you don't get it, that only goes to show you didn't want it badly enough.

This is no place for specific advice on marketing your novel. Market conditions change constantly. Annual editions of *Writer's Market* and marketing columns in *Writer's Digest* will keep you in touch with these changes as they occur. If you're writing category fiction, your own day-by-day research at bookstores and newsstands will let you know just who's publishing exactly what.

A few marketing observations, however, might be useful.

It's been a trend of late for publishers to adopt a policy of declining to read unsolicited manuscripts. This doesn't mean they're all a bunch of flint-hearted old dogs. It simply means that more and more of them are finding that the cost of reading over-the-transom submissions is unaffordably high, given the infinitesimal number of such submissions that wind up getting published. By limiting their reading to agented manuscripts and others that have come recommended, publishers can save thousands of dollars a year.

What does this mean to you? First, let me say that it's not as disastrous as it looks. It certainly doesn't transform the business of novel writing into a closed shop. You don't need a track record, or an agent, or even a membership card in Author's League in order to have your novel considered for publication.

What you do need is permission to submit your novel, and what I would suggest is a query letter. Let's suppose you've written that gothic novel of the windswept moors of Devon and your market research has led you to believe that it would have its best chance of acceptance at any of six paperback houses. You've checked *Writer's Market* and learned the name of the editor at each house who's likely to be in charge of gothics. Now you sit down and write each of the six editors a letter, something like this:

> *Dear Ms. Wimpole,*
> *I have recently completed a gothic novel with the working title of* Trefillian House. *Its setting is Devon, its heroine a young American widow hired to appraise antique furniture in a creaky old mansion on the lonely windswept moors.*
> *Would you be willing to look at a copy of the manuscript? I'm enclosing herewith a self-addressed stamped envelope for your reply, and I'll look forward to hearing from you.*

I would suggest you write a letter of this sort whether or not the house in question reads unsolicited manuscripts. You'll get a reply, and a much faster reply than if you submitted a complete manuscript, as it takes rather less time to read a letter than a novel. If the reply tells you thanks but no thanks, that they're no longer an active market for gothics, that they're over-inventoried with books set in Devon, or any other sort of negative reply, you'll have saved the cost of submitting your novel to them and the time they'd take returning it.

If the editor agrees to consider the manuscript, you've cleared a hurdle. *Trefillian House* is no longer an over-the-transom submission, no longer pure slush. It's instead a manuscript an editor has agreed to read.

This doesn't mean Ms. Wimpole's going to buy your book. It doesn't mean you should get your hopes up, only to be deflated when the manuscript comes winging back to you. But it does mean that you've improved your odds a little bit.

Your query letter will have served another purpose. In it you've already described what you're sending—not the nature of your novel, but the nature of your submission. You've labeled it not *the manuscript* but a *copy of the manuscript,* and that's precisely what you're going to submit.

To several publishers. Simultaneously.

Publishers, like everybody else in this imperfect world, like to have things their own way. For years they managed this by somehow getting the word out that it would be unethical for an author to submit his work to more than one publisher at a time. Never mind the fact that a manuscript could languish on a publisher's desk for months on end. Multiple submission, one was given to understand, was underhanded and unfair.

The hell with that noise. The only possible argument against simultaneous submission is that it's improper to lead someone to believe he's the only person considering a novel if this is not in fact the case. By describing what you're sending as a copy, both in your query letter and in the covering letter that accompanies your manuscript, you eliminate this possible source of unpleasantness, and you do this without displaying an unpleasantly aggressive manner. You wouldn't want to say, "I'm sending this novel to ten other guys at the same time, so you better hop to it if you want to get there fastest with the mostest." That just might rub Ms. Wimpole the wrong way.

It should go without saying that we're talking about a clean legible copy of the manuscript, a photocopy equal in quality to the original. Not a carbon copy. Not one of those old-fashioned photocopies on smelly purplish plasticized paper. If that's the best you can do, you'll have to do better.

I would suggest that you have between four and six copies of your novel in circulation. More than that gets confusing. When you submit the novel, describe it again as a copy and make it clear that the editor has encouraged you to send it. Don't take it for granted that she'll recall your name or anything else about you. It may be hard for you to grasp this, but at this stage of the game Ms. Wimpole plays rather more of a role in your life than you do in hers.

You might write something like this:

> *Dear Ms. Wimpole,*
>   *Thanks very much for your letter of February 19th. As you suggested, I'm enclosing herewith a copy of my gothic novel,* Trefillian House. *I hope you like it and that it will fit your publishing requirements.*
>   *SASE enclosed.*

It's virtually impossible, when submitting to more than one publisher at a time, not to project a fantasy in which two or more of them accept the book the same day. There are three things to keep in mind when this fantasy strikes:

(1) It won't happen.
(2) It should be your biggest problem.
(3) Your agent will handle it.

• • •

Nowadays, of course, most submissions are electronic. All you need to do is attach a file.

That saves you postage when you submit, and additional postage on the SASE you no longer need to enclose. It also saves the cost of making all those photocopies.

That's the good news. The bad news, which comes in the same package, is that everybody who's managed to write a novel can submit the hell out of it without any real investment of time and expense. Editors, all of whom are heroically overworked, have less time for over-the-transom submissions and more of them to deal with.

Does this mean you should submit to one publisher at a time, in an effort to lighten their load? No, because they can still take forever to get to your book, and may never get to it at all. A physical manuscript, back in the day, took up space in an editor's office; along with other submissions, it loomed balefully, giving that editor one more thing to feel guilty about. Sooner or later, that guilt-ridden editor would act to get those manuscripts out of his office. He might not go so far as to read the bloody things, but at least he'd mail them back in those handy SASEs.

Nowadays there's no pile of manuscripts, just a slew of emails with files attached. An editor who'd draw the line at throwing unread paper-and-ink manuscripts in the trash may be more sanguine about saying the hell with it and hitting the Delete key.

Or, should you inquire about your novel's fate months after you submitted it, is the editor likely to search through hundreds of unanswered emails, looking for your letter and attachment? Or will he just type "Sorry, your novel's not quite right for us," hit SEND, and forget you or your book ever existed.

No, you won't get this treatment everywhere. And yes, you've improved your odds by getting Ms. Wimpole to greenlight your submission. But none of this changes the fact that, ninety-nine percent of the time, whatever you submit is a burden and a nuisance, and its chances of getting a warm reception are pretty slim.

Which serves as a good lead-in for the next question . . .

• • •

Speaking of agents, do you need one? And, if you do, how do you get one?

It's possible, certainly, to represent yourself, just as it's possible for you to act as your own attorney or remove your own appendix. And there's less potential hazard than you'd face in the courtroom or the hospital.

Some very successful authors act as their own agents, making their own deals and doing quite well at it. They let their publishers act as their representatives in the foreign market (usually at a higher commission than most agents charge) and generally remain with one publisher for many years.

Personally, I think they cost themselves money, but it's hard to prove it to them. They see the 15% commission they're saving and they don't see the money they're *not* earning by going it alone. They don't see the clauses in their contracts that a decent agent would insist be changed. They don't see the higher advances and better rates they might be receiving. But that's their business. My business is writing, and I'm pleased to leave the dollars-and-cents side of it to my agent.

For a novice writer, it would seem that an agent would be all the more desirable. He's in daily contact with the market, knows what editor is looking for what sort of material, and can pick up a phone and set wheels in motion. What he can't do—and this is worth stressing—is get an editor to buy a book he wouldn't want in the first place. He can lead the horse to water or carry water to the horse, but that's as far as it goes.

How do you get such a person? The same way you bring your manuscript to the attention of an editor. By writing a query letter of the sort you wrote to Ms. Wimpole, explaining a little about your book, detailing whatever previous writing experience you've had, and asking if the agent would be willing to have a look at what you've got. *And,* let me remind you, enclosing a stamped self-addressed envelope.

The agent may already have a full house. He may not have any interest in representing the type of material you've written. If he's willing to look at the script, send him a copy. If he reads it and expresses a willingness to represent your work, you've got an agent.

Let's suppose you've managed to connect with an editor all by yourself. You've submitted a novel to Ms. Wimpole and she writes back that she'd like to publish it. Perhaps she presents terms. Perhaps she encloses a contract. Perhaps she asks for revisions without saying anything about terms or a contract. Perhaps . . . .

Perhaps you need an agent *now*.

You may feel it goes against the grain to seek representation now that you've already done the hard part of finding a publisher. But it's at this stage of the game that not having an agent can really screw you up. Before you sign anything, before you do any further work on speculation, in short before you make any conclusive move, you should have professional counsel. The commission you'll pay is a small price.

Sounds like a good idea. But won't Ms. Wimpole get steamed if I tell her I don't want to do anything without an agent?

She shouldn't. If she's a competent editor working for a respectable publisher, she'll probably welcome the news; she knows it's easier to deal with a professional agent than with an unknowledgeable and perhaps scatterbrained amateur writer. She may even suggest of her accord that you avail yourself of an agent.

Even if she doesn't, she'd be a good person to ask advice from on the subject. I know any number of writers who selected agents largely on the basis of their publishers' recommendations.

It's true, though, that some publishers are more reputable than others. While all the major houses play it straight, you might wind up breaking into the business writing for some graduate of the Ring Around The Collar School of Business Ethics. You may be assured that you don't need an agent, that the publisher's more comfortable not dealing through agents, and you may be given the impression that insisting on an agent may blow the whole deal.

If that costs you the deal, you're better off without it.

Where do I find an agent—assuming I don't have an editor to recommend one?

There's a list of them in *Writer's Market*. That's one sensible place to start.

If you know anybody who knows an agent, so much the better. The agents I've known have always gotten a large number of new clients through referrals from other clients. Any third party whose name you can conveniently use can make it easier for you to get a positive reply to your query—and that's all connections can ever do for you. After that, the book has to sell itself.

• • •

Writer's Digest Books publishes annual print and electronic editions of both Writers Market and Guide to Literary Agents—and there's no end of additional information available in book form and online.

Over the years, I've learned that writers conferences have hooked up quite a few writers and agents. Any agent who attends one of them is at the very least open to signing new clients—really, why else would they go? I don't know that you ought to start signing up for conferences in order to get an agent, but if there's already one you've been considering, that motive might tip the scales.

I should add that not everyone agrees that an agent is desirable, let alone necessary. Kristine Kathryn Rusch argues persuasively that most agents do more harm than good, and it's probably true that a majority of writers who publish their own work leave their agents behind as they move into the indie world. For my part, I continue to cherish my agent, and make him a part of my self-publishing ventures as well as my traditionally published work.

• • •

What about reading fees?

Forget about reading fees.

Some agents charge prospective clients a fee to cover the cost of reading and evaluating their work. The rationale here is that the agent has to be compensated for his time, but more often than not the tail winds up wagging the dog. The great majority of agents who solicit reading fees barely have a professional client list worthy of the name; without reading fees, they'd have trouble swinging the monthly light bill.

As a result, you wind up paying a fee in the hope that you'll be represented by a person who, if anything, has negative clout with the publishing industry. Furthermore, the criticism he gives you can't be trusted, because he has a vested interest in encouraging you to keep on writing—and to keep on sending in manuscripts with checks attached.

• • •

I know whereof I speak, having worked for such an agent back in 1957–8. I wrote at some length about those days in *The Crime of Our Lives*.

• • •

In some instances, the fee agent is in the editing business as well. The fee's not all he wants from you. He'll also offer to rewrite the manuscript, for a price.

Not all agents who charge fees are quite so venal about it, and I suppose there are a few who are really just trying to cover the overhead while assembling a list of professional clients. Even so, why pay an agent when you can find another agent to perform the same task for free?

The fee agent, of course, is a sure bet. You won't have to write him a query letter and wait with bated breath for his reply. And, after he's read your book, you can be fairly sure of a courteous letter praising various aspects of your writing. An agent who reads your work at no charge may send it back with a brief not-for-us note.

Think about it. Do you want to pay fifty or a hundred bucks so someone'll write you a nice letter? We're supposed to get paid for what *we* write, not to pay for what other people write to us. Remember?

I suppose you feel the same way about subsidy publishers?

You bet.

There is some justification for paying to have your work published if you are a poet or a writer of nonfiction. For most poets, that's the only available avenue for publication. And, since poetry doesn't make money anyway, there's no particular stigma attached to paying for publication.

Some nonfiction deserves publication and can be commercially viable, but it may be too highly specialized to interest a commercial publisher. This is particularly likely with regional material.

In such cases, there's no reason why an author would be ill advised to underwrite the cost of publishing his book. I personally believe that self-publishing is a much better plan than paying a subsidy publisher to do the job for you, but that's by the way. We're talking about novels, and it just doesn't make sense for a novelist to pay for publication of his book. The only possible reason for it is vanity.

The novel you publish with a subsidy publisher will not do much of anything but cost you money. It will not get reviewed in any significant media. It will not be handled by stores. It will not sell enough copies to amount to anything. It will not even do much for your vanity, really, because knowledgeable people will look at the book, note the subsidy house's imprint, recognize it for what it is, and know that your novel is one you had to pay to have published.

•   •   •

Vanity Presses were always a horrible idea, and many of their business practices skirted the brink of larceny. One of the happiest fruits of the ebook revolution has been the disappearance of vanity publishers. (Even so, it should be noted that the core principle of the vanity press—"We make our money by screwing our clients"—lives on in some of the murkier byways of self-publishing. A truly contemptible operation like Authors Solutions is an example of this latter-day parasitism.)

•   •   •

You can avoid the last pitfall by publishing the book yourself, using some *ad hoc* imprint. And, if you want to have a small edition of books made up in this fashion so that you can pass out copies to friends, there's really nothing wrong with that. Writing's a fine hobby, and if the novel you produce turns out not to be commercial, there's no reason why you can't indulge yourself a little and see your work in print. You'll still spend considerably less annually than an amateur photographer, say, would part with for equipment and film.

Self-publication's okay, then, if you can afford it. And if you know that it's not the road to wealth, fame or professional status.

And what is the road to all those good things?

You just keep punching. You must submit your manuscript relentlessly, shrugging off rejection and sending it on to another publisher the day it comes back. You simply cannot let rejection get you down, whether it comes in the form of a printed slip, a personal note, or a refusal to read your book in the first place. You can remind yourself that all a rejection means is that one particular person decided against publishing your book. It doesn't mean your book stinks. It doesn't even mean that particular editor *thinks* it stinks. And it certainly doesn't mean *you* stink.

You can remind yourself, too, that most novels have taken awhile to find a publisher, that many smash best sellers were turned down by ten or twenty or thirty publishers before someone recognized their potential. And you can tell yourself that success doesn't hinge upon merit alone, that the determination to keep marketing your book is equally essential if you're going to get anywhere.

You already showed you've got determination. It takes plenty of it to get a novel written from the first page to the last. You're not going to quit now, are you?

No trick, then? No handy household hints to make it easier?

One trick.

One way of taking your mind off rejection.

Get busy on another book. Get deeply involved in another book, so much so that the rejections the first one piles up won't hurt nearly as much. You'll be amazed, I think, by how much easier the second book is to write—and by how much you've grown as a result of the work that went into the first one.

One of the functions of an agent is to spare you the hassle of marketing your own work, not only because he's better at it than you are but so that you don't have to concentrate on two things at once. Until you acquire an agent, you'll be wearing two hats, an agent's peaked cap and a writer's pith helmet. To keep the marketing process from taking your mind off your writing, make the business of getting your manuscript in the mail as automatic as possible. And, to take the sting out of the rejections your novel accumulates along the way, throw yourself into your second novel as completely as you can.

• • •

While just about every aspect of the publishing world has changed enormously in recent years, nothing's as utterly changed as self-publishing.

Consider what I just told you: Self-publication's okay, then, if you can afford it. And if you know that it's not the road to wealth, fame or professional status.

Well, I couldn't write those two sentences today. Because acting as your own publisher is something virtually everyone can afford. It's not quite free, but it comes surprisingly close. And there are more than a few writers for whom it has led directly to wealth and fame and professional status.

Which is why it deserves a chapter of its own.

Chapter 15

The Case for Self-Publishing

Publishing one's own work is nothing new. A number of famous writers published their own books—though fewer than a couple of deceptive websites would suggest. Back when Stephen Crane published his first novel, *Maggie: A Girl of the Streets,* that involved finding a printer and paying him to print a certain number of books, then persuading booksellers to give the books space on their shelves. I don't suppose Crane made any money with *Maggie*, but it probably got him some attention, and commercial publishers brought out all of his subsequent work, including the novel everybody remembers, *The Red Badge of Courage.*

("Write what you know," remember? Crane, who'd never been to war, wrote a brilliant novel of the experience of battle, one that still rings true a century later. But I digress . . .)

Self-publishing has always been a better idea than patronizing a vanity press, or subsidy publisher, and as noted in the preceding chapter, it's made more or less sense for a lot of writers, according to their aims and circumstances. For the personal memoir or family history, written with a small focused audience in mind, self-publishing has always been the best option. For most poets, except for the handful who have a sufficient following or critical reputation to interest a commercial publisher or university press, publishing one's own work is a good choice—and often the only choice.

Was it apt to be profitable? No, probably not. But it had to be satisfying to have one's work in print, and the cost wasn't all that high. The self-published grandfather had something to hand to his grandkids, and might do so with the expectation that his words would be read by an as-yet-unborn generation as well. A self-published poet would have a published book to his credit, thus enriching his academic credentials; he'd also be able to sell copies at readings and public appearances.

I published a book of my own in 1986. Not a novel at all, it was a book for writers called *Write For Your Life*. I'd already published two books for writers, *Telling Lies for Fun & Profit* as well as the first edition of *Writing the Novel,* and I might very well have found a commercial publisher willing to bring out *WFYL*.

I never even looked for one. I'd long entertained muted fantasies of publishing my own work, and this book was clearly an ideal candidate. At the time, my wife and I had spent a couple of years traveling around the country with an interactional seminar for writers—called, you'll be astonished to learn, *Write For Your Life*—and I wanted to put the seminar in book form, so that it would be available to people unable to attend in person.

That made it a natural to sell directly—at the seminar, and via advertising to the seminar's potential audience. While nobody could expect the book to be a hot ticket in bookstores, it ought to do well in that capacity.

And, too, time was of the essence. I didn't expect to be offering the seminar for more than another year or so, and I wanted to strike while the iron was lukewarm. If I were to find a commercial publisher for *WFYL*, it would be at least a year before the book was on sale. That was longer than I wanted to wait.

I asked around, and learned that publishing employees who handled book production from 9 to 5 sometimes took on freelance work by the light of the moon. I found such a fellow, and for a modest fee he shepherded my manuscript through the production process. I got to make all the decisions, but he helped inform my decisions, and did all the heavy lifting. I wound up with 5000 books in my storeroom, and I set about selling them, and all but a carton or two were gone within the year.

We made a profit, albeit a modest one. But it took an investment of time and money, and it was a lot of work, and for a while our house was full to overflowing with bright yellow copies of *Write For Your Life*. There was never a moment when I regretted the venture, but neither was there a moment when I was tempted to repeat it. Not with another book for writers, and certainly not for a novel.

That was then.

In 2011, I got out a blog post on self-publishing, specifically of e-books. (I called it "A Tip of the Hat to John Locke, and a Wink to Russell Blake," and I won't reproduce it here, but it's still out there for you to find; just go to lawrenceblock.com and hunt for it.)

Now my blog has never had enormous readership, and very likely never will, but that particular post drew a remarkable reaction. Last I looked, there were 127 responses, and many of them were at least as interesting as what I'd written. Here's one of my favorites:

> *. . .Your book* Write For Your Life *is probably responsible for my writing career. When NY started sending me the message that my romantic comedies just didn't fit their marketing view, I read your book again – even though my new dog had demolished the cover years before. I wrote the affirmations. That kept me going and believing in my writing.*
>
> *Eventually, after the world revolved enough times and the Kindle was invented, I had a means to test my belief in my writing. Guess what? I was right. There was a market for my books! I have 4 romantic comedies on ebooks. In less than 4 months, I've sold more than 80,000 copies.*

> *True, that's nothing like John Locke's sales, but it gives me great satisfaction and joy to have readers appreciating my writing.*
>
> *I don't do very much with FB or Twitter, but I do blog every day . . .*

Yes, you read that right. Joan Reeves sold 80,000 ebooks in four months, books she'd shopped around for years without getting anywhere. I just checked her Amazon listings, and at present she's got 15 romantic comedies eVailable, most of them priced at $3.99. I don't know how much she's writing these days, or how well her books are selling, but that's sort of beside the point. Here's a woman who couldn't get arrested, and then ebooks and self-publishing came around, and everything changed.

Not too many months after my blog post, I looked at the novelettes and short stories I'd written about my series detective, Matthew Scudder. There were ten of them, enough for a book, especially if I could write one more.

I knew right away I wanted to publish the book myself. While one of my regular publishers might be persuaded to take the book, there's no way they could be expected to give it more than short shrift. It was nobody's idea of a hot property, and if the chains even carried it, they'd tuck it away in a corner.

Long story short, I wrote an eleventh story. My friend Brian Koppelman, an ardent Scudder enthusiast, volunteered to contribute an introduction. I found a company specializing in the production of e-books and print-on-demand paperbacks; they worked on a straight work-for-hire basis, so that 100% of the book's earnings would come directly to me.

I wrote some checks, and spent a couple thousand dollars, as opposed to starting out with a check in hand for a publisher's advance. I ran the numbers, and decided I wouldn't have to sell too many books to come out ahead.

It was a wonderful experience. In almost no time at all I had an ebook for sale on Kindle and Nook and Kobo and Apple, and shortly thereafter I had a handsome trade paperback for sale online at Amazon and Barnes & Noble. I am not getting rich, but four years later *The Night and the Music* continues to sell, as an ebook and as a paperback, and brings me income every month, with no signs of slowing down.

If a commercial publisher had brought it out, it would have long since been remaindered. But the publisher would cling like a barnacle to the ebook rights, and would pocket three-fourths of the eRoyalties until the end of time.

Well, the hell with that.

So I guess you're completely sold on publishing your own work, right?

Nope. I've published some books myself since *The Night and the Music*. I've published some with commercial publishers. And in a couple of instances I've done a combination deal, with a publisher bringing out the book's print edition while I've retained ebook (and occasionally paperback) rights for myself.

My greatest self-publishing leap of faith was two years ago, when I wrote *The Burglar who Counted the Spoons*, the first new book about Bernie Rhodenbarr in quite a few years. I knew I could have secured a substantial advance from any of several traditional publishers, but the desire to do it myself was a prime motivator in getting the book written, and I felt I owed it to myself to follow through with it.

I brought it out in three forms—as an ebook, as a trade paperback, and as a deluxe leather-bound limited collector's edition. All three editions were profitable, and all three continue to sell, but it's fair to say my results were mixed.

Here's the downside: Except for those mystery specialty

bookshops who elected to carry it, the book did not get into stores. And, except for online media and the blogosphere, the book did not get reviewed. (A year after publication, Bill Schafer at Subterranean Press brought out a hardcover trade edition, aiming largely at libraries, and that edition did get reviewed by *Publishers Weekly*, and went on to sell a heartening number of copies.)

So get to the bottom line, will you? Did you come out ahead by doing it yourself?

Hard to say. I could have secured a large advance for the book, and even if it never earned out, it would have put a lot of money in my bank account. I'm sure I wound up behind in the short run, but the book continues to sell strongly, and I'm inclined to believe that I'll come out ahead in the long run.

Well, you'd want to believe that, wouldn't you?

Good point.

So here's another question. Are you glad you did it yourself? And would you do it again?

That's two questions. And the answer is yes and no. Yes, I'm very glad I published *The Burglar who Counted the Spoons* myself. And no, should I write another book about Bernie (or Matt Scudder, or Keller, or indeed any A-list novel that might excite a commercial publisher and elicit a substantial advance) I don't think I'd be tempted to do it myself.

But, see, I've already done it. And, like the magnificent Mae West, when faced with a choice of two evils, I always like to pick the one I haven't tried yet.

By recounting my own experiences with self-publishing, I've tried to show how it can be a viable choice for an established writer. Even as my half century in the business would suggest that I don't have to act as my own publisher, some readers will infer that an old hand like me has an edge in this new world.

"You have a track record and a following," one fellow wrote me. "Whoever publishes your book, you or Alfred Knopf, you've got a dedicated fan base and a built-in audience. But nobody ever heard of me, so how can I hope to sell any books without a powerful established publisher behind me?"

I get the point. But in fact it's new writers who are far and away the most active in publishing their own work.

It's true that no end of veteran writers are dipping their toes in these new waters. Some are pros with solid track records whose modest sales numbers are no longer profitable for an increasingly corporate publishing industry; dropped by their publishers after years of steady sales, their only real alternative is to go it alone. A growing handful of others, still prized by their publishers, have grown sick of the way the business works and hate to see the lion's share of their ebook earnings get siphoned off before it reaches them.

But most writers are staying with corporate publishing. It's not hard to understand why. They get big advances. They get taken to lunch in expensive restaurants. They're served by a whole team—editor, copy editor, publicist, marketing specialist, and on down the line. Bookstores, both chains and independents, order great quantities of their books, and display copies in the window.

That's a lot to give up, and it shouldn't be surprising that most writers with a choice elect to stay put.

But you, Gentle Reader, are not in that enviable position. You've written a first novel, and nobody knows you from Adam (save those in a position to know that you have a navel, as Adam of course does not).

Let's assume that you've written to Ms. Wimpole and her colleagues, and that you've submitted your book to she and the five other editors who've agreed to look at it. Now, three months down the line, three of them have assured you that the book is not quite right for their needs.

The other three have yet to respond, so you send out follow-up emails, and learn that Editor D has left the company to spend more time with her family, and no one in the office knows anything about your submission. Editor E is silent for two weeks, then sends an email saying he hasn't had a chance to read *So Grows the Tree* yet, and will be in touch when he does. You find it somewhat disquieting that he's spelled your name wrong, and that your title was *Once More With Zombies*.

You never hear anything from Editor F.

You could keep going. You've read enough stories about books that were turned down by twenty or thirty or fifty consecutive publishers, only to be snapped up by #51 and wind up spending a year and a half on the bestseller list. True, it doesn't happen very often, but who's to say it couldn't happen to you?

You have faith in the book, right? And you have faith in the notion that a good book will eventually find a publisher. But with every passing day you're beginning to feel a little more like a Christian Scientist with appendicitis. Your faith is undiminished, in your book and in the publishing process, but maybe it's time to see a doctor.

Why you should publish your own book:

1. You'll be published.

That's obvious enough, isn't it? Hell, it's essentially tautological. Of course your book will be published if you go and publish it yourself.

But, obvious or not, it's what you've been aiming for from the beginning. The goal of seeing your book in print is what kept you going from the first page to the last. And it's something that doesn't seem to be happening going the conventional route. You're beginning to wonder if the book is any good, and thinking that maybe you ought to set it aside and write another. And indeed you probably should write another, but how much enthusiasm can you summon up for the task with this first book sprawled across your desk like a corpse?

Won't it be easier to write a second book once the first one's found a home? And isn't that just as true if you're the one paying the rent?

2. It's quick.

Traditional publishing takes time. If your book is accepted by the first publisher who sees it, it's still going to take a minimum of a year and often closer to two years before you see it offered for sale.

It's way faster when you do it yourself. You can have your novel on sale as an ebook in a matter of weeks. Add another couple of weeks for publication as a print-on-demand paperback. Your self-published novel will be in readers' hands or on their Kindles in very little time.

3. You get paid faster.

Sometime in late March, you get paid for all your sales recorded in the month of January. Thirty days later, you get paid for February. And so on—once a month, the platforms on which your books are sold pay you, generally by direct deposit into your bank account.

With a commercial publisher, on the other hand, you generally get paid twice a year; in April, for funds received by your publisher between July and December, and in October, for funds received during the first half of the year.

4. You get paid more.

Quick math: Your Kindle ebook is priced at $9.99. A customer buys it, Amazon collects $9.99, pays you 70% of their receipts. Net to you: $6.99

Your publisher prices the book at the same $9.99. A customer buys it, Amazon collects $9.99, pays your publisher 70% of their receipts, or $6.99. As per your contract, your publisher pays you 25% of his receipts. Net to you: $1.75.

5. You control the design, the marketing, the price.

A commercial publisher has access to quality artists and book designers, so that your book will look good inside and out. His marketing and publicity departments can develop a promotional campaign designed to maximize your sales. And they'll set the book's price to bring the best possible return.

Maybe.

Except yours is just one of the titles they're working on that month, and if the others are by Stephen King and Clive Cussler and Danielle Steel, how much of a priority is yours gonna be? If you're low man on the totem pole, you'll take what cover they give you, and you'll probably be afraid to say you don't like it. (And if you do, they'll explain to you why you're wrong, and assure you the sales force is crazy about it.)

And so on. They'll price the ebook too high, explaining that they don't want it to cut into your hardcover sales, whatever the hell that means.

I don't want to make this a horror story, because a lot of the folks in publishing are very bright and very capable, and sometimes they do everything right. But all too often they don't, and you have a lot more control plus a whole lot more flexibility when you do it all yourself.

You can hire an artist and get a cover made. Lots of artists do this sort of thing, and a couple of hundred bucks should get you something more than decent. If you have a flair for it, you can do this yourself. Many of my own best covers started out as stock photos; I used Picasa to crop and add type, and if I knew how to use Photoshop I could do even more. My cost on those covers was $4.98 for the stock photo, plus . . . well, plus half an hour of my own labor. The whole deal set me back about the same as a mocha latte.

Will your cover be as good as a publisher's? Probably not, because they're professionals and you're not. But it can easily be good enough. It might be different if your book were going to be out there on the front octagon at Barnes & Noble, but the only place anybody's going to see your cover is on the web. You don't need Chip Kidd or Milton Glazer to design a book cover that's only going to show up online.

You mentioned flexibility . . .

I did, didn't I? And here's what it means. You can, in a half hour's time, change the price of your ebook or POD paperback. You can raise it or lower it with ease, and within a matter of hours the new price will show on the various online platforms.

A couple of my books, *Catch and Release* and *Defender of the Innocent*, were published in hardcover by Subterranean Press, while I retained paperback and eRights. I published my ebook of each title when Subterranean's hardcover came out, and set the price of the ebook at $9.99. After they'd had six months lead time to sell the book, I dropped the ebook price to $4.99—and witnessed a comforting spurt in sales.

With certain backlist titles, I've decided over time that the covers I stuck on them weren't so hot. In several instances I invested another $4.98 and another half hour, crafted a new cover, and swapped it for the dud; in a matter of minutes the deed was done, and in not too many more minutes the new version was live online at Amazon and B&N.

The flexibility extends to the inside of the book, incidentally. As long as I've been writing, I've had occasional notes from readers calling attention to an egregious typographical error or, worse, a mistake of my own making. In one of the Burglar books I identified a song from *My Fair Lady* as having been from *Brigadoon*. (Or maybe it was the other way around. You'd think I'd remember which it was, because you wouldn't believe how many helpful readers were moved to call the error to my attention.)

When that happens in a publisher's printed book, what you can do is drop your editor a note, and it'll go into a file, and if they do another printing, or reprint in paperback, and if your editor remembers, maybe it'll be changed down the line.

If it's a publisher's ebook, it's a little quicker and easier. You email the editor, and she passes the word to their ebook division, and maybe somebody makes the change. Or maybe not.

When *you're* the publisher, you pull up the ebook file, make the change yourself, go to your Kindle Direct Publishing account, upload the corrected file, then do the same thing on other platforms. It takes time, and it can be annoying if you have to do it very often, but by the day's end the task is done.

Okay, I'm sold. Publishing my own work is clearly the only way to go. What do you say to that?

What do I say, pilgrim? I say not so fast.

CHAPTER 16

THE CASE AGAINST SELF-PUBLISHING

There's another side to the story, and it deserves its own chapter.

Why you should *not* publish your own book:

1. There's a world of difference between a published writer and a self-published writer.

In the public mind, that is, and very possibly in yours as well. Bragging rights are vastly different. Imagine the following two sentences, spoken in your mother's voice:

> "My daughter Mallory's novel, Had I But Known, was just published by Random House. It's in all the stores, even the Barnes & Noble on Brookshire Boulevard!"

> "My daughter Mallory's novel, Had I But Known, was just published. Actually, she published it herself, and you can buy it on Amazon, whatever that is . . ."

Well, you get the point. When you identify yourself as a writer, the first thing people ask is if you've had anything published. Many will react differently, depending on your response, and the reaction of more than a few will echo that of Mallory's mom. Even among your more knowledgeable acquaintances, self-publishing has a distinct Rodney Dangerfield aspect to it. It don't get no respect.

Will this change? It's already done so, to an extent, but the process will take a while. What you have to decide is how much it matters to you.

And that's entirely an individual matter. I know a woman who's been trying to get her first novel published for many years now. A lot of people have admired it, some of them quite extravagantly, but that hasn't led to a publishing deal.

Along the way, her mother died. She too was a writer, and had published a couple of books some years ago. She'd completed a new novel shortly before her death, and my friend made it her business to get it edited and published. Rather than buck the fierce odds against finding a publisher for it, she published it herself as an ebook and POD paperback.

I don't know that it sold many copies, but that wasn't the point. She wanted it out there, and it's out there.

She's still trying to get her own novel published. This has been an uphill battle from the start, and it's pretty clear the ascent is only going to get steeper.

She could, of course, publish it herself. She knows this, and when that course is recommended to her she rejects it. "I need the validation of being accepted by a real publisher," she says.

If you have the same need, self-publishing probably won't work for you.

2. You won't make any money.

There are exceptions. Quite a few of them, actually. There are also people who buy a $1 lottery ticket and collect a seven-figure prize. The odds are a lot better in self-publishing, but you can't expect to get rich—or even come out ahead—by publishing your own work.

If a commercial publisher accepts your work, you'll receive an advance against future earnings. Even if it's minimal, it's actual money. A $5000 advance may very well amount to $5000 more than the profit you'll see by publishing it yourself.

I'm not sure how heavily this consideration ought to weigh in your decision. Did you honestly sit down and write a first novel with an expectation of substantial profit?

3. You'll have to do a whole lot of things yourself.

This is the flip side of the fifth argument in favor of doing it yourself—i.e., you're in control. The reason you're in control is you're the only one there.

When you sign with a publisher, his people pretty much take over. You can sign the contract and book passage on a freighter to Pusan, knowing that while you're gone somebody will produce a cover, somebody else will copy edit your manuscript, somebody will schedule the publication date and send out review copies and sell the book to bookstores—and so on.

They may do this well, or they may make a dog's breakfast of it, but it'll be done and you won't have to worry your pretty little head over it.

If you self-publish, you'll have to either learn how to do a slew of onerous tasks yourself, or else assemble your own team to assist you with them. (We'll see how that works in the next chapter.) Either way, you'll have things to do and decisions to make.

Even if you're good at it (and you may be) and even if you enjoy it (and there's a lot about it that's enjoyable) it's going to take a great deal of time and effort. One's allotment of time and effort, while sometimes elastic, is ultimately finite. What you spend on publishing your first novel is time and effort you're unable to spend on writing your second.

As a writer, and particularly as a new writer, the most important thing you can do is write. You've written a novel? Then you ought to be writing another.

Self-publishing the first may provide positive reinforcement, fueling the fires for the next book. That's ideal, and as good as it gets. But if instead it drains the energy that ought to go into your next book, it may be a bad idea.

4. Your book won't be in stores or libraries. It won't get reviewed in the *New York Times*. And you won't get to promote it on the Tonight Show.

This might seem to echo the first point, but it's not just about image. It's also about sales.

While brick-and-mortar bookstores (as opposed to the online variety) are no longer the only place where books are sold, they're still important. If your book's on the shelf at the local chain or independent, a prospective reader who's never heard of you or of it may spot its eye-catching cover and pick it up. That can't happen if your book's not on the shelf in the first place, and it won't get there if you publish it yourself.

(Well, okay, it might. You can order a few cartons at wholesale from the POD printer, load them into the trunk of your car, and call on local stores, persuading them to display a few copies. Sometimes this works. In the case of John Erickson, who chronicles the adventures of Hank the Cowdog, it worked brilliantly; he drove around the Southwest peddling his books to feed stores and turned it into a career. I tell John's story in my blog post: just go to lawrenceblock.com and search for *All Changed, Changed Utterly*. His approach will work reasonably well with books, fiction or nonfiction, of considerable local interest. But even when it works, it's a far cry from having stacks of books in bookstores all over the country.)

Similarly, you may well persuade your local newspaper to review your books. But maybe not—much of the printed media has a fairly firm policy against reviewing self-published work.

I know whereof I speak. When I bring out a book with a commercial publisher, it gets store space and reviews. When I publish one myself, it doesn't. Period.

Libraries order their books from publishers' catalogs, from trade reviews in *Publishers Weekly* and *Booklist* and *Kirkus*. Library interest in ebooks is increasing, a trend which seems likely to continue, but the way things are now, they couldn't order yours even if they wanted to.

(Though that may be in the process of changing. EbooksRForever, a new enterprise organized by indie guru Joe Konrath, is being set up to broker self-published ebooks to libraries. If it works it'll be a godsend to all concerned—but that's a big if.)

As for TV, I was Craig Ferguson's guest on *The Late Late Show* on CBS for an astonishing ten times, and at least once the book I was there to promote was one I'd published myself. But that was a special case. Craig was a big fan of the Scudder novels, and that's why he had me on the first time, and over the years we became good friends. By the time I self-published *The Burglar who Counted the Spoons*, it almost went without saying that I'd get to talk about it on the show. The only difference was that this time, instead of sticking the publisher with the cost, I had to pay my own airfare.

Which leads to the next point:

5. You'll have to spend some money.

Not a whole lot. You can, of course; you can pay a ton of money to a cover artist and you can hire a publicist and you can send out a score or a gross of review copies. You can do the latest version of the Vanity Press experience, signing on with some exploitative outfit like Author Solutions, who'll overcharge you while underperforming. You can spend big money on advertising.

You can even buy five-star reviews, if your gorge doesn't rise at the very idea.

And so on.

But even if you avoid all this openhanded excess, you'll still be out of pocket. How much depends on how wisely you shop around and how much you manage to do for yourself, but you'll certainly be a few hundred dollars out of pocket, and possibly as much as a couple of thousand.

With, as noted, no certainty that you'll ever earn it back, let alone make a profit.

Gee, and it seemed like such a good idea a mere chapter ago.

It's still a good idea, for some of you if not for others. I must think it's a reasonable option myself, or I'd be looking for a publisher for this book. After all, it had a run of almost forty years for Writer's Digest Books. How hard would it be to find a legitimate trade publisher for this updated and expanded edition?

I'll never know, because I see no point in looking. I've known all along that I want to self-publish this one, and I'm more than willing to pass up reviews and bookstore sales in order to do so.

Perhaps, after weighing the options and considering them in the context of your book and your own nature, you have come to believe that publishing your own book might suit you.

In the next chapter, we'll examine how to go about it.

CHAPTER 17

How to Be Your Own Publisher

In this chapter, we'll assume you've weighed the pros and cons in the two preceding chapters and decided to publish your novel yourself. If that's not the case, feel free to skip this chapter altogether.

Still with me? Wonderful! But first, a cautionary note: Everything in this chapter may be out of date by the time you read it.

And it could hardly be otherwise. Every sphere of publishing is changing and evolving at a dizzying pace, and nowhere is that more the case than in the indie world. (Note that I'll be using indie here interchangeably with self-publishing. In another context, independent bookstores also carry the label. This can be confusing to indie authors when they look at what purports to be an Indie Bestseller List—only to find exclusively the books of traditional commercial publishers.)

Because everything's changing so rapidly, most of what I write here will be designed less to tell you what to do than to suggest where you can find what to do. You'll have to search for up-to-date information on your own, I'm afraid, but I can at least point you in the right direction.

Let's see now. You've finished your book. Now what?

Editing what you've written.

You've told your story. You've gone over it and polished it, and as far as you can tell it's in good shape. If you were going to submit it to a commercial publisher, it would be ready to send in.

(In fact you may well have sent it in, once or twice or twenty times, and the fact that it keeps bouncing back has helped inform your decision to go the indie route. That's fine. Either way, you're satisfied with the manuscript—even if so far you're a minority of one.)

But if you did submit it to a publisher, and if that publisher did handsprings over it and offered you a contract, this wouldn't mean the editing process was completed. An editor would read it and make a batch of suggestions—cut this, build this up, you're using this word too much, this dialogue is wooden, di dah di dah di dah. And you'd do some things and resist doing others, but by the time this process had run its course, your manuscript would be at least a little bit different.

Probably for the better. Not always, some editors wind up making some books worse, but the odds are the book would have been improved by editing.

But if you're publishing it yourself, how do you get it in the best possible shape?

Well, you could hire an editor.

This is sometimes not a bad idea even if you plan to submit to a traditional publisher. There was a time when publishing was a more leisurely occupation, and when editors had time to work on manuscripts. What they did was called line editing, and the thing to remember about line editing is that almost nobody does it anymore. An editor's job these days consists of finding the right books to publish and championing them in marketing and sales meetings and seeing the book through the publication process.

You know how Maxwell Perkins took the young Thomas Wolfe in hand and helped him carve *Look Homeward, Angel* and *Of Time and the River* out of a couple of cubic yards of manuscript? Well, Maxwell Perkins went on to that chop shop in the sky a long time ago. Nobody's around these days with either the time or the talent to perform similar cosmetic surgery on your masterpiece.

Nobody riding a desk in a publishing house, that is. But, because publishers keep acquiring one another, and downsizing their staffs accordingly, and because creative management these days consists in good part of replacing seasoned workers who know what they're doing with younger people who'll work for less, a lot of the best editors in the business can't find work in publishing.

For a long time, many former editors have set up shop as literary agents. More recently, quite a few have found a way to remain editors—by offering their editorial services on a freelance basis. They get referrals from publishers and agents, for manuscripts that would be publishable if only they were in publishable condition.

And, increasingly, they're sought out by writers who recognize that their books need professional attention.

A friend of mine, a longtime editor with an illustrious résumé in publishing, has been a freelance editor for the past decade. Last time I saw him, he confided that more than half his business these days was with writers who intended to publish their work themselves.

"At first I thought they were deluding themselves," he told me, "and signing on for this generation's equivalent of those legendary vanity publishers, Dewey Shaftham & Howe. But I've come to see that they're making a sound decision. And God knows it makes my job easier and more emotionally rewarding. I can focus entirely on shaping their material into the best possible book, without having to concern myself with whipping up something that will tickle the ironic sensibilities of some 23-year-old Wellesley grad at Random Penguin. All I have to do is produce a book that will please a reader, because I can take it for granted it will be published."

How do I know if I need this guy? And how do I find him?

An internet search will turn up a great many people doing this type of work. Before you pick one, you'll want to check out the track record and experience of various prospects. And, at least as important, you'll want to consult the great community of indie authors.

In fact, you'll want to do this time and time again. Probably the first thing you need to do, even before you make a firm decision to publish your own novel, is to begin immersing yourself in that community. That means spending a lot of time following blogs and hanging out in online cafés where self-publishing is a central topic.

You are going to have no end of questions, far more than I could begin to address here. And the good news is that there are hundreds of people happy to answer them. You'll get better advice from some people than from others, so part of your job will be sifting what you're told, but isn't that always the case?

Follow these bloggers immediately:

Joe Konrath. The Passive Guy. Dean Wesley Smith. Kristine Kathryn Rusch. Barry Eisler. Hugh Howey. Lee Goldberg.

That'll get you started, and one thing will lead to another. There'll come a time when you realize you're spending too much time in these internet byways, at which time you can cut back; meanwhile, you'll learn a lot, and it has to be more useful than watching cat videos and having arguments with strangers.

Uh, what I was asking—

Right, let's get back to that. How do you know if you need an editor?

You have to get somebody to read your book, somebody with sufficient discrimination to evaluate what you've written and sufficient detachment to tell you the truth. For openers, rule out anybody with whom you share either DNA or a bed (or both, for who am I to judge you?). Pick someone who reads a lot, and whose reading taste includes books similar to what you've been trying to write. If you're in a writing group, pick someone whose reaction to your work is at once favorable and cold-eyed.

And pose your question properly; instead of asking *Do you think this is any good?* ask *Do you think I need the help of an editor?*

If so, sort through the pool of freelance editors, and find out what members of your indie internet community have to say about their experience. When you've found someone you've got a positive feeling about, send him/her an email about your book. If the editor expresses interest, you'll probably have to pay for an evaluation, because no editor can know what your book needs without reading it carefully, and that takes time for which compensation is only appropriate.

Copy editing and proofreading.

Let's assume you've managed to come up with a book that's in no need of heavy editorial attention. Your plot is sound, your characters are fully realized, your prose flows and your dialogue rings true.

Congratulations! You're almost there.

But not quite, because you probably need the services of a copy editor, someone who will be able to make sure that what winds up on the page, physical or virtual, is grammatically correct and stylistically consistent, that it's truly professional.

I feel funny urging you to seek out a copy editor, because I've so often battled with them over the years. I think of a copy editor as the very person Emerson had in mind when he noted that a foolish consistency is the hobgoblin of small minds, a ninny who corrects grammar in dialogue, an anal-retentive pest who plucks out my carefully positioned commas and puts them where I don't want them.

When I self-published *Write For Your Life* in 1986, my book production guy told me I'd have to budget $300 for a copy editor. "Wait a minute," I said. "You mean I can spare myself the aggravation of fighting with a copy editor, and save three hundred bucks in the process?"

And that's what I did, and it's entirely possible I made errors of consistency, and that some work is hyphenated in one chapter and not in another, and I have to tell you I don't care.

But just because I'm a reckless brute doesn't mean I'd recommend that you follow in my paw prints. Someone in the online indie community will be able to steer you to an affordable copy editor, or one amenable to barter.

An exchange of services is even more likely when it comes to proofreading, that last line of defense against everything from typographical goofs to errors of fact.

And it's all too easy for the occasional howler to survive the scrutiny of one pair of eyes after another. I told you about my own *Brigadoon–My Fair Lady* fumble, and just the other day someone asked me about one of Donald E. Westlake's Dortmunder capers, in which his happy band of thieves depart from Grand Central Terminal on a train bound for Long Island. Now Long Island trains all leave from Penn Station, and while you'd have to be a New Yorker to know that, Don was a New Yorker, and I'm a New Yorker, and so were all the book's editors and publishers, and twenty years went by before anybody noticed.

(And, within a week or so of the fellow's email, the *New York Times* has just reported on the eleven miles of tunneling currently under way, designed to connect the LIRR to Grand Central; the projected completion date is 2022.)

Of course you'll read your work many times over before you publish it. And you'll very likely find a lot of things to fix. But you won't find everything, because one simply can't be a good proofreader of one's own work. You wrote it, and you know what you meant to say, and that's what your eyes will see.

Spell-check programs are an enormous help, and it's shocking when an error slips through that Spell-Check would have caught—a sentnece lkie htis, for exmaple. But no spell-check app can save you from writing cant for can't, or mold for mould, or dog for cat.

You may know someone who'll be happy to proofread your book, and who'll accept a listing in the acknowledgements in lieu of cash. Or you can exchange proofreading services with another indie writer, the two of you doing for one another what neither of you could effectively do for yourself. (It helps, incidentally, if neither of you is dyslexic . . .)

Formatting your novel for ePublication.

The various ebook sales platforms—Kindle, Nook, Apple, Kobo, Smashwords, Draft2Digital, etc.—have user-friendly sites designed to enable anybody with minimal smarts and opposable thumbs to publish an ebook. Most of them are set up to handle virtually any Word file you upload, transforming it into the requisite EPUB or .mobi file.

That's not good enough.

If an ebook's going to be read with enjoyment, it has to be properly formatted. Unfortunately, most people preparing manuscripts for ebook conversion don't know what they're doing—and the mass of ebooks rendered essentially FUBAR by bad formatting includes a disheartening number of titles foisted on the public by A-list traditional publishers.

(I know. They charge way too much for an ebook, and share too little of the take with the writer, and justify all of this because of their professionalism. And then they can't even turn out an ebook anybody can read. I read one the other day that was double-spaced between paragraphs. All paragraphs. You can imagine what a page of dialogue looked like. I read another where everything was in italics.)

How do I make sure that doesn't happen?

There are two ways. You can hire a formatter or you can do it yourself.

It's not impossible to learn. Joel Friedlander offers a batch of books for the self-publisher, and covers all aspects of book design, including formatting. Jaye W. Manus (QA Productions) is a brilliant formatter and production person, who has taught herself no end of improved ways to navigate the formatting process; astonishingly, she blogs regularly, giving away all her secrets to anyone with the sense to follow her blog.

I suggest that you at least investigate the possibility of doing your own formatting. You may find the whole business absorbing and enjoyable, in which case you can not only save yourself time and money but may even wind up with a sideline business, formatting work for other indie authors.

Or you may decide in short order that the whole business is way too much trouble, that you'd rather leave it to somebody who's far better at it than you could ever hope to be.

My sentiments exactly. Now how do I find a formatter?

The same way you find most of what you need in the brave new world of self-publishing. You ask your friends, new and old. You work the message boards and check the blogs and websites. You compare services offered and rates charged, and you make your choice.

One thing to watch out for:

Pick someone who operates on a work-for-hire basis. Work for hire means they put a price on their services and you pay it and it's all yours. When you're writing something, the last thing you want to do is sell your material as work for hire; you wrote it and it's yours and you want a permanent ongoing stake in its earnings.

But when you're dealing with formatters and marketers and publicists, you don't want to saddle yourself with a partner.

I can see where you might be tempted. If any of these folks will work with you for a percentage of future earnings, you don't have to come up with money in front. And their stake in your book's success will motivate them to do their best work, right?

The hell with that. The only people worth working with will do their best work regardless. And you'll pay them a fair price. And you'll own 100% of your book.

Getting a cover.

A cover will set you back anywhere from a few dollars (if you purchase a stock photo and adapt it yourself) to a few hundred (if you commission an artist to produce a wholly original cover specifically for your book). On balance, I think this is an area in which it's sensible to save money.

How important is the cover? As we noted earlier, it's very important for a book on a shelf or table in a bookstore. Somebody did a study a while back, determining the percentage of customers who, having picked up a book for a closer look, wind up carrying it to the counter and paying for it. It was a high percentage, as I recall, and it was impressive, but the flip side is even more convincing: not a single sale resulted from all those people who didn't pick up the book.

The cover's by no means the only factor in whether or not a bookstore browser picks up your book. Your name is a factor, as is whatever publicity or word of mouth the book has generated. Still, every time somebody picks up a book, that book's cover is doing its job.

That's in a bookstore. But you essentially gave up bookstore sales when you opted to be your own publisher. So how important is that cover in the online marketplace where your book will be offered for sale?

Less important, clearly. For one thing, it won't be the size of a book, not on the computer screen where it shows up. For ebook sales, you want the title and author to be readable, and you want the type of book to be immediately evident. It's a plus if the cover's attractive, but I don't know that a gorgeous cover makes anybody desperate to own an ebook.

For a POD paperback, the cover's a little more important, in that it winds up existing as a physical object. It may be the same little thumbnail picture that the prospective purchaser sees, but when he opens the envelope and takes out the book, there's the cover, big as life. He's already paid his money, he's not likely to send the book back if the full-size cover's a disappointment, but a superior cover may increase his pleasure in your book.

I've published many books with Hard Case Crime, and without question their superb covers drive sales—in bookstores, certainly, but also in online bookstores. Those customers most responsive to the covers buy the physical book, but even so the Hard Case covers are a real factor in generating ebook sales.

Publishing your ebook.

When you've got everything in hand—an edited, formatted, and proofread manuscript, and a finished cover—you're ready to publish.

You'll most likely choose to bring out a Print-On-Demand paperback edition. But it's absolutely certain that you'll want to publish an ebook. It's ebooks that created the contemporary universe of self-publishing, and with very little effort on your part you can offer your novel for sale throughout the world.

The various ebook publishing platforms make the self-publishing process quite easy. Kindle and Nook, while different from one another, are quite easy to follow. Kobo is also quite straightforward. Apple can be more challenging, and I've found Google Plus such a muddle that I still haven't figured it out.

My suggestion would be that you publish directly on Kindle and use an outfit like Draft2Digital or Smashwords to offer the book on Nook, Kobo, Apple, and the various smaller platforms.

Or you may decide to publish on Kindle exclusively. Amazon would certainly prefer that you do so, and toward that end they extend certain benefits to indie authors who click the box for Kindle Select, thus giving Amazon sole rights to distribute the book for a specified period.

It's confusing. What do you think I should do?

I have no idea.

What???

I know, I know. But I'm writing these words in November of 2015, and unless you're standing behind me and reading them over my shoulder, there's a time lag involved. By the time you get your hands on this book and reach this chapter, it's impossible to guess what the world of indie publishing will look like.

Let me give you a little personal history:

Sometime in 2009, I began experimenting with Kindle Direct Publishing, making some of my backlist titles, long out of print, eVailable in the new medium. My efforts at formatting and cover design were crude at best, and sales were certainly modest, but I was over the moon at the notion that my old books were finding new readers, and that I was even picking up a couple of bucks every month.

The following year, I had an approach from a new business, Open Road Integrated Media. The creation of a top publishing professional, Jane Friedman, ORIM proposed that they take over the handful of titles I'd published and add all my other backlist books. They'd do all the work, getting the books scanned and proofread. They'd design covers, they'd upload on all ebook platforms, they'd shoot elaborate videos for promotional purposes, and in return they'd split all income evenly (after recovery of initial costs).

That looked like a good deal. And it was a good deal, and my agent was savvy enough to insist on a five-year time limit in the contract, and at the end of 2015 the time is up, and I knew I didn't want to renew. Because the business has changed, and it's now much easier and not very expensive for me to do for myself what Open Road has been doing for those books of mine that they publish. (In fact I've been doing just that for books that weren't part of the Open Road deal, and have been pleased with the results.) I'd rather have the control, and I'd rather be able to use my own covers rather than the rather generic sort they've been using, and I'd like to adjust the prices as I wish.

And, duh, I'd rather have 100% than 50% of earnings.

Things change. Especially in a field as fiercely volatile as this one. If I recommend a company to you, it may be out of business by the time you read about it. Or it may still exist, but be doing business differently.

It seems confusing.

You bet.

But here's the thing—you'll figure it out. Let's be clear on this: You could have written your novel without any help from me, and you'll be every bit as able to navigate the turbulent waters of indie publishing without my holding your hand. You'll work out how to publish your ebook, and if you make a mistake or two you'll figure out how to fix it.

And you'll probably do just fine with your POD paperback, too.

Publishing your paperback.

I would be surprised if you didn't decide to publish a Print-On-Demand paperback edition as well as an ebook. There's something about a physical book that makes the whole publishing process a lot more real. You can hold it in your hands, you can turn it this way and that, you can place it on a shelf or coffee table and gaze upon it with admiration.

And you can give copies to friends and relatives. (And yes, it's possible to give ebooks as gifts, even as it's possible to remember your mother's birthday with an e-card. But it's somehow not the same, is it?)

And just how are you going to autograph that ebook?

It's the ebook revolution that gave birth to contemporary self-publishing; it made it easy and inexpensive to publish one's own work, and possible to reach an audience. Following close on its heels, Print-On-Demand has made it easy and affordable to bring out one's books in paperback.

In 1986, when I published *Write For Your Life*, I had to order five thousand copies from my printer and write him a check for payment in full. Some months ago, when I published *The Crime of Our Lives* via Amazon's CreateSpace division, my only costs were the prep work my formatter did, producing pdf files of the book's cover and interior. (And this is a little more complicated than formatting an ebook. I wouldn't want to try it on my own—although CreateSpace and Ingram's Lightning Source are quite good about guiding one through the process.)

I didn't have to pay for any printing, because no copies were printed. Print-On-Demand means precisely that—copies are printed as books are ordered, with the printing costs of each book covered by a portion of what the buyer pays.

Once your POD paperback is up and running, it's as blissfully maintenance-free as your published ebook. You'll receive monthly statements and payments, and online retailers will no more run out of stock of the paperback than they do of the ebook. On the one hand it's a physical reality, composed of paper and ink instead of electronic impulses, but in another sense it's more of the same; it exists as a dormant seed in dry ground, and then somebody clicks a BUY button and waters it, and the desert blooms.

Publishing your audiobook.

I never said a word about audiobooks in this book's original edition, and for a fairly good reason: they barely existed. Aside from Talking Books for the Blind—recordings one could obtain on loan from the Library of Congress—reading was not something you could do with your ears.

This has changed to a remarkable degree, with audio emerging as an important part of the novelist's market, and audio publishers springing up everywhere—and, like their cousins in print publishing, gobbling up one another with boundless appetite. The business keeps changing—does that sound familiar?—and technology continues to evolve, from cassettes to CDs to MP3 audio downloads.

And the audience keeps growing.

I haven't discussed audio in earlier chapters because, however increasingly important it may be, it remains a subsidiary right. Your contract with your traditional print publisher will almost certainly bestow audio rights upon him, with the two of you splitting audio income. Your share will initially be credited against your outstanding advance; if and when your book earns out, you'll receive audio royalties along with your other earnings, at the usual six-month intervals.

And if you self-publish?

Well, theoretically you could try to sell audio rights to an audio publisher, but I think you'd have better luck selling ice in Antarctica. A first novel is a tough sell for audio even with a major publisher behind it, but at least an acquisitions editor will give it a look. An indie first novel won't get that much.

So I forget about audio, right?

You can probably forget about audio publishers. But that leaves you an option you've already chosen for the ebook and print editions: i.e., you can do it yourself.

At present, I know of only one way to manage this feat—but that's one more than existed just a couple of years ago. ACX is the self-publishing division of Audible, the leader by far in the field of downloadable audiobooks. (Audible is itself now a division of Amazon.) ACX is to Audible as KDP is to Amazon/Kindle, and their user-friendly site will explain, far better than I can, exactly how it works.

You have two options at ACX: You can set up a home studio and record the book yourself, or you can team up with an ACX narrator who will narrate and produce the audiobook, either on a work-for-hire basis or for an equal share in the royalties.

Unless you're really good at reading your own work aloud, and unless you've got the savvy to record and edit the work, you're well advised to team up with a narrator/producer. If you can find someone willing to work on shares, you save having to come up with a couple of thousand dollars. As to which is better in the long run, well, that depends on how well the audiobook sells—and that's never easy to predict.

If you're going to publish your own novel, an ebook is a must, a POD paperback is almost certainly indicated—and you may want to hold off on audio. It's something you can always add down the line, if your book does well enough to suggest an audio version might have a real audience.

That, in a nutshell, is how you self-publish your novel.

Or perhaps that should be not a nutshell but an eggshell, because even as I've typed the last few chapters, I've been struck by the fragility of my words and sentences. At the risk of belaboring the point, I'll stress once again how rapidly the game is changing.

This book's first fourteen chapters, concerned specifically with the process of turning your desire to write a novel into upwards of sixty thousand words of prose and dialogue, are not all that different from what I wrote and published in 1978. There have been enough changes in the publishing world to justify my enlarging upon what I'd written, but replacing a typewriter with a computer doesn't alter the basic nature of the writing process. The vital part remains what it's always been—thinking up what happens next, figuring out how best to express it, and staying with it until you've accomplished what you set out to do. It hasn't changed that much since 1978, and I doubt it'll change much in the next twenty or thirty or forty years.

I can't say the same for the material covered in this chapter and the two before it. Will ebooks continue to increase their audience? Or will it shrink? The other day an early ebook enthusiast told me he's buying more and more paper-and-ink books these days, and likens the ebook experience to listening to a CD, and a printed book to a vinyl recording. I know what he means, though not quite well enough to explain it. I also know that the period of rapid evolution in publishing has not stopped with the present moment.

If there's one thing I hope you'll take away from these chapters, it's that you have to learn the game on your own. And that's not only true in the indie world. Even if you decide to place your book with a traditional publisher, and even if you're successful in so doing, you'll be expected to generate much of the book's publicity.

Resources for Self-publishing

Blogs:

Joe Konrath/Newbie's Guide to Self Publishing
jakonrath.blogspot.com

The Passive Voice
www.thepassivevoice.com

Dean Wesley Smith
www.deanwesleysmith.com

Kristine Kathryn Rusch/The Business Rusch
kriswrites.com/category/business

Barry Eisler
barryeisler.blogspot.com

Hugh Howey
www.hughhowey.com/blog

Lee Goldberg
www.leegoldberg.com/blog

JW Manus/QA Productions
jwmanus.wordpress.com

Joe Friedlander/The Book Designer
www.thebookdesigner.com

Online Retailers:

Amazon/Kindle Direct Publishing
www.amazonkdp.com

Barnes & Noble
www.nookpress.com

Kobo
www.kobo.com/writinglife

Apple:
www.apple.com/itunes/working-itunes/sell-content/books/book-faq.html

Ebook Distributors:

Smashwords
www.smashwords.com

Draft2Digital
www.draft2digital.com

Print on Demand Services:

Createspace
www.createspace.com

Lightning Source/Ingrams
www.lightningsource.com

Audio Books:

ACX/Audible: www.acx.com

Chapter 18

Doing It Again

And, to take the sting out of the rejections your novel accumulates along the way, throw yourself into your second novel as completely as you can.

• • •

That's how Chapter Fourteen ended, leading directly if predictably into a chapter on following a first novel with a second.

This time around, of course, three chapters on self-publishing got there first. Now it's time to resume, but first I should probably recount a conversation I had perhaps a dozen years ago over dinner with an acquisitions editor for a major audio publisher. He was aggrieved to report a statistic he'd come upon recently. "I just learned this," he said. "Of all the people who publish a first novel, ninety-five percent never follow it with a second."

"That," I said, "just may be the most hopeful news I've heard in years. Now if we can just get those numbers up a little higher, we'll really have something to crow about."

It took him a while to realize I was kidding.

But let's see what I had to say . . .

• • •

It's a lot easier to begin work on a second book if some eager publisher snapped up the first one ten minutes after it left your typewriter. But it doesn't happen that way very often. As I suggested earlier, a great many of us write first novels that turn out to be unsalable. And many who do go on to produce salable second novels—but that only happens if we get that second novel written.

There's no reason to assume that your first novel will turn out to be unpublishable. But there's every reason in the world to expect that it will take a long time finding its way into a publisher's heart and onto his spring list. That time will pass much faster and be put to far better use if you spend it writing your next book.

Among other things, plunging into your next book may help you deal with the old My-Novel's-Finished-And-I-Wish-I-Were-Dead Blues.

I almost hesitate to mention the depression that so frequently follows the completion of a novel for fear of making it a matter of self-fulfilling prophecy. I'd hate to think that, having finished your book in high spirits, you'll now go sit in the corner and sulk so you can be just like the pros. I think it's better overall, though, to be able to allow for this sort of thing. We writers tend to regard ourselves as unique specimens of humanity, so it may be reassuring to know that one is not the first person in the world to have finished a novel and wanted to throw up.

It does indeed happen to most of us, and I'm sure it's not limited to writers. This sort of after-work depression seems to be the typical aftermath of any arduous long-term creative endeavor. Indeed, it's quite obviously equivalent to the syndrome known as Post-Partum Depression, the feeling of emptiness and purposelessness so many mothers go through immediately after childbirth. For nine months they've defined themselves in terms of this life growing inside of them. Their whole purpose has been to carry their child to term. Now the child's born and the mother's chore is completed, and what's she supposed to do for an encore?

Sound familiar?

It's a little worse for a writer. The mother's got a cute little baby to play with, and if changing him's a bore, there's still a certain amount of satisfaction in having it around the house. If nothing else, everybody who sees it is going to make admiring noises. Even if the kid looks like a monkey, nobody's going to hand it a banana. They'll all assure the mother that her kid's a beauty.

Pity the poor novelist. Nobody comes over to visit his book and bring it a squeaky toy or a cuddly stuffed animal. His friends read it out of a sense of obligation, and what praise they offer has a suspiciously hollow ring to it. Agents and editors, meanwhile, have the effrontery to tell him thanks but no thanks. His child doesn't fit their needs at the moment, he's assured, although this is not to say that the little brat lacks merit.

> *My book's no good,* the novelist concludes. *Therefore I'm no good. Therefore I'm a failure, and therefore I'll be a failure forever, and if I had any brains I'd blow them out. If I had the guts to do it, which I don't, because I'm worthless. So I guess I'll drink myself to death, or go eat worms, or really get into daytime television watching.*

There's not much point in attacking this position logically. Logic doesn't have a whole lot to do with it. Post-novel depression is just as likely to strike when the book's a hit, and it's absolutely devastating when the novel scores a really impressive success.

Does that seem strange? Here's how the writer's mind adds it all up:

> *The book's a success. Gee, that's terrific. But wait a minute. It can't really be that good. I know it can't be that good, because I'm the guy who wrote it, and I'm not that good, so how good can it be, huh? Now sooner or later they're gonna find out it's not as good as they think it is, and where'll I be then? And anyway, what difference does it make if it's good or not? Because one thing's sure. I couldn't possibly write anything that good again. Matter of fact, I don't think I could write anything halfway decent again. Come to reflect on it, I'm pretty sure I couldn't write anything again, decent or otherwise. I think I'll throw my typewriter out the window. I think I'll throw myself out the window. I think . . . .*

I think you get the idea.

Does this really happen? You bet it does. I've written more novels than I can shake a stick at—though some of them deserve it—and I still experience a letdown when I finish a book, one composed of many of the thoughts presented above. After all this time, I recognize what I feel as symptomatic of Post-Novel Depression. You would think this recognition would help, and once in awhile it does, but often it doesn't.

Some years ago, finishing a book was a signal for me to reach for a bottle. I put myself under considerable pressure in my work and felt that alcohol would do a good job of relieving that pressure when the work was done. What booze does, of course, is not so much relieve tension as mask its symptoms. When post-novel depression set in, I'd go on drinking in an attempt to alleviate the depression.

This wasn't wise. Alcohol is clinically a depressant, and pouring it into a depressed writer is like pouring oil on troubled fires. It does exactly the opposite of what you hope it will do, deepening and exacerbating the underlying depression. A few celebratory "Hey-the-book's done" drinks may be a great idea, but the kind of medicinal drinking some of us get into can be ruinous.

I don't drink any more, and that helps. Another thing that makes my post-novel depressions easier to bear is that I don't have as much of a high to crash from these days. I don't write as intensively as I used to, having settled down to a steady and comfortable pace of five pages or so per day. I'm not panting when I get to the finish line, and that seems to make a difference.

When I finish a book nowadays, I take good care of myself. For a couple of weeks I take plenty of time off. I read fiction—something I often can't do while I'm writing it. I take long exploratory walks, recharging my batteries for the next book. I buy myself a present. If I can afford it, I try to get away for a week.

During this period, I recognize my own emotional frailty. I've learned not to be surprised if my eyes begin to tear while I'm watching reruns of the Mary Tyler Moore show, I make it a point to eat properly, to get plenty of exercise, to keep reasonably regular hours. Sometimes I even try fasting for a few days.

Before very long, my mind begins to remember that I'm a writer. It starts sending up signals, playing games of What If?, knitting little plot fragments like a subtle wife turning out tiny garments. I can't avoid knowing that, to strain the metaphor, the honeymoon is over. It's time to get back to work on the next one.

You write the second book the same way you wrote the first one—hatching an idea, shaping it into a plot, outlining or not outlining as you prefer, and turning out the book itself one day at a time. In a sense, every novel's a first novel—because you haven't written it before. You'll be ever so much more at ease the second time around, and you'll probably display considerable technical proficiency compared to your maiden effort, but that doesn't mean it's going to be a piece of cake. Listen, it's *never* a piece of cake. No matter how many books you've done.

Should your second book be similar in type to your first? Having written *Trefillian House*, would you be wise to embark on another gothic while Ms. Wimpole's reading your first one?

That's your decision to make. And it's possible your unconscious mind will make it for you. After I wrote my first novel, years passed before I was to write another lesbian novel—not because I wouldn't have been delighted to do so, but because my mind didn't produce any ideas in that vein. If I hadn't been so goddam young and stupid I might have cudgeled it some, but I guess I just figured I'd exhausted the subject and ought to go on to other things—which may have been the right decision for me at the time.

You may find that *Trefillian House* was your ultimate statement in the world of gothic novels. Or you may decide that you're simply ready for something else; while you had fun writing the book, you now regard it as a warm-up exercise for something more ambitious and artistically satisfying. On the other hand, you may have found your métier, and your mind may be teeming with ways to write the same book different—and better this time around.

Remember that the choice is yours, and that it doesn't involve signing any long-term contracts. You can try something else with your second book, then return to gothics at a later date. Conversely, you can write a second gothic without typing yourself irreversibly as a writer of gothics and nothing else. Your second book is just a second book. It's not a career.

Even if you do write a second gothic, it's not too likely that we'll be seeing more of *Trefillian House's* young widow. Gothic novels don't run to series heroines. Their lead characters are generally well supplied with house and husband by the time the book is over.

Series characters, however, are frequently met with in some other fiction categories—suspense novels, first and foremost, but westerns and science-fiction novels as well.

I've worked with three series characters over the years—Evan Tanner, Matt Scudder and Bernie Rhodenbarr. Obviously, I enjoy doing this sort of thing, developing a character over several books, learning more about him as he makes his way through plot after plot. When I get hold of a character who really engages me, I'm loathe to let go of him.

Should your second novel feature the same character as your first? Again, that's up to you. If you find that the lead of your first book has a sufficiently strong hold upon your imagination so that you want to write a second book about him, by all means go ahead and do it. Bear in mind, though, that you can always write your second book about some other character and come back to the first one in a later book. You may want a change of pace.

It's important, if you do embark on a series, that you not presuppose the reader's acquaintance with any previous books. Your second novel—indeed, each of your series novels—ought to be complete in and of itself. You're writing a second book about a particular character, not Volume Two of a trilogy; the reader shouldn't have to have read your first book in order to appreciate your second.

At the same time, there shouldn't be so much duplication in the second book that someone who has read the first will be bored. Don't worry overmuch about this last, however. It's been my observation that the sort of reader who likes series books doesn't mind being reminded of certain things. The sense of the familiar evidently appeals to him; he gets the feeling that he's an insider, already acquainted with characters who must be described for noninsiders.

One problem with a series is that you have to remember who's who and what's what. The same readers who most enjoy series novels are most insistent that the writer avoid inconsistencies. It may be no particular problem remembering that your lead has blue eyes, but what color are his girlfriend's? And where did I mention the names and ages of Scudder's kids?

Arthur Maling has a particular dilemma along these lines, and one that serves to illustrate just how complicated the business of series novels can be:

> *The Price, Potter and Petacque books have given me particular problems. Instead of having just one series character, I have a cast of fifteen or sixteen major and minor characters that move from book to book—Brock Potter and everyone in the company—and I have a hell of a time remembering the color of everyone's eyes, the names and ages of everyone's kids, etc. A fellow mystery writer and friend of mine, James McClure, made a chart for me, listing all the Price, Potter and Petacque characters and their relationships, and it's been helpful; but I keep forgetting to enter the pertinent details, which means that I frequently have to dig through several finished books or a couple of hundred pages of manuscript to find what I said about one or another of the characters a year or two or four previously.*

A problem with a series, albeit one you're not terribly likely to face in the second book, is boredom. Most series writers run into this sooner or later. Dorothy Sayers is supposed to have told Agatha Christie how sick and tired she was of writing about Lord Peter Wimsey; Christie in turn confessed to a deep-seated desire to kill off Hercule Poirot, and proved it by doing precisely that in the "final" Poirot novel, written in the '40s and not published until after the author's own death.

I stopped writing the Tanner series not because I grew tired of the character but because the books themselves seemed to have a deadening sameness about them. It seemed to me that Tanner kept going to the same kinds of places, meeting the same sorts of people, having the same kinds of conversations, and dealing with the same kinds of plot problems. I've since come to realize that there's nothing necessarily wrong with that. My awareness of this sameness was inevitably more acute than a reader's would be, since I was spending a couple of months writing something he would read in as many hours. Besides, readers want a series book to be pretty much like the last one; if they hadn't liked the last one in the first place they wouldn't have bought the second, or the third, or the fortieth.

The fact that you've created a strong character doesn't mean you should write a second book about him. It seems as though some writers are geared to write series books and others are not. Sometimes success will tend to force a series upon a writer. That sort of thing has been happening ever since Shakespeare wrote *The Merry Wives of Windsor* because Queen Elizabeth wanted to see another play about Falstaff. At this stage of the game, however, it's not too likely that you'll have to launch a series as a command performance for royalty. With one unpublished novel to your credit, you still have the freedom to make your own decisions.

• • •

Ah, series novels. Let me take a moment to tell you a story. It's not about novels, or writers. It's about elephants.

> Two guys run into each other on the street. "You're just the man I wanted to see," says Virgil. "I've got something to sell, and you'd be the perfect customer."
>
> "Oh?" says Horace. "What have you got?"
>
> "An elephant."
>
> "An elephant? You want to sell me an elephant? Are you out of your mind? I live in two rooms on Pitkin Avenue, I

haven't even got a backyard. Where would I keep an elephant? What would I feed it? How could I clean up after it? Seriously, Virgil, what the hell could I possibly want with an elephant?"

"I see what you mean," says Virgil, "and I'm sorry to hear it. See, I've actually got two elephants, and I could offer you a really good price for the pair."

"Ah," says Horace. "Now you're talking!"

Something very close to this happens all the time in our business. An agent submits a novel to a publisher, and gets a note or a phone call saying something like this: "I really love this book, but before I pitch it to the editorial board it'd help to know if your client's planning more books about the character. Because we're a lot more likely to be interested if it's the beginning of a series."

One elephant? Pfui. Two elephants? Hmmm . . .

In genre fiction, series have been popular for a long time, with readers and with publishers. And this has never been as true as it is now.

For readers, a series provides a sure thing ("I liked two of the books about Siobhan Gronkowski, Forensic Librarian, so I'm positive I'll like a third.") and the chance to relax with old friends ("I don't even care whether Siobhan tracks down that overdue library book. It's so much fun eavesdropping on her conversations with Erasmus Dichotomy, and when those two finally get it on, I want to be there!")

For a publisher, a series gives you a built-in audience for future books. Getting somebody to try something new is difficult. Getting that person to try something that's "the same only different" is much easier. A series allows all concerned to have a pleasurable experience again for the first time.

Series, I should point out, are more of a factor in some genres than in others. Traditional romance fiction lends itself to series less reliably than, say, traditional westerns; the rawboned cowhand can ride off into the sunset, bound to have another stirring adventure in the next town over the horizon, while the young woman who finds true love in the last chapter of one novel can't be expected to transfer her affections to another handsome dude in Book Two.

It seems evident that ebooks and internet commerce have boosted the tendency to read, write, and publish books in series. The series is tailor-made for binge reading, and ebooks and online booksellers make it easy for the reader who wants to knock off one book after another. While mass-market paperbacks have largely disappeared from brick-and-mortar bookstores, online booksellers can supply any title that's in print and most that aren't, and can deliver in a couple of days.

4 reasons why your second book should be a sequel to the first.

1. It's an answer to the question of *What should I write next?*
2. Having a series makes it easier to get your books noticed by publishers and readers.
3. You had so much fun writing about your character that you'd like to see what's next in his/her life.
4. You already know you can write this kind of book about this character, so you'll be confident of your ability to do it again.

4 reasons why your second book should *not* be a sequel to the first.

1. You're just getting started. How are you going to grow as a writer if you insist on repeating yourself this early on?
2. You got a terrific idea for a new book while you were writing the first. But there's no way it'll fit into a series. Why abandon it when it's what you really want to write?
3. Your character died in the last chapter of your book. Of course you could quickly bring him back to life, but the death was the right ending artistically. And besides, truth to tell, you were

getting a little sick of the sonofabitch. Are you sure you want to do CPR at this late date?
4. Why exactly did you get into this business in the first place? To cater to the baser impulses of publishers and readers? Or to expand your own horizons and enjoy yourself?

I'm confused.

I should hope so. But remember that it's your choice, and what's sauce for one goose is something else for another. Circumstances alter cases, and your mileage may vary. The only real advice is, as it's so often been, to do what you want.

When I first met Sue Grafton, she'd just published her second Kinsey Millhone mystery, *B is for Burglar,* and she was already very clear on what the future would look like. She would go through the alphabet, all the way to Z, for a total of 26 books. And then she'd stop.

I was stunned. How could she possibly look so far ahead with such indomitable assurance? How could she know she'd be *able* to go on writing about Kinsey, let alone *want* to?

But she did know. And, last I looked, she was up to the twenty-fourth volume, which breaks the pattern slightly with the title *X*. (Not X is for Xylophone, or Xray, or X-rated. Just plain X. Live with it.)

It's worked for her commercially, and that's not a trivial matter, but it's clear that it's never been the main consideration for Sue. It's also worked artistically for her, has in fact worked superbly in that respect. As she somehow was given to know it would right from the jump.

Donald E. Westlake's first book about Parker, the armed robbery guy, ended with the antihero dead. Bucklin Moon, editor at Pocket Books, called Don with a question: Would it be possible for Parker to survive, and star in at least two more novels?

"You know, the guy's got a cast-iron constitution," Don told him. "I somehow sense that he's recovering even as we speak." Parker pulled through, and Don went on to write a couple dozen books about him. A lot of people would contend that they were his finest work.

• • •

The journeyman novelist occasionally has the opportunity to produce books of a sort we haven't yet discussed—tie-ins, novelizations, and books in someone else's series.

I haven't mentioned them previously because they're the sort of thing a publisher is likely to hand out as an assignment, and it's highly unlikely your first novel will be assigned to you. Later on, though, when publishers are familiar with you and your work, or when you have an agent who can recommend you for assignments, some of this work may come your way.

Books of this sort aren't much fun to write. You can't display a hell of a lot of creativity, nor are you likely to earn substantial sums from them. Writing paperback novels about the Brady Bunch will not make you rich. Turning Grade "B" movie scripts into Grade "C" novels won't make your name a household word. And there's a limit to how much pride you can take in having been one of fifty people to write under the umbrella pen name of Nick Carter.

All the same, any assignment that brings the novice novelist money for writing fiction is not all bad. And writing the books can sharpen your craft considerably, whatever the ultimate merits of what you write. There's a point, certainly, when you should stop accepting these assignments and concentrate instead on your own work, but you can burn that bridge when you come to it.

The tie-in is a book based on someone else's characters. You generally furnish your own plot, although the publisher or someone from the network may have suggestions to throw into the hopper—which is probably the right place for them.

I wrote my first detective novel this way. Belmont Books had a deal set for a tie-in novel based on *Markham,* a series starring Ray Milland. The book I wrote turned out rather well, and my agent agreed it was a shame to waste it as a tie-in so he showed it to Knox Burger, then at Gold Medal. Knox liked it, whereupon I had to redo the book, changing Roy Markham to Ed London and otherwise altering the character. That done, I had to go write yet another book about Markham, which Belmont did indeed publish.

Novelizations are easier in that the whole plot is laid out for you, scene by scene. You've got a movie script in front of you and your job is to turn it into prose. It's very rare that this is anything more than a purely mechanical task, which explains why knowledgeable readers shun those paperbacks that carry notices indicating they were based upon a screenplay. They're almost invariably lifeless.

The fact that the books sell so well all the same indicates too how few readers are all that knowledgeable, or all that sensitive to writing quality. Sad to say.

Some writers are better at novelizations than others. A pro who can turn out solid acceptable novelizations regularly can count on a decent steady income. A handful have acquired reputations; Leonore Fleischer, for one, is able to demand high advances and preferential royalty rates because of her reputation for delivering a quality product.

• • •

Tie-ins and novelizations are essentially a form of adaptation; just as screenwriters are occupied with adapting novels into film and TV scripts, so are novelists occasionally called upon to turn movies and television shows into prose fiction. Opportunities of this sort most frequently come to one through one's agent.

It may strike you as onerous hackwork not worth your time and creative energy, or you may find it an interesting and challenging way to hone your writing chops while getting paid for it.

Lee Goldberg, a capable novelist as well as a TV writer and showrunner, made a good thing of tie-ins with the *Monk* TV series.

Graphic novels, essentially comics in book form, have emerged in recent years as a viable category of fiction. While the graphic artist is an indispensable component, so is the person who writes the dialogue and narrative; Duane Swierczynski and Greg Rucka both flourish in the dual roles of prose and graphic novelist. As far as adaptation is concerned, books are more likely to be adapted into graphic novels than the other way around—but that could change, and might become an opportunity for a developing novelist.

• • •

Writing books in somebody else's series is just what it sounds like. I couldn't say how many people have launched literary careers by being Nick Carter for a couple of books. Here again, the work can strike you as thankless and ill-paying, but it's a way to learn your craft while you get paid for it, and that's not the worst thing that ever happened to a writer.

• • •

Most of the apparently unending Western and Male Adventure series—The Destroyer, The Executioner, Longarm, etc.—are begun by an individual writer, who tires of the chore after a certain number of books and subsequently hires ghost writers to keep the series going. Sometime it's a packager who dreams up the series, and in a sense there is no original writer; the packager slaps a pen name on the books, and hires ghostwriters from the start. Either way, the ghost's compensation is almost invariably work for hire.

A fairly recent phenomenon has elevated this sort of ghostwriting to a higher and far more lucrative level. It's very clearly the result of market conditions, specifically of the publishing industry's recognition of the importance of brand names. A bestselling author is just that, a Brand Name, and after decades of taking it for granted that one book a year was as much as the market could absorb from any writer, publishers discovered that they were completely wrong. If readers really liked a particular author, they'd buy books as fast as he could write them.

Or even faster, if he could find somebody else to do the heavy lifting.

This has been going on quietly and in a limited way for some time now. Newly discovered books by dead authors, books written from "extensive notes and outlines they left behind"—the degree of absurdity varies from case to case, but one way or another the implication has been that the Big Name Author actually wrote the book himself, or would have if he hadn't been inconsiderate enough to drop dead.

What's new is that the anonymous ghost has evolved into a credited and well-compensated co-writer. "By James BrandName and Andrew UpAndComer," the joint byline reads, and if the Brand Name's name is in larger type, and he alone is pictured on the rear flap, well, what would you expect? More to the point, Andrew UpAndComer gets a flat fee for his work-for-hire contribution. It may run well into six figures, which is a lot more than anybody ever made ghosting Executioner novels for Don Pendleton, but it's one fee and out, and the Big Name gets the royalties, foreign and domestic, and any ancillary income from TV or films or audio or T-shirts.

In some cases, the Brand Name has written one or two books of a series, and reviews the co-writer's outline and text along the way, calling for changes when they seem required. James Patterson, who with his co-authors produces more books every year than many people read, is said to supply his co-author with a detailed chapter-by-chapter outline, sometimes running sixty or eighty pages; his co-authors are apt to report that they learned an astonishing amount from the experience of working with him.

It's not easy to get a gig like this. They're a cut above entry-level, and some credited co-authors published a long list of their own novels before they went to work sharing a byline with a star. But the work is out there, and it's not a trend that's likely to reverse itself anytime soon. If you publish a novel or two, and if the right person has the right reaction to it, you may find yourself presented with such an opportunity.

• • •

A second novel, whatever sort you choose, is the best thing to do after you've done your first novel. You'll learn from it, even as you have learned from the first. You'll be able to see your own increased facility. You'll be doing the best thing possible to cure the post-novel blahs. And, once you've finished it, you'll have two manuscripts out to market. While this may bring rejections at double your usual rate, so too will it more than double your chances of eventual acceptance.

Finally, there's one more argument for writing a second novel. If you don't, how can reviewers complain that it doesn't fulfill the promise of your first novel?

Chapter 19

Now It's Up to You

Well, I'm done.

Has this helped any?

I wonder, looking over what I've written, whether I've done what I set out to do. I'm often similarly uncertain when I write the last words of a novel, skip a few spaces, and type "The End" in the center of the page. Does the story hold up? Are the characters interesting? Is the book I've written the book I wanted to write in the first place? It never quite is, perhaps because one's reach always exceeds one's grasp, but is it at least a good book?

Maybe you'll get something out of it. I don't know. In the final analysis, you can no more learn the gentle art of novel writing from a book than you can learn how to ride a bicycle from studying the owner's manual. The only way you really learn is by doing it yourself, and you may fall off a lot before you get the hang of it.

I wish you luck.

I won't read your manuscript, or recommend an agent, or put you in touch with a publisher. In 1978, I promised to answer letters—if I can make the time, and if you enclosed a stamped self-addressed envelope. Nowadays I promise I *won't* answer letters, and I trust you won't write me any. What I will do is answer emails, insofar as time permits, and I'm happy to let you have my email address, which is lawbloc@gmail.com.

But that's as much as I'll do. You have to do the rest yourself. That, I'm afraid, is how it works in this business.

I hope you write your novel. I hope you write a lot of them, and that they're very good books indeed. Not because I would presume to regard your work as a sort of literary grandchild of mine—let's face it, you'd write it whether or not you read this book.

But simply because, while there are far too many books in this world, there are far too few good ones.

And I don't ever want to run out of things to read.

Acknowledgements then and now...

In 1978:

Before this present volume was in the planning stages, I circulated a questionnaire on writing methods with the intention of doing a magazine piece on the subject. A large number of writers of fiction and nonfiction alike were kind enough to reply at some length. While my article was not ultimately published, the replies to my questionnaire were of inestimable value to me when it came time to write this book on the novel. I've had occasion to quote from several of the replies I received; all of them in one way or another enlarged my understanding of how writers do whatever it is that we do.

This book's defects are mine alone. For its strengths, I should like to acknowledge the assistance of all those who replied to my questionnaire, to wit:

Mary Amlaw, Poul Anderson, Mel Arrighi, Isaac Asimov, Michael Avallone, Jean L. Backus, Eugene Franklin Bandy, D.R. Benson, Robert Bloch, Murray Teigh Bloom, Barbara Bonham, Jon L. Breen, William Brittain, Barbara Callahan, William E. Chambers, Thomas Chastain, John Cheever, Mary Higgins Clark, Virginia Coffman, George Harmon Coxe, Linda Crawford, Clive Cussler, Dorothy Salisbury Davis, Richard Deming, F.M. Esfandiary, Stanley Ellin, Harlan Ellison, Robert L. Fish, Patricia Fox-Sheinwold, Lucy Freeman, Anne Freemantle, Tonita S. Gardner, Brian Garfield, Herbert Gold, Arthur Goldstein, Joe Gores, Marilyn Granbeck, Russell H. Girran, Irving A. Greenfield, Isidore Haiblum, Joseph Hansen, Joyce Harrington, Tony Hillerman, Edward D. Hoch, Peter Hochstein, James Holding, Hans Holzer, Dorothy B. Hughes, Beatrice Trum Hunter, Bel Kaufman, Richard Kostelanetz, Eda J. LeShan, Elizabeth Levy,

Robert Ludlum, John Lutz, Arthur Lyons, Arthur Maling, Harold Q. Masur, John D. MacDonald, Ross Macdonald, Gregory McDonald, Thomas M. McDade, Patricia McGerr, William P. McGivern, James McKimmey, Francis M. Nevins, Donald Newlove, Stephen R. Novak, Al Nussbaum, Dennis O'Neil, Robert B. Parker, Don Pendleton, Judson Philips, Richard S. Prather, Bill Pronzini, Tom Purdom, Robert J. Randisi, Malcolm Robinson, Willo Davis Roberts, Sam Ross, Sandra Scoppettone, Justin Scott, Henry Slesar, Martin Cruz Smith, Jerry Sohl, Jane Speed, Aaron Marc Stein, Richard Martin Stern, Ross Thomas, Lawrence Treat, Louis Trimble, Thomas Walsh, Stephen Wasylyk, Hillary Waugh, Sol Weinstein, Edward Wellen, Helen Wells, David Westheimer, Donald E. Westlake, Collin Wilcox and Chelsea Quinn Yarbro.

... AND NOW:

It's harrowing to read through that list and realize how many of the writers on it are no longer with us. I could trot out a bit of tripe about how they live on in their work, and some of them do, but that's often cold comfort, isn't it?

I may have their responses somewhere, but maybe not. Letters in my possession tend to have a shorter lifespan than their authors. My favorite was a note from John Cheever, on his letterhead and in the self-addressed stamped envelope I'd provided. It read as follows: *"Dear Mr. Block, I find I am unable either to respond to your questions or to waste your stamp."*

And whom ought I to acknowledge this time around? The *Writer's Digest* editors—John Brady and Bill Brohaugh—who for fourteen years encouraged me to spend time thinking about and writing about this curious business of making up stories. And the late Donald I. Fine, who published my second book for writers, *Telling Lies for Fun & Profit,* and somehow persuaded Book-of-the-Month Club to take it as an alternate selection.

Nor would I care to forget Jerrold Mundis, Patrick Trese, Nona Cleland, Barbara Morris, Sheila Walsh, Alex Segura, Dennis Broe, Janet Capron, Erin Mitchell, Diana Gould, Bootsie Martinez, Summer Shohfi, Dan Swanson, David Tereshchuk, Paul Vlachos, Nancy O'Hara, Linda Nathan, Michael Simon, Cheryl Morrison, Quincy Long, Kate Lardner, Trebbe Johnson, Bill Hoffman, Alexandra Bonfante-Warren, Nick Bryant, Anne Flournoy, all either regular or occasional providers of mutual support and encouragement at the Thursday Afternoon

Chowder & Marching Society. (And Edward Hannibal and Charles M. Young, who've moved on to another meeting.)

Two good friends, Brian Koppelman and David Levien, gave me the use of an office at the very moment when I needed a home away from (but within walking distance of) home. My expanding-and-updating chores would have taken me twice as long.

But for the remarkable efforts of Jaye Manus, this book and many of its fellows would be no more than a Word file on my computer, wasting its digital essence on the desert air.

And it would not even be so much as a string of electronic impulses but for the timely prompt of Alex Kourvo, who, when not busy writing fine novels of her own, is a perceptive and enthusiastic reviewer of books on writing. She emailed me to say that *Writing the Novel from Plot to Print* was one of her favorite books, and to point out gently that it needed to be updated.

Somehow her words got through to me. If you find *Writing the Novel from Plot to Print to Pixel* helpful, you have Alex to thank.

Lawrence Block's Books for Writers

1. **Writing the Novel from Plot to Print to Pixel.** That's this one, and the title says it all.

2. **Telling Lies for Fun & Profit: a manual for fiction writers.** LB's most popular book for writers, perhaps because it's blessed with such a good title. It's drawn from the first several years of his *Writer's Digest* column, and deals with all aspects of fiction.

3. **Spider, Spin Me a Web: a handbook for fiction writers.** A sequel to *Telling Lies*. Fewer people have read it over the years, perhaps because *Fun* and *Profit* are more appealing buzzwords than *Spider* and *Web*. Sheesh—*now* you tell me!

4. **Write For Your Life: a home seminar for writers.** This might as easily have been called *The Inner Game of Writing* and grew directly out of a day-long interactional seminar for writers that LB presented nationwide during the mid-1980s. It centers on the writer within, and is designed to help you get out of your own way and get your best words on paper.

5. **The Liar's Bible: a compendium for fiction writers.** Its forty chapters include *Make No Misteak, Getting By on a Writer's Income, The Guts of the Fiction Writer, Overcoming the Ultimate Writer's Block,* and *Pieces of String Too Small to Save.*

6. **The Liar's Companion: a field guide for fiction writers.** Chapters include *No, but I Saw the Movie, No Tense Like the Present, Bouncing One Off the Fourth Wall, Are You Sure Chandler Started This Way?* and *Stop Making Sense.*

Years after LB gave up the *Writer's Digest* column, Terry Zobeck pointed out that *Telling Lies* and *Spider* were drawn from the column's early years, and that many of his best pieces on the subject were thus not included. Terry, a collector, had copies of what magazines LB was missing, and he found himself able to put together this volume and *The Liar's Companion*. (And, having learned his lesson with *Spider,* LB had little trouble coming up with titles. He did, however, have a memory lapse when it came to subtitles, with the result that *The Liar's Bible* started life with the subtitle *a handbook for fiction writers,* a line he'd already used for *Spider, Spin Me a Web.*)

7. **The Crime of Our Lives.** This is more a book *about* writers, specifically writers of crime fiction. Includes essays and recollections of Fredric Brown, Donald E. Westlake, Robert B. Parker, Raymond Chandler, Dashiell Hammett, Charles Willeford, Evan Hunter, Al Nussbaum, and more.

Staying in Touch With LB

By email:

Because I enjoy hearing from readers, I've chosen to make my email address public information. It's lawbloc@gmail.com, and you can feel free to write me at will. You'll very likely get a response, probably from me but occasionally from my Indispensable Assistant. Understand, though, that I'm not able to engage in lengthy correspondence or answer elaborate questions.

What I absolutely will *not* do:

—Read something you've written, whether published or unpublished.

—Give you a blurb. (I don't give *anybody* blurbs. Period.)

—Allow you to send me books to be signed and returned. (I do offer signed copies of some of my works through LB's eBay Bookstore—more on that below—and booksellers like The Mysterious Bookshop, VJ Books, and Seattle Mystery Bookshop often have signed books of mine for sale.)

—Meet you for coffee.

—Provide you with information you can readily dig up for yourself. You want a list of the Matthew Scudder novels in chronological order? While I applaud you for wishing to read the books in order, you can find that list readily online at any of a number of sites Google will direct you to, not least of all my website.

My website:

The url is www.lawrenceblock.com, and if you forget it, well, you can probably find your way there without much trouble. There's a lot of information on its various pages, including the various series in order, with order buttons should you care to add something to your library.

There's also a blog, wherein I or my Marketing Goddess or my Indispensable Assistant post in an irregular manner, and there's a doohickey—that's the technical term—that allows you to sign up to receive blog posts by email.

My newsletter:

I get out an email newsletter at unpredictable intervals, but rarely more often than every other week. I'll be happy to add you to the distribution list. A blank email to lawbloc@gmail.com with "newsletter" in the subject line will get you on the list, and a click of the "Unsubscribe" link will get you off it, should you ultimately decide you're happier without it.

My bookstore:

I've accumulated spare copies of many of my books over the years. In more innocent times one needed a supply for overseas submissions, etc., but in today's world, with virtually all submissions electronic, they're less essential. Thus LB's eBay Bookstore, where autographed copies of my work are available at reasonable prices. (Some are as low as $9.99 with free shipping; collector's items run as high as $100. And especially rare items, including the occasional original manuscript, are offered periodically in eBay auctions.) The url is stores.ebay.com/LBs-Bookstore/

Social media:

My twitter handle is @LawrenceBlock
My Facebook fan page is
www.facebook.com/LawrenceBlockOfficialFanPage

Cheers!

www.ingramcontent.com/pod-product-compliance
Lightning Source LLC
Chambersburg PA
CBHW060459090426
42735CB00011B/2038